The Struggle for the Arab World

The Struggle for the Arab World

Egypt's Nasser and the Arab League

TAWFIG Y. HASOU

KPI

London, Boston, Sydney and Henley

First published in 1985 by KPI Limited
14 Leicester Square, London WC2H 7PH, England

Distributed by
Routledge & Kegan Paul plc
14 Leicester Square, London WC2 7PH, England

Routledge & Kegan Paul Inc
9 Park Street, Boston, Mass. 02108, USA

Routledge & Kegan Paul
c/o Methuen Law Book Company
44, Waterloo Road,
North Ryde, NSW 2113
Australia and

Routledge & Kegan Paul plc
Broadway House, Newtown Road,
Henley-on-Thames, Oxon RG9 1EN, England

Produced by Worts-Power Associates
Set in Times by Margaret Spooner Typesetting
and printed in England by Redwood Burn Ltd, Trowbridge

ISBN 0-7103-0080-8

Acknowledgements

I am indebted to numerous people for their advice and contributions which have made the completion of this study possible. Throughout the research and writing of this book I have benefited from the wise counsel and insightful advice of my former graduate school advisor at the University of Virginia, Professor Rouhallah K. Ramazani. Professors Ramazani and Kenneth W. Thompson of the University of Virginia and James Piscatori of the Australia National University made a great impact on my education and in the production of this book.

I owe so much to a number of other individuals who, since beginning the research on this book, have provided me with many thought-provoking comments, insights and ideas: Abdalla Alnafeesi, Douglas Cassell, Inis Claude, Alfred Delasia, Robert Evans, Robert Fegan, Rentaro Hashimoto, Robert Heany, Peter Heller, Giri Horak, Ravic Huso, Ghassan Hussein, Whittle Johnston, David Jordan, Christopher Joyner, Ahmed Kamil, Clyde Lutz, Charles Macdonald, Osama Marar, Hamid Mayhoub, Mark Peterson, Kamal Qanbariyeh, Vladimir Reisky de Dubnic, Abdel-Munim el-Rifai, Eric Rouleau, Ghanim Saleh, Amin Salty, Salem Sari, Shafqat Shah, Ahmed Shikarah, Hasan Suleiman, Hasan Taha, Robert Wood and Kim Worts.

The Institute for the Study of World Politics of New York and the Graduate School of Arts and Science of the University of Virginia provided financial support for field research in the Middle East for this study. In Egypt, in 1978, I greatly benefited from several individuals. Sayed Nofal and Tal'at Hamed of the Arab League provided me with the necessary documents (some of which have never been seen before by scholars) and with information on the League; at *al-Ahram* Lewis Awad, Hedeit Abdel-Nabi and Zakaria Niel were helpful; Hussein Hassouna and Amina Rizkallah were of assistance during my stay in Cairo.

My thanks to the staffs of the following libraries who provided me with the necessary materials: University of Virginia's Alderman Library, Columbia University's International Affairs Library, the Library of Congress (Middle East Section), Dar al-Kutub Library in Cairo, the Library of the League of Arab States (Cairo) and the United Emirates' Library.

The book, in its initial form as a Ph.D. Dissertation, was improved by careful reading of all or part of various drafts by Rouhollah K. Ramazani, Kenneth W. Thompson and James Piscatori.

My sincere thanks to Peter Hopkins, chairman of KPI, and his staff and associates who were helpful and efficient throughout.

Finally I would like to express my gratitude to Jennifer Backman who typed various drafts of the manuscript. Salam-Hameed provided assistance in typing matters.

For the assistance of all these individuals and institutions I am truly grateful, but it should be noted that all errors of analysis, facts, or interpretations are solely mine.

Tawfig Hasou
Al-Ain, United Arab Emirates

Foreword

Hasou's study is essentially about Nasser's policy vis-a-vis the Arab League. To fit the subject of this study in its wider perspective, one has to recall the three levels of political activity. There was the local Egyptian level, the Arab level, and lastly the international level. Locally — that is on the Egyptian level — Nasser was a dictator, using all means of repression at his disposal to crush all forms of opposition. His story with the Muslim Brothers, the Communists, the Egyptian press, and the Egyptian universities speaks for itself. On the Arab level, he used both the Arab League and his enormous propaganda machine to further his domination over the Arab masses. His international role rotated around the invitation of Soviet influence in the area to counter-balance the western influence, but the end result — much to his surprise — was to strengthen both.

Nasser was a charismatic leader. Most writers who studied this period agree with that; whether it be Baker, Dekmejian, Copeland, Dawisha or Lacouture. Any interpretation of this period that does not emphasise this charismatic nature of his leadership might mistakenly view him as an Arab Nationalist, or a Socialist, or for that matter a Communist. Nasser was none of these. He was a 'Blangui', to use Engels. A Blangui is essentially a political revolutionist. He is a 'socialist' only out of sympathy. Nasser was basically a 'man of action', who believed that a small, well-organised minority, acting at the proper moment, could lead the masses. The movement he built in the Arab world was a charismatic one. It had no administrative organs, but was based on an irrational emotional form of communal relationship. Among his followers there was an absence of defined hierarchy, and the staff of his movement were not recruited on the basis of rational requirements, but on the basis of an emotional irrational experience open to all. Even his relationship with the Arab masses was charismatic. A charismatic relationship is one in which A is able to lead B because B believes he has a duty to follow A, as the result of some personal qualities of A. It is not necessary for the observer to accept the validity of the attributed qualities as long as he can see others — in this case, the masses — respond to the charismatic individual as if he has these qualities. Such was the relationship between Nasser and the Arab masses. This charismatic nature of his leadership — in fact — shaped his politics, his views, his actions, and maybe even his conceptual framework.

Having that in mind, one would agree with Hasou's findings about Nasser's endeavours to dominate the Arab League. To Nasser, the Arab League was not a unifying organisation, rather he viewed it as an instrument of Egyptian foreign policy. Hasou's explanation of that is very valid. The author lists several indicators of Egyptian predominance in the League: the highest position in the League, the Secretary-Generalship, was consistently occupied by an Egyptian citizen, the predominance of Egyptian nationals in all ranks of the regional machinery, the substantial Egyptian financial contributions to the League's budget, and the location of the headquarters of the League in Cairo. The cases through which the author shows Nasser's manipulation of this favourable position are several, i.e. Baghdad pact 1955, Lebanon 1958, Syrian complaint 1962 and the Yemeni War 1962-1967. All through, Hasou shows how Nasser effectively used the Arab League to pass resolutions aimed at constraining the policies of rival Arab governments. This study is a valuable addition to the few objective studies devoted towards an understanding of Nasser's policy on the Arab level.

Abdalla F. Alnafeesi

Contents

Appendices

To
the memory of my father

Introduction

International regional organizations are created to serve the interests of the member states. The Arab League, the second oldest continuously existing regional organization of its kind (only the Organization of American States has a longer history), was established in 1945 to serve, in the view of the founding fathers, the interests and aspirations of the Arab people. Prior to its establishment Arab leaders were actively engaged in the affairs and interests of the Arab world as a whole. The talks of Arab unity dominated their interest and activities. But after attempts that were unsuccessful due to rivalries, among other factors, the 'independent' Arab states settled for a lesser plan, namely the Arab League, which they conceived to be a first step towards realizing this unity. The 'special relationship' among the member states, all of them being parts of the Arab nation, has given the League a distinctive character.

Because of internal as well as external factors, as we shall see, the Arab League turned into a regional organization that reflects Arab rivalries, contradictions, and the seemingly endless disputes among the Arab states. Thus the Arab League was rendered ineffective and intrinsically too weak to solve Arab disputes harmoniously. One of the reasons for its weakness is member states' lack of confidence and trust in it because of the widely conceived Egyptian domination of the Arab League. Perhaps every member has voiced this belief at one time or another. This view hardened during the presidency of the former Egyptian president Gamal Abdel-Nasser, whom many accused of using the Arab League as an instrument of Egyptian foreign policy. They argued that President Nasser used the League to influence other Arab states' foreign policies. Indeed their argument is beyond any doubt convincing. Egyptian predominance in that organization made it appealing for Nasser to use the League in his attempts to make other Arab states' foreign policies compatible with those of Egypt's foreign policy objectives. In several specific cases Nasser hoped to bring other Arab states' foreign policies in line with that of Egypt through the Arab League.

Nasser had several main foreign policy goals, but his primary goal was the preservation of Egypt's sovereignty and the enhancement of Egypt's self-respect and prestige under his leadership. Because of his personality and charisma and his appeal to the people, he was able to exercise the primary decision-making power. In handling the Arab masses he possessed and exhibited great skill, and this made him the most effective Arab leader. He was also able to exert influence on other Arab leaders. Initially he believed Egypt's greatest enemies were 'imperialists', who at the time (early 1950s) dominated much of the Arab world, including Egypt, where British civilians and forces were stationed. Also, to undermine his rivals and thus enhance his position among the Arabs, Nasser often said that moderate, pro-Western Arabs were agents of 'imperialism' in the Arab world. To increase his influence in the Arab countries, Nasser during the 1950s repeatedly said that to serve Arab interests (actually his own) he wanted to defeat 'imperialism' and the 'reactionary' (pro-Western) forces in the Arab world. While these two goals were separable, in Nasser's mind they were closely related. The battle against 'imperialism' could not be fought until the fight against 'reactionism' was won, Nasser insisted. To achieve this however, Nasser was forced at times to shift his tactics. In this struggle against the 'reactionary' forces in the Arab world the regional machinery was instrumental in the attempts to advance, cover, and support President Nasser's foreign policy. Actually, his struggle was for Egypt's independence and Egypt's predominant power over the other Arab states. For example, Nasser used Egypt's centrality in the League to pass resolutions aimed at constraining the policies of 'reactionary' and rival Arab countries. Moreover, through the League's secretary-general, Nasser influenced the behaviour of other Arab states in an effort to bring these states' policies into line with that of Egypt.

It is widely believed, as we shall see in this study, that Egypt was the dominant power in the League for many years after it was established in 1945. Between that date and 1979 there were three secretaries-general, all of them Egyptians. Because of its predominant political position, important financial contribution, location, and number of employees in the League, as well as some of its tactics, which included political isolation of other Arab states (i.e. breaking diplomatic relations), President Nasser not only managed to persuade those states to elect whom Egypt wanted for that crucial job, but also often to go along with his initiatives. It is believed that the three Egyptian secretaries-general showed their loyalty to their mother country through their actions. Indeed, the first Arab League secretary-general, Azzam Pasha, put 'the cause and safety' of Egypt ahead of the rest of the Arab countries.

This 'Egypt first' attitude became more evident during Nasser's era. One of the indicators of this attitude was Nasser's perception of the League, which he evidently regarded as an extension of his foreign ministry. Another indication of President Nasser's use of the League to influence other Arab states' foreign policies was through the encouragement and adoption of resolutions concerning inter-Arab relations in the League's assembly. Nasser successfully used Egypt's predominance in the regional machinery to solicit the League's members' support against rival Arab governments, as was the case in 1955 when Egypt succeeded in isolating Iraq from the Arab world as a result of the Baghdad Pact.

The Lebanese case of 1958 was another example of Nasser's use of the League. Lebanon was reluctant to entrust its problem to the Arab League because it recognised that, under the influence of Nasser, the regional body was more inclined to promote than prevent its isolation. In fact when the League's council met at Benghazi, Libya, to consider the Lebanese complaint of outside intervention (Egypt) in Lebanese internal affairs, the council was not eager to respond to Lebanon's insistent pleas for the League to put an end to the alleged Egyptian activities in Lebanon. Ultimately, the League's secretary-general succeeded in having the UN General Assembly adopt a resolution favoured by Cairo, but not necessarily by Lebanon.

Nasser also brought pressure to bear on the Arab states through the League by boycotting the organization itself and by withholding the substantial Egyptian financial contribution to the expenditure of the League. Such policy led to Arab support of Egypt's position, as was the case at the Shtoura meeting in 1962, which met at the request of Syria to look into its complaints against Nasser's alleged interference in Syrian internal affairs. Egypt stood firm in its opposition to the Syrian regime in power at the time until it was toppled and then, to appease Nasser, the Syrian complaint against Egypt was withdrawn from the Arab League.

Finally, unlike the previous cases where Egypt was successful in the League, in the case of the conflict in Yemen Egypt, due to several factors which we shall examine later, could not effectively utilize that body's machinery to serve Egyptian foreign policy ends. However, at the request of Nasser, the League arranged an Arab summit meeting in 1964, mainly to help Egypt extricate itself from the Yemeni war.

In short, the main objective of this study is to show that regional organizations are often used by the major regional powers to advance their foreign policy goals, as the case of Egypt in the League of Arab States during the tenure of President Gamal Abdel-Nasser clearly shows.

In chapters I and II, I shall examine the historic background of the Arab League and consider to what extent Egypt's role was dominant in its creation. I shall examine indicators of Egyptian predominance in that regional organization including the role of the secretary-general, Cairo's financial share in the League's budget, the significance of the League's location and its employees' nationalities, and the influence of Nasser's personality on the League's policies and on the Arab masses and leaders.

Chapter III will be devoted to Egyptian foreign policy goals under President Nasser. I will examine Nasser's role in ending the British presence in Egypt and the manner in which he capitalized on Arab sentiments against the widely mistrusted Western 'imperialism' to serve his own interests, as in the enhancement of Egypt's position in the Arab world. Chapters IV, V, VI, and VII will illustrate how these goals were advanced. These will include an examination of the Iraqi case, 1955; Lebanon, 1958; Syria, 1962; and the Yemeni episode, 1962-67. Although such cases reflect important differences, the League's methods of handling these situations were different in the cases of Iraq and Yemen and similar in the cases of Lebanon and Syria. But overall Cairo sought in the League's meetings to deal with the issues at hand and seek results that were not contrary to Nasser's foreign policy goals.

Finally, I will conclude by seeing how and when the League was effectively used by Nasser; when it was not effectively used; whether the instrumental effectiveness of a regional organization depends on the position of the regional power, or the types of foreign policy goals pursued, or both.

Chapter One

Egypt, the Arab World, and the Arab League: A Historical Overview

The Egyptian connection with the Arab world goes back to ancient times, reinforced by economic and strategic interests. The people of the Middle East were in communication with each other even before it was Arabized, particularly in relations between the ancient Egyptian state and the peoples of Syria and Palestine. The rule of Pharaoh Tuthmosis III (1502–1448 BC) was extended to the banks of the Euphrates in Mesopotamia.[1] The pharaoh made military alliances with various Asian kingdoms. His successors followed similar policies such as the first recorded treaty between two sovereigns which Ramses II concluded with Hattusilis, the Hittite king.[2] The purpose of the treaty was to keep peace and fraternity between the Hittite and Egyptian empires, including a part of south Syria conquered by the Egyptians.[3]

Cultural relations did not commence until the seventh century AD when Muslim Arabs conquered the whole Middle East and Egypt became Arabized and the majority of its population was converted to Islam;[4] the population of Egypt was largely of Christian Copts before the Arab conquest. Egypt's dominance in the Arab empire came about during the Fatimid caliphate in the period 909–1171 AD, in which 'Cairo became the capital, and Egypt the base, of a magnificent civilisation that extended to Syria, Yemen and Hijaz and included the holy cities of Mecca and Medina.'[5] Egypt's hegemony continued until the Ottomans conquered most of the Arab lands, including Egypt, in 1517.[6] The effectiveness of the Ottoman empire continued until an

1

Albanian officer, Muhamad Ali, became the ruler of Egypt in 1805, and his son Ibrahim assumed the governorship of Syria in 1830.[7] Between 1830 and 1840, Muhamad Ali and his son ruled much of the Arab Middle East including Mecca, Medina, Jerusalem, and Damascus. During this period, the idea of Arab revival was born again among the Arab intelligentsia in Syria and Egypt.[8] Moreover, during the Ottoman rule, the North African Arab states became the target of European colonialism. France occupied Algeria in 1830, Tunisia in 1881, and Morocco in 1912; Britain occupied Egypt in 1882; and Italy conquered Libya in 1911.

With the exception of Aden, the Arab Middle East continued to be ruled by the Ottomans until World War I, when the Ottoman empire disintegrated and the modern state of Turkey emerged. Contrary to Allied, particularly British, promises to Sherif Hussein of Hijaz, the British and the French divided the Arab Middle East between them.[9] The Arab nationalist drive against the two Western powers was ineffective. This Arab ineffectiveness was partly due to the Arab weakness and divisions and the Egyptian resort to 'Egyptian nationalism' against the British. For at this time Arabs still were under foreign rule. Indeed, when Shukri al-'Asali, a Syrian nationalist leader, visited Cairo, he did not find any support in Egypt in 1911 for a call for the unity of Syria and Egypt. Sa'ad Zaghlul, an Egyptian nationalist, told Arab leaders who approached him in 1919 with the idea of uniting their efforts in the Paris Peace Conference, that 'our case is an Egyptian and not an Arab one.'[10] In other words, though Egypt, by and large, is an Arab country in terms of language, history, and religion, yet it has its own distinct character. Unlike other Arab lands, Egyptian civilization is several thousands years old. The Egyptian identity of *Iglimiyyah* (Egyptian nationalism) seems to come ahead of Egyptian Arab *Qawmiyyah* (pan-Arabism).

None the less Egypt continued its involvement in Arab affairs. Egypt had become the centre of several pan-Arab societies. Moreover, prior to World War I and afterwards, it 'led the Arab intellectual awakening. Egyptian printing presses, periodicals, schools, radio and cinema greatly contributed to this revival. Its impact was not immediately felt, but gradually led to an Arab cultural and political awakening in which Egypt played a leading role.'[11] For example, in 1909, 1910, and 1912, three secret Arab societies were established in Egypt.[12]

Such societies led to closer associations between Egypt and the rest of the Arab world. Sayed Nofal wrote that the Egyptian revolution of

1919 attracted attention and support from the rest of the Arab states. So did the Iraqi revolution of 1921, and the Syrian revolution of 1925, as well as other Arab national movements.[13] This feeling of closeness among the Arab states continued throughout the 1930s. Arab attitudes became, more than ever before, oriented toward 'Arab unity', at least in rhetoric. In 1931 at a pan-Arab conference in Jerusalem, an Arab covenant was drawn up by Arab nationalist figures 'as a guide post for future unity'. Article I of the covenant declared: 'The Arab lands are a complete and indivisible whole, and the divisions of whatever nature to which they have been subjected are not approved or recognized by the Arab nation.' Moreover, the Arab leaders pledged themselves to concentrate their efforts 'towards the single goal of their complete independence.'[14] Furthermore, in 1936 a treaty of brotherhood and alliance between Iraq and Saudi Arabia was signed, and a similar treaty between Saudi Arabia and Egypt was also signed in the same year during which the king of Egypt 'stressed the need for consolidating relations with the "sister" Arab countries.'[15]

During the 1930s the incursion of Zionism in Palestine worried the Arab nationalist leaders. For example, in response to Zionism the Arab Company to Save the Palestinian Land was created; Egypt increased its involvement in its northern neighbour's affairs; and the Palestine revolt broke out in 1936 — a revolt which was accentuated by the contiguity of Palestine to Egypt and by the belief that the Arab cause there merited support both on Arab and on Islamic grounds.[16] Also a higher committee for the relief of the Palestine victims was formed late in 1936, including prominent Egyptians, like Hasan al-Banna and Dr Muhammad Hussein Haykal. The Palestinian issue became an Egyptian domestic issue as, for example, Mustafa Nahas championed the Arab cause and Nahas Pasha, the leader of the Wafd party, was interested in Arab unity as far as it could serve Egyptian interests. Nahas favoured the promotion of economic and cultural inter-Arab relations as he believed that such relations if successful could lead to 'political co-operation' by which each country retained its political identity in accordance with its special circumstances and needs.[17]

On the foreign relations level, in 1937 the Egyptian prime minister emphasized in the League of Nations 'that because of neighbourhood, history, language and civilization, Egypt is concerned about the Palestine Cause.'[18] Furthermore, in 1938 an Egyptian parliamentary committee called for an Arab parliament conference, which was held in Cairo and discussed the Palestine question.[19] Until World War II similar Arab conferences continued to be held, mostly in Cairo.[20] Britain, a major party involved in the issue, called the Arab 'governments' for a conference, which was held in London in February 1939, to discuss Palestine. The conference ended in failure.[21] By the time World War II broke out, there were anti-British movements in the Arab world like Ali Maher's government in Cairo, which refused to enter the war on the side of the Allies, and Rashid Ali al-Kaillany's movement of 1941 in Iraq.

By the early 1940s, the Egyptian intelligentsia became more outspoken in favour of the 'Arab idea'. A prominent Egyptian, Fuad Abadah, organized *al-Ittihad al-'arabi* (the Arab Union) in 1942. *Al-Ittihad* called for closer relations among the Arabic-speaking people. Its members included prominent intellectual and political leaders. Nahas Pasha, then prime minister of Egypt, wrote to the Union's president in 1943 that 'the government takes great interest in the affairs of the sister-Arab-nations, and is always ready to defend their interests and rights. It also views with great interest the question of Arab unity.'[22] Nahas was not alone in his 'interest' in Arab unity. Other Arab leaders were also interested in some form of an Arab union. Indeed, the Arab sense of belonging to one nation and to one destiny led to the creation of the League of Arab States in 1945.[23] The establishment of the League in 1945 has been the nearest approximation to the Arab quest for unity.

Britain's Role in Creating the Arab League

At the outbreak of World War II the Arab world was mostly under foreign rule. The Arab nationalist leaders attempted to defend the Arab cause by reuniting into political parties calling for the end of colonialism. Allied forces, particularly the British, tried to win the Arabs to their side and promised them independence after victory. Anthony Eden, the British foreign minister, declared to the House of Commons on 6 May 1941, and again in an address at the Mansion House on 29 May 1941, his support of the Arab people in achieving their unity through the institution of a body that looked after their interests and tightened their ties. Britain claimed that Arab strength and friendly relations with London were crucial to the interests of Britain because of the Suez Canal, Middle East oil, and the threat of Soviet infiltration. The British saw Russia as 'coming right across the throat of the British Commonwealth' and Arab unity appeared to aid

Britain against Soviet advances in that region.[24] Moreover, Britain's interests were threatened by the growing influence of the Axis powers and by the Arab nationalist movements, such as that of al-Kaillany of Iraq in 1941 which was directed against the British.[25] Furthermore, Britain saw the French as rival in the area and wished to get them out of Syria and Lebanon. The best way to accomplish these goals was through regaining Arab friendship. Great Britain was soon to announce its support of Arab unity.[26] Such a gesture first came in Eden's speech at Mansion House in which he said:

> The Arab world has made great strides since the settlement reached at the end of the last war, and many Arab thinkers desire for the Arab peoples a greater degree of unity than they now enjoy. In reaching out towards this unity they hope for support. No such appeal from our friends should go unanswered. It seems to me both natural and right that the cultural, and economic ties, too, should be strengthened. His Majesty's Government for their part will give their full support to any scheme that commands general approval.[27]

Eden reiterated these assurances throughout 1942 and in 1943.[28]

The Greater Syria Plan

British signals were welcomed by a number of Arab leaders. The Hashemite dynasties of Trans-Jordan and Iraq hailed the idea of unity. The ambitions of King Abdallah of Jordan to rule a reunified Trans-Jordan-Syria, Lebanon and Palestine had been known since the 1920s. The British support for Arab co-operation encouraged the king to be more vigorous in his quest for Greater Syrian unity; he was the first Arab leader to respond to Eden's statement on May 1941. On 1 July 1941, the cabinet of the prime minister of Jordan, Tawfiq abul-Huda, passed a resolution calling for the reunification of Greater Syria.[29] In April 1943 the king called on the Syrian leaders to help him to achieve his aim, while criticizing those who charged that he was looking after his own interests.[30] Nevertheless King Abdallah's efforts proved to be fruitless — the Syrians suspected his motives and argued that Abdallah's kingdom should be annexed to the Syrian republic since it had been a Syrian province during the Ottoman empire.[31]

The Fertile Crescent Scheme

Iraq had been one of the most active exponents of Arab unity since the end of World War I. Having attained its independence in 1932, Iraq became a centre of pan-Arab agitation. Eden's statements of the early 1940s were welcomed in Baghdad and Prime Minister Nuri al-Sa'id concentrated on creating an Arab League in which Iraq would be the leader. Al-Sa'id preferred a Fertile Crescent project,[32] calling for the reunification of Syria, Lebanon, Palestine and Trans-Jordan, into a Greater Syria, and for its union with Iraq in an 'Arab League'. In 1942 Nuri al-Sa'id forwarded his famous 'Blue Book' to Richard Casey, then British minister of state in Cairo; this 'Blue Book' embodied his scheme for Fertile Crescent unity. The Iraqi prime minister's plan was to have a permanent council nominated by member states and responsible for defence, foreign affairs, currency controls, communications, customs, education, and the protection of minority rights.[33] Nuri's scheme excluded the countries of the Arabian Peninsula and Egypt. The Arab League envisaged by the Iraqi prime minister failed, however, 'largely' because of Egyptian opposition, and because of the objections of Arab nationalists[34] like Shukri al-Quwatli who reportedly said, 'Syria will never allow a flag higher than her own to be raised in her sky, save that of Arab Unity.'[35] Thus, Nuri's plan suffered a similar fate to that of King Abdallah's.

Egypt and the Creation of the League of Arab States

Britain believed that Egyptian participation in an Arab League was essential. Egypt was the wealthiest, most populous, technologically most advanced, and on the whole the most powerful of the Arab states. In terms of location and culture, Egypt was a bridge between Western Europe and the Arab world. Since Egypt was still ruled by Britain it could serve British interest better than any other Arab state.[36] Even though King Abdallah and Prime Minister Nuri al-Sa'id were under the influence of Britain, London did not favour their schemes and instead encouraged Egypt to take the lead with British blessing.

It was generally conceived that Egypt had little, if any, interest in pan-Arabism. However, Cairo took the lead in the projected Arab League, 'because it [was] conscious of the immense tangible advantages to be gained, especially if Egypt itself should become the leader of a block of Arab countries whose prestige would be enhanced at the peace conference as well as in any future international organization in which the Arab countries will take part.'[37]

Mustafa Nahas, a British friend and the leader of the Wafd party who was made prime minister in 1942, was very supportive of the Arab cause in Syria and Palestine. He started his exploratory talks with the Arab leaders immediately after he became prime minister, as evidenced by his talks with several Syrian and Lebanese leaders.[38]

On 30 March 1943 Sabri Abu Alam Pasha, minister of justice, on behalf of Prime Minister Mustafa Nahas Pasha, stated the position of the Egyptian government on Arab unity as follows:

I have been long ago interested in the affairs of the Arab countries and in the cöoperation for the realization of their aspirations towards independence and freedom . . . In this respect I have been able to reach some successful steps; one of them was that the system of government in certain Arab countries has been modified in order to fulfil their real national aspirations.

Ever since Mr. Eden had made his declaration I have given [the problem of Arab unity] my consideration; and I thought that the matter should be undertaken by the official Arab Governments themselves. I came to the conclusion that it would be better if the Egyptian Government itself should take the initial official steps in this respect. First, the opinions of each Arab Government would be sounded as to what would be its aspirations. Then [the Egyptian Government] would endeavour to bring together and reconcile the various opinions as much as possible. [The Egyptian Government] will then proceed to invite [the Arab Governments] to a friendly meeting in Egypt in order that the movement towards Arab unity would proceed to an effective agreement. Should such an agreement be reached, a conference will then be called in Egypt, presided over by the head of the Egyptian Government, in order to continue discussions of the subject and to make certain proposals for the realization of the objects aimed at by the Arab countries. These are the best possible steps to be taken in order that the scheme would be successful.

Last Saturday I discussed the matter with His Excellency

Tahsin bey Al-Askari, Iraq's Minister of Interior, and His
Excellency Jmil bey al-Midfai . . . Moreover, I sent an
official invitation to His Excellency Nuri al-Sa'id Pasha,
Prime Minister of Iraq, who, should he agree with this
procedure, will study the matter from the Iraqi point of view
politically, economically, and socially, but especially from
the political point of view. Then I shall send invitations to
the various Arab Governments to send their representatives
to Egypt in order to sound out their views respectively on
the same subject.

When such preparatory discussions have been completed
and, I hope, will have been successful, the Egyptian
Government will then invite [the Arab Governments] to a
conference to be held in Egypt.[39]

On the recommendations of Great Britain[40] Prime Minister Nahas
Pasha began at once to carry out his proposed plan. He asked the
various Arab governments to send their representatives to Cairo. He
opened his discussion with Nuri al-Sa'id of Iraq in July and August
1943, with Tawfiq abul-Huda of Trans-Jordan in August and
September, with Yousef Yassin, personal representative of the king of
Saudi Arabia, in October, with Sa'adallah Jabri, prime minister of
Syria, in October and November, with Riad al-Sulh, prime minister of
Lebanon, in January 1944, and with Sayed Hussein al-Kibsi,
representative of the imam of Yemen, in February.[41]

Nuri and Nahas agreed on co-operation among the Arab states for
the sake of 'unity', provided that each state retained its sovereignty.[42]
Nuri characterized his talks with the Egyptian prime minister as
merely 'an exchange of personal views on the project'.[43] His views
merely repeated what he announced earlier in his famous 'Blue Book'
(see under the Fertile Crescent Scheme). Despite Nuri's statement
playing down the talks, Nahas' views, as we shall see later, prevailed
over those of the Iraqi leader.[44]

Tawfiq abul-Huda's talks in Cairo were similar to those of Nuri. He
simply reiterated King Abdallah's plan for Greater Syria. However,
abul-Huda agreed with Nahas on 'general lines' for an 'Arab union'.[45]
Sheik Yousef Yassin, the Saudi representative, in his talks with
Nahas, expressed reservations towards the Hashemite projects. The
Syrian delegation to Cairo expressed similar views to those of Saudi
Arabia. However, Prime Minister Sa'adallah al-Jabri let it be known
that Syria stood for 'full Arab union', and that, as noted earlier, it

would 'refuse to have raised in her sky any flag higher than her own, save that of an Arab union.'[46]

Riad al-Sulh, the Lebanese prime minister, did not support the idea of 'full Arab unity', but expressed his intention to co-operate with the rest of the Arab states for the establishment of an Arab League.[47] The Yemeni representative, Sayed Hussein al-Kibsi, expressed his government's interest in being only an observer in the projected Arab League; he 'hardly contributed any positive plan to the scheme of Arab unity.'[48]

Arab leaders' conversations in Cairo led to the general consensus that the Egyptian prime minister, Mustafa Nahas, would call for an Arab conference. On 12 July 1944, in answer to a question raised in the Egyptian senate, Nahas declared:

> I am still immensely interested in the project of Arab Unity
> and any efforts in a liaison capacity for its success
> continue . . . I have recently written to the governments of
> Iraq, Transjordan, Saudi Arabia, Syria, the Lebanon, and
> Yemen, notifying them of the formation of a Preparatory
> Committee to record the views agreed upon in our
> preliminary meetings, to complete any investigation required
> on any particular subject, and to prepare for a general Arab
> Conference . . ..[49]

At this stage in the process of consultation, the Arab states, particularly Syria, Lebanon, and Saudi Arabia, consented to Egyptian leadership of the Arab countries. Thus, Mustafa Nahas summoned the Arab leaders to Alexandria for his proposed conference, 'officially identifying Egypt's definite decision' with the rest of the pan-Arabists.[50]

On 25 September 1944 Nahas presided over and opened a preparatory committee of the plenary Arab conference at the Antoniades Palace in Alexandria. In addition to the Arab states who participated in the initial conversations, Musa el-Alami, a representative from Palestine, attended the meeting as equal member with the rest of the delegates. Nahas opened the conference in a speech in which he called on the delegates to work out a general scheme of unity acceptable to all particpants.[51] The delegates were to discuss the kind of structural organization that would be established.

The participants, particularly Syria, Lebanon, Trans-Jordan and Iraq, reiterated their previous positions. The new participant, el-

Alami of Palestine, stressed the gravity of the situation in Palestine owing to Zionist activities there, and asked that Palestine be a trust of the Arab world.[52] Nahas' active role helped to clarify and crystalize delegates' views and succeeded in bringing them closer to Egypt's stand. The participants agreed:

1   to reject full union and central government under the existing circumstances;
2   to recognize the independence of Lebanon within its present border;
3   to drop the Greater Syria and Fertile Crescent schemes.[53]

The Egyptian position was that each of the states would retain its sovereignty. The majority rule would apply to matters relating to defence, foreign policy, and settlement of disputes. Resolutions of the proposed organization should be binding only when voting was unanimous.[54] Egypt saw majority rule as 'an unavoidable necessity' to get the general Arab consensus. It saw that 'the unanimous adoption of resolutions on all issues would impede the work of the Council and would not help in realizing the objectives of the organization and fulfilment of the obligations and principles upon which it was founded.'[55] Egyptian proposals indicated that it was taking a middle position between those who wanted a full union and those who preferred to maintain their dynastic privileges. It was believed that such a middle course would give Cairo more freedom of action within the proposed organization, and, thus, put Egypt in a position where it could serve its own interest rather than be tied down with a full union where it could not act towards its goals. When it became certain that Egyptian leadership was accepted by the rest of the Arab countries, and that Cairo would be the headquarters of the new organization, Nahas declared Egyptian acceptance of the discussed 'protocol' and proclaimed the establishment of the Arab League in October 1944.[56]

The preparatory discussion led to the adoption of those proposals which were generally accepted by the participants. The conference, accordingly, decided to establish a League of Arab States, composed of the independent Arab countries. Binding procedures for settling disputes were to be established, and arbitration before the League council was to be voluntary.[57]

On 7 October 1944 the preparatory committee ended its meetings by agreeing on what came to be known as the 'Alexandria Protocol', which formulated the aims and proposed constitution of the League of Arab States which was entrusted to a subcommittee.[58] The proposed

League was to have a council which would meet periodically to implement agreements reached by the states among themselves, to co-ordinate their political plans, and 'generally to watch over the affairs and interests of the Arab peoples'. Council decisions 'were to be binding upon those states which accepted them, except in cases where conflict had arisen between two member states, which would then have to accept the Council's decisions'. Member states were free to conclude special agreements with a member state or with other powers, provided that such agreements did not contradict the text or spirit of the pact of the League. However, the protocol stated firmly that 'In no case will the adoption of a foreign policy which may be prejudicial to the policy of the League or an individual member state be allowed.' It also provided for close co-operation between member states on economic, cultural, and social matters, and recommended the setting up of commissions of experts in each field to elaborate programmes of joint action.

Two special annexes of the protocol dealt with Lebanon and Palestine. The independence and sovereignty of Lebanon within its present borders was to be respected by the other Arab states. The second declared Arab solidarity with Palestine and pledged full support to the Palestinian people.

A formal Arab conference met in Cairo and signed the pact of the Arab League on 22 March 1945 (see Appendix A). The original members were Egypt, Saudi Arabia, Syria, Iraq, Lebanon, Yemen, Trans-Jordan,[59] and a representative for the Palestinians. It should be noted, however, that the legal status of some of these original states, was either only *de facto* independent or not independent at all. This would explain their reluctance during the preparatory conversations to give up their sovereignty and independence in favour of a full union with a central authority.[60] Instead, the conferees agreed to establish a barely loose association for the agreed purpose of 'strengthening bonds of friendship between the members and the co-ordination of their political action with the object of safeguarding their independence.'

Originally, the Arab League comprised three categories of bodies: the council, the specialized commission, and the general secretariat, the last comprised of a secretary-general, assistants, and other officials. The League's headquarters, as mentioned earlier, was to be in Cairo. The council of the League, however, was the supreme body of the organization. Thus, as noted above, the original members exercised great caution to avoid imposing binding commitments on the members. As an outcome of such consensus, members were free to withdraw at any time. Each state had one vote. The League was made up of a council composed of the representatives of the member states. The council was to have no army or police force, nor any means of making its decisions obligatory for a state. Article 7 of the pact stated that 'unanimous decisions of the Council shall be binding upon all member states of the League; majority decisions shall be binding only upon those states which have accepted them.' In other words, each member state was always free to act according to its *own will* and *interest* and was not obligated to follow the majority rule.[61]

However, the council was entrusted with the task of achieving the goals of the new organization. The League aimed at close co-operation of the member states in economic and financial matters, communications, cultural affairs, matters connected with nationality, and travel, social welfare issues and health matters. A special committee was to be created for each of the above areas to deal with issues of concern, as article 4 states.[62]

The provisions outlawed resort to force for the settlement of disputes between member states, and the council was to deal with any dispute that might arise between one member and another. The Council decision was to be obligatory except in matters involving the sovereignty, independence, or territorial integrity of the members. Any threatened state had the right to request the Council to take the necessary steps to repel the aggression.

Although the idea for the Arab League was a brain-child of the British, the above analysis shows that Egypt played the leading role in creating the League of Arab States. According to one observer, the Arab League 'was conceived in 1943, not in amity, but in a contest of wills and struggle for prestige between the then Prime Ministers of Iraq and Egypt, Nuri Pasha al-Sa'id and Mustafa Pasha al-Nahas.'[63] Egypt was in favour of a loose organization in order to serve its interests best. 'In the outcome', wrote Cecil Hourani, 'the Arab League was formed, not as Nuri al-Sa'id had at first envisaged it, but on a more general and looser pattern, and with Egypt taking the lead.'[64] Egypt exploited the rivalries among the other Arab states to establish its own domination of the League through its charter. Egypt has used the League to serve its interests since its early days, or to put it differently, it has treated the League 'virtually from the start as an instrument of her national policy'.[65]

Notes to chapter one

1 A. I. Dawisha, *Egypt in the Arab World, the Elements of Foreign Policy*, London, Macmillan, 1976, p. 1.
2 B. Y. Boutros-Ghali, 'The Arab League 1945–1955', *International Conciliation*, no. 498 (May 1954), p. 387.
3 See Muhamad Hafiz Ghanim, *Lectures on the League of Arab States*, (in Arabic) Cairo, Institute of Higher Arabic Studies, 1960, p. 28; see also Philip K. Hitti, *A Short History of the Near East*, London, Van Nostrand, 1966.
4 Boutros-Ghali, p. 387.
5 Dawisha, p. 2.
6 Ibid.
7 Boutros-Ghali, p. 388; see also, Ahmad M. Gom'a, *The Foundation of the League of Arab States: Wartime Diplomacy and Inter-Arab Politics 1941–1945*, London, New York, Longman, 1977, p. 30.
8 Bernard D. Weinryb, 'The Arab League: Tool or Power?', *Commentary*, vol. 1, no. 5 (March 1946), pp. 50–57.
9 See Ghanim, pp. 29–31.
10 Gom'a, p. 31.
11 Anwar Chejne, 'Egyptian Attitudes toward Pan-Arabism', *Middle East Journal*, Vol. 11, no. 3 (summer, 1957), p. 256.
12 Mahmoud Kamel, *al-Dawlah al-Arabiyyah al-Kubra* (The Great Arab State), Cairo, Dar al-Ma'arif, 1967, p. 425.
13 Sayed Nofal, *al-'Amal al-Arabi al-Mushtark* (The Joint Arab Activities), book I, Cairo, Ma'had al-Bihouth wal-Dirasat al-Arabiyyeh, 1968, p. 40; see also Gom'a, p. 33.
14 Paul Seabury, 'The League of Arab States: Debacle of a Regional Arrangement', *International Organization*, vol. 3, no. 4 (November 1949), p. 635.
15 Ibid. See also Gom'a, p. 36.
16 Ibid. See also Nofal, pp. 40–41.
17 Gom'a, p. 49.
18 Nofal, p. 41.
19 Ibid., p. 42. Mohamed Amarah, *al-Aummah al-Arabiyyeh Wa-Qadiatt, al-Tawhid* (The Arab Nation and the Unity Issue), Cairo, Dar-al-'Ahd aljadid, 1966, p. 16. See also *al-Ahram*, 21 July 1977, p. 7.
20 Nofal, pp. 41–42, and Amarah, pp. 16–18.
21 Ibid.
22 Chejne, *op. cit.*, p. 258.
23 Boutros-Ghali contends that it is a mistake to consider that the 'Arab

State' is based on a racist concept. Indeed, he said, if the Arabs can be counted, pure Arabs are no more than 10 per cent and the remaining 90 per cent are simply 'Arabized', or Arabic-speaking, Berbers, Copts, Nubians, a mosaic of races fashioned in the Arab melting pot. 'Arabism' is based on the concept of an open society. Boutros Boutros-Ghali, 'The Arab League 1945–1970', *Revue Egyptienne de Droit International*, vol. 25 1969, p. 70.

24   Weinryb, p. 51; see also Sidney B. Fay, 'Egypt and the Arab League', *Current History* (August 1947), p. 84.

25   Ahmad Farid Ali, *al-Jami'ah al-Arabiyyeh Bien al-Qowa al-Rij'iyyah wa al-Qowa al-Sha'biyyah* (The Arab League Between the Reactionary Forces and the Popular Forces), Cairo, al-Moassasah al-Misriyyah al-'Amah, 1972, p. 22.

26   Ghanim pp. 34–35; Ali, p. 23.

27   Hussein Hassouna, *The League of Arab States and Regional Disputes: A Study of Middle East Conflicts*, Dobbs Ferry, N. Y., Oceana, 1975, p. 4; Fay, p. 84.

28   Nofal, pp. 58–59; Ali, p. 25; Fayez A. Sayegh, *Arab Unity*, New York, Devin-Adair, 1958, p. 119; Muhamed Abdul Aziz, 'The Origin and Birth of the Arab League', *Revue Egyptienne de Droit International*, vol. 11 (1955), pp. 48–51; Sami Hakim, *Mithaq al-jam'ah wal wihdah al-'Arabiyyeh* (The League Pact and the Arab Unity), Cairo, al-Matba'ah al-Fanniyyah al-Hadithah, 1966, p. 17; Vernon McKay, 'The Arab League in World Politics', *Foreign Policy Reports*, vol. XXII, no. 17 (15 November 1946), pp. 208–09.

29   Hakim, p. 11.

30   *King Abdallah Ibn al-Hussein Memoire*, Beirut, n.p., 1965.

31   Majid Khadduri, 'Toward an Arab Union: The League of Arab States', *American Political Science Review*, vol. 40, no. 1 (February 1946), pp. 96–97. King Hussein of Jordan contends that his grandfather, King Abdallah, 'was particularly grieved by the partitioning of natural Syria, in consequence of the Sykes-Picot Agreement [which was agreed upon secretly at the time by France and Britain in 1916], which vivisected natural Syria into zones of mandates and influence between France and Britain. King Abdallah's adversaries, in their relentless and unabashedly self-seeking efforts to abort his efforts toward restoring the God-created and timeless unity and territorial integrity of Syria, tried to denigrate his endeavors by distortive descriptions such as the "Greater Syria plan", to connote the idea of aggrandizement'. *(Middle East Journal*, vol. 32, no. 1 (winter, 1978), p. 80)

32   Khadduri, *op. cit.*, p. 92; Hassouna, p. 5; Ali, pp. 28–29.

33   Hakim, pp. 15–16; Fayez A. Sayegh, *op. cit.* p. 118; Robert W. MacDonald, *The League of Arab States*, Princeton, N. J., Princeton University Press, 1965, p. 35.

34   Boutros-Ghali, 'The Arab League 1945–1955', p. 389; Cecil A. Hourani, 'The Arab League in Perspective', *Middle East Journal*, 1, no. 2 (April 1947), pp. 128–29.

35   Majid Khadduri, *Independent Iraq*, London, New York, Oxford University Press, 1951, p. 254, quoted in Aziz, p. 53.

36   Ali, pp. 29–30; John Marlowe, *A History of Modern Egypt and Anglo-Egyptian Relations 1800–1956*, Hamden, Conn., Archon Books, 2nd edn, 1965, p. 322.

37   Khadduri, *op. cit.*, pp. 92–93.

38   Ibid. Gom'a, p. 153.

39   Khadduri, *op. cit.*, p. 93. See also *Muthakarat Abdel-Rahman Azzam*, Cairo, Matba't Al-Ahram al-Tijariyyeh, 1977, pp. 262–63.

40   *Muthakarat Abdel-Rahman Azzam*, p. 263.

41   For detailed discussion of the Cairo conversations see Hakim, pp. 15–32.

42   Nofal, p. 60.

43   Khadduri, *op. cit.*, p. 94.

44   Habib Jamati, '*Wiladat Wa-Nommo al-Jam'ah al-Arabiyyeh*', (The Birth and Growth of the Arab League), *al-Mussawar*, (March 1964), pp. 47–51.

45   Ibid.; Khadduri, *op. cit.*, p. 94; Nofal, p. 61.

46   Ibid.; Khadduri, *op. cit.*, p. 95; Nofal, p. 62.

47   Ibid.

48   Ibid.

49   Khadduri, *op. cit.*, pp. 95–96.

50   Ezzeldin Foda, *The Projected Arab Court of Justice*, The Hague, Martinus Nijhoff, 1957, p. 6.

51   Hassouna, p. 5.

52   Khadduri, *op. cit.*, p. 97.

53   Nofal, pp. 63–64.

54   Hassouna, pp. 6–7.

55   Foda, p. 9.

56   Fikri Abada, '*Jam'at al-Dowal al-Arabiyyeh*', (The League of Arab States), *al-Mussawar*, (March 1964), p. 6.

57   Hassouna, p. 7.

58   Fayez A. Sayegh, *op. cit.*, p. 120.

59   Today, in addition to the original members, the following states have joined the Arab League: Libya (28 March 1953); Sudan (19 January 1956); Tunisia (1 October 1958); Morocco (1 October 1958); Kuwait (20 July 1961); Algeria (16 August 1962); South Yemen (12 December 1967); Bahrain (11 September, 1971); Qatar (11 September 1971); Oman (29 September 1971); United Arab Emirates (6 December 1971); Mauritania (26 November 1973); Somalia (14 February 1974); Palestine (9 September 1976); Djibouti (4 September 1977).

60   Hassouna, p. 16; Ismail Maglad,'*Al-Jam'ah al-Arabiyyeh*' (The Arab League), *al-Ahram el-Iqtisadi*, no. 543 (1 April 1978), p. 64.

61   Weinryb, p. 54; Nofal, *al-'Amal al-Arabi al-Mushtarak*, (The Joint Arab Activities) book II, (Cairo: Ma'had al-Bihouth Wal-Dirasat al-Arabiyyeh, 1971) p. 111; Fayez A. Sayegh, *op. cit.* p. 123.

62   Khadduri, *op. cit.*, p. 98; Muhammad Khalil, *The Arab States and the Arab League*, vol. II, Beirut, Khayats, (1962), pp. 57–59. For significant differences between the 'Alexandria Protocol' and the League's Pact see Cecil A. Hourani, pp. 132–33; Mahmoud Kamel, *Mithaq al-Jam'ah*, pp. 334–35.

63   A. D., 'The Arab League: Development and Difficulties', *World Today* (May 1951), p. 188.

64   Cecil A. Hourani, p. 129.

65   A. D., pp. 188–89.

Chapter Two

Indicators of Egyptian Predominance in the League of Arab States

Egyptian predominance in the Arab League was evident since the establishment of that organization. There are several indicators of Egyptian predominance, including Cairo's long-running monopoly of the office of secretary-general; it substantial financial contribution to the League's budget; the location of the Arab League headquarters in Cairo and the predominance of Egyptian employees; and, finally, President Nasser's personality which influenced the attitudes and orientation of the League's policies.

The Secretary-General and Secretariat

Article 12 of the League of Arab States declared in part that:

> ... the League shall have a permanent Secretariat-General,[1] consisting of a Secretary-General, Assistant Secretaries, and an appropriate staff of officials.
>
> The League Council shall appoint the Secretary-General by a majority of two-thirds of the states of the League. The Secretary-General, with the approval of the Council, shall appoint the Assistant Secretaries and the principal officials of the League.[2]

The influence of Egypt and the secretary-general in the Arab League is apparent from the start. Article 15 of the League's pact states that: 'The Council shall be convened in the first occasion at the instance of the Head of the Egyptian Government, and subsequently, at the instance of the Secretary-General.' In theory the pact does state that the Secretary-General shall be a servant for all Arab states.

Let us first look at the secretaries in other international organizations. International organizations tend to be, by and large, international. Inis Claude, an authority on international organizations, wrote that members may control an organization, but the staff is the organization: 'The Secretariat is the major organ that best expresses the permanence and vitality of the whole, as distinguished from its parts. In international organization, the member states are "organized", but the staff is the "international" component.'[3] He adds that in international organization, 'the secretariat may be conceived in the dual role of staff and executive, with the Secretary-General serving as chief bureaucrat and prime minister, but this is an anomalous and delicate position; as one commentator has put it, the secretary-general of the League had to try to get his budget "voted by a parliament where everyone belonged to the opposition".'[4] In the case of the League of Nations, 'the members of the Secretariat, once appointed, are no longer the servants of the country of which they are citizens, but become, for the time being, servants only of the League of Nations. Their duties are not national but international': members of the secretariat 'pledge "to discharge their functions, and to regulate their conduct with the interests of the League alone in view," and binding them not to "seek or receive instructions from any Government or other authority external to the Secretariat of the League of Nations."'[5] Were these pledges carried out?

> Experience shows that a spirit of international loyalty among public servants can be maintained in practice. It shows also that maintenance of such spirit is an essential factor in the activity of an international service, since this alone can ensure to it that confidence without which it cannot function as it ought . . . National interests must be represented and defended, of course, but representation (in the diplomatic sense) and defence should not be the function of secretariat officials.[6]

In the case of the United Nations, the picture, to some extent, is different from that of the League of Nations. The major member seems to enjoy influence over the secretariat. For example, at the urging of the USA, the first secretary-general of the UN eliminated suspected American Communist officials working at the UN secretariat. The action by the secretary-general to satisfy Washington

> has weakened the capacity of secretariat heads to resist the proposition that the international employment of any person who fails to meet the standards of political allegiance defined by his own government is of doubtful propriety, thus impeding the full realization of the ideal international civil service immunized against national pressures and autonomously devoted to international functions.[7]

The Arab League seemed to be an organization dominated by the major member, namely Egypt. The secretariat-general, 'the centre of gravity' of the League, was, by and large, run by Egyptians. The staff were largely citizens of Egypt, as we shall see later. The most important job, secretary-general, was held by an Egyptian.

The highest position in the Arab League is that of the secretary-general. Although the duties of the secretary-general are of an administrative and financial nature, none the less he plays a very significant role in the policies of the League. Through his position he can exert considerable influence on the member states in the interest of his mother country.

The pact did not specify the secretary-general's duties except those of an administrative and financial nature. However, history shows that he enjoyed considerable freedom to act on his own, particularly in important cases. Political initiatives of the first two secretaries-general of the League in inter-Arab relations were very significant. According to the pact, the secretary-general prepares the council's agenda, and presents a report on the secretariats to every session. He brings members' attention to any political issue he might deem necessary; he attends the council's meetings.[8]

By a two-thirds majority, the council appoints the secretary-general. With the council's approval, he appoints the undersecretaries-general and other top officials. To be selected the secretary-general has to be a distinguished Arab personality who has held high positions in his native country.[9] The Egyptian nationality of the candidates for secretary-general played a fundamental role in their selection.[10]

To guarantee the secretary-general's allegiance to the League and not to any particular country, the following should be noted:

1 He has to make an oral oath of allegiance to the League in the presence of the League's council: 'I swear to be faithful to the League of Arab States and to carry out my duties in trust and honesty.'[11]

2 He should not request or receive instructions from any government or authority except the League when carrying out his official duties. He should not bow to any pressure or outside influence, and he should refuse to receive any orders from his native government or from any other government in the course of his work in the League. He should not implement policies of any governmental authorities in any state and should make the necessary decisions in an independent way.

3 He should be similar to a judge — patient and neutral in relation to the facts. He should not expect all member states to agree with his decisions. And he should put his self-interest at the service of the interest of the League.[12]

These comments indicate theoretically and legally the duties, character, and allegiance of the secretary-general of the Arab League in accordance with the pact. But what about the practice? Does the secretary-general actually live up to the spirit of his organization's constitution? It is very difficult to dissociate a person from his native land. One commentator states that it is not necessary for the secretary-general to discontinue his connection with his state or to suspend his allegiance to it; the League is not a state above its member states and his appointment in the League's system cannot restrict his inherited allegiance to his native country.[13]

The relationship between the secretary-general and his native country has two sides. First, the emotional and moral attachment to his country cannot be ignored. What strengthens his emotions is that the secretary-general is a citizen of the country where the League is located, where he will work and live his private life, as was the case of the first two secretaries-general. Second, his appointment in the League does not void his status as a citizen, rather it discontinues some of his rights and duties; he enjoys diplomatic treatment and privileges in accordance with the pact and its internal regulations. Except for these privileges, he has to observe his country's laws. For example, some of the agricultural, commercial, and financial laws announced by the Egyptian government after the 1952 revolution were applied to the second secretary-general, Hassouna.[14]

Members of the Arab League were aware of these facts. Some of them criticized the secretary-general's allegiance to Egypt first. King

Abdallah of Jordan, for example, observed that Abdel-Rahman Azzam, 'would not hesitate in destroying anything facing him, even his son, for the safety of Egypt.'[15] Azzam, who before and during his years at the League was a staunch pan-Arabist, admitted after he was forced to resign, that he was an Egyptian first: 'We are Egyptian first, Arabs second, and Muslims third.' He added that:

> I do not deny, and no one denies, that Egypt is the first nursery of mankind. God singled it out above all other nations. This is a characteristic of Egypt, and this is what always made of Egypt the shining place of the world. For here in Cairo, if we are angered, the whole world is angered. If we are contented, mankind from all shades of color or ideology — whether they are the negroes of Africa, or the white people of the North, whether they are Muslims or Christians, whether they respect our culture or are opposed to our ancient thousands of years old — is also contented.[16]

Azzam, who before becoming the first secretary-general, was a devoted pan-Arabist, said that each person has a 'duty towards his country as a citizen' and a duty towards the Arab nation, but a person's duty ought to be towards his country first.[17]

One of the first member states openly to criticize Azzam's behaviour was Trans-Jordan. He was even accused of being responsible for the Palestine tragedy when he was put in charge of supervising the Palestine 'war' affairs through the political, military, and financial committees which were formed for that purpose.[18] In 1948 Azzam visited Amman, Jordan, to pay £250,000 from the funds of the Arab League earmarked to meet the cost of the Palestine war, as a first instalment of an amount of £3,000,000 which was to be issued to Jordan from the Arab League fund. When Jordan's Arab Legion was facing difficulties in the war, Azzam refused to pay additional sums from the fund in spite of his promises.[19] Sir Alec Kirkbride, who then served as envoy extraordinary and minister plenipotentiary of the British Foreign Office in Amman, met Azzam and Glubb, the then commander of the Arab Legion. He wrote,

> Both Glubb and I sensed that Azzam shared the hostility which the Egyptian authorities showed toward King Abdallah and his followers. Azzam was entirely unhelpful in the scandalous case when the Egyptian army seized a

shipload of ammunition at Suez which was consigned by the British ordinance depot to the Arab Legion. This high-handed action was all the more reprehensible because the consignment in question proved to be the last opportunity for the Legion to replenish its stocks before the general embargo on the issue of supplies and money was imposed by Great Britain with regard to all the belligerents. The only explanation offered by the Egyptian Government for stealing this ammunition was that they were in urgent need of it themselves . . .. Azzam declined to intervene in the matter and the Egyptians refused to return the stores or to refund their value to the Jordanian Government.[20]

Such behaviour by the first secretary-general angered Abdallah who accused him of being no more than a servant of the Egyptian interest.

Another country which strongly deplored Azzam's actions was Iraq. As in the case of Jordan, Iraqi hostility to the secretary-general arose from a dispute with the League regarding the financing of the Palestine volunteers. Speaking in the Iraqi chamber of deputies on 3 May 1949, Fadil al-Jamali, then the Iraqi foreign minister, attacked the first secretary-general, who 'came to control and dominate the policy of the League.' He went on 'Azzam Pasha is thus acting as an independent head of State, supreme over the Foreign Ministers of the Arab States, making statements and negotiating with regard to political matters as he himself deems fit, without caring whether or not this policy satisfies all the Governments of the Arab States by which he is employed.'[21]

Underlying these charges was a more fundamental issue: the Fertile Crescent scheme, espoused by Iraq (see chapter 1), which would have been under the sway of the Iraqi king. Reflecting on Egypt and the secretary-general in early May 1949, Assad Dagher, League press officer, publicly opposed the Iraqi plan: 'The realization of either [the Iraqi scheme] would fatally create discord among the Arabs. This would destroy their influence and create a feeling of hatred which would be most harmful to the League.'[22]

In the face of increasing Arab criticism, by the early 1950s the first secretary-general began to follow a line more independent of Egyptian policy. For example, as the Cairo press reported, Azzam protested against the prime minister's statements in which he attacked the secretariat officials. He told the then prime minister, Hussein Sirry, that he hurt the dignity of those international officials, asking him to reconsider his statement.[23] The new leaders of the July 1952 revolution viewed Azzam's activities as not in line with that of the new revolutionary mood. According to Azzam, Nuri al-Sa'id asked Cairo to remove him from the League if there were to be an improvement in relations with Baghdad. Azzam said that Rashad Mhana, a member of the revolutionary council, called him to tell Azzam that the council viewed his resignation as secretary-general of the Arab League a matter of necessity. Azzam replied that he worked for all member Arab states and that he was not an Egyptian employee. Mhana retorted, 'But you are an Egyptian first.'[24] Mhana's request was followed up by another revolutionary council member, Salah Salem, who visited Azzam at his home to tell him the decision of his colleagues in the council. 'He purposely appeared as if he was ordering me to resign, and that I should immediately implement his instructions,' Azzam wrote. He replied 'I shall think of the matter.' 'We said you resign. That means you resign,' Salem snapped back.[25] Finally, Azzam had no other choice but to accept the new Egyptian leader's decision and on 9 September 1952 he handed in his resignation as secretary-general of the Arab League.[26]

The second secretary-general, Abdel-Khaliq Hassouna, pursued policies similar to those of Azzam. The Egyptian government selected Hassouna as the candidate for that job, and he remained in office until 1972, when a third Egyptian, Mahmoud Riad succeeded him. Hassouna desired to leave his job in 1957, but he agreed to Cairo's suggestion to continue for another five years. In 1962 and in 1967 he was again selected for further five-year terms.

Under Hassouna the League grew into a large and complex organization. The permanent staff quadrupled during his tenure, and the second secretary-general's role in Arab disputes, especially those between Egypt and other members, grew to be significant. Apart from the secretary-general's constant support of Nasser's policies toward Israel, there were serious issues within the Arab world in which member states' trust in him was weakened. He was deeply involved in the 1961 Iraqi-Kuwaiti dispute and in the Algerian-Moroccan conflict of 1963. His role in these disputes included conciliation and fact-finding and was less controversial, but in other conflicts, such as the 1958 dispute between Egypt and the Sudan, that involved Egypt and other members of the League, his role proved to be more questionable.

In the 1955 crisis of the Baghdad Pact, the secretary-general preferred not to call for a prime ministers' meeting. Egypt overruled the League even though the secretary-general claims that he preferred that Egypt deal with that problem.[27] Moreover, Hassouna supported Nasser's 'non-alignment' position at the Bandung Conference of 1955, and he recommended, in his report to the Arab League council, that the secretariat, as Robert MacDonald wrote, 'should act as a coordinating center in the Near East for Afro-Asian activities and that the League's office in New York should perform the same function at the United Nations.'[28]

In the Lebanese case of 1958, the secretary-general succeeded in getting the UN Security Council to agree to refer the case to the League,[29] and finally succeeded in having Lebanon agree to a resolution favoured by Cairo. By this time, the secretary-general was pursuing Nasser's pan-Arabist policy. In September 1958, for the first time, Hassouna opened the League council session 'in the name of God, Arab nationalism, and Arab unity'.[30] Hassouna repeated his pan-Arabist sentiments in March 1960, at the inauguration of the new secretariat building in Cairo, when he called for full Arab union. Lebanese leaders were angered and some politicians called for Hassouna's resignation.[31]

In 1961 Secretary-General Hassouna was deeply involved in attempting to settle the Syrian-Egyptian dispute of that year. He succeeded in getting Syria to agree to an exchange of military forces after Syria broke with the United Arab Republic. However, his role at the Shtoura meeting had encountered heavy Syrian resistance, which led to Cairo's withdrawal from that conference.

In the Yemeni case of 1962–67, the secretary-general attempted to mediate between Egypt, on the one hand, and Saudi Arabia and Jordan, on the other. His visit to those two countries in 1963 did not produce an agreement acceptable to Egypt, and his mission was not successful. His efforts continued throughout 1964, 1965, and 1967. The Egyptian defeat in June 1967 led, however, to Egyptian troop withdrawal from Yemen.

In 1972 a new secretary-general was appointed by Egypt, Mahmoud Riad, former foreign minister of Egypt. Egypt refused to let other Arab states submit candidates for this office.[32]

In 1972 a new secretary-general was appointed by Egypt, Mahmoud Riad, former foreign minister of Egypt. Egypt refused to let other Arab states submit candidates for this office.[32]

In sum, these three secretaries-general were clearly closer to the Egyptian policy line than to that of any other member state. Indeed, during disputes where Egyptians were involved, their acts were supportive of Egyptian interests. Recognizing this fact, Boutros Boutros-Ghali, then an international legal authority on the Arab League, suggested that the League ought to have an international Arab official 'who thinks in a comprehensive Arab mentality and not in a narrow mentality of his local nationality.'[33]

Financial Contribution and the League's Budget

A country that contributes more to an organization's budget than any other member usually tends to enjoy more influence in that organization. The USA played a dominant role in the UN until its contributions were greatly decreased. In other organizations such as the Organization of American States, the World Bank, and the International Monetary Fund, Washington still enjoys dominance, due in part, to the size of its contribution.

Similarly, Egypt, from the establishment of the League until the early 1960s, paid the lion's share in the League's budget and thus was able to enjoy a predominant role in that organization. Article 13 of the pact stated that the secretary-general shall prepare the League's budget, and that 'The Council shall fix the share of the expenses to be borne by each state of the League. This share may be reconsidered if necessary.'

Throughout the 1950s and early 1960s, Egypt was viewed as the wealthiest of all Arab nations. Egypt willingly paid almost half of the League's budget when it was formed. This high Egyptian share, which continued into the mid 1960s, increased the influence that Egypt used to exercise in the League. One cannot expect, say, Jordan to have a similar role in the League, when it contributes only 3 per cent as against Egypt's 42 per cent. Regardless of the member states' importance in terms of size, population, and wealth, the pact attempted to treat them all 'equally' in the League's decision making by giving each member an equal vote.[34] In practice, however, size, wealth, and strength were taken into account. Moreover, if an armed attack occurred against a member state, the shares of the defending parties would not be equal. The bigger members would have to shoulder a larger burden than the smaller ones.[35] This would give a big power more weight in the League's policies.

Originally the shares of the members used to be assigned and allocated through decisions by the League's council and on the basis of 'brotherly' agreement between the member states. This method was later changed, and in September 1970 the council assigned the shares on the basis of 'scientific study', based on the Gross National Product, population, and per capita income of the League's member states.[36]

Table 2.1, based on data mainly from official League documents, shows a steady increase in the Arab League secretariat's ordinary annual budget from 75,000 Egyptian pounds in 1945 to 1,064,681 Egyptian pounds plus 4,347,760 American dollars. The table illustrates

Table 2.1 *Member shares of Arab League budgets*

Country	Date Ratio Established					
	1945[a]	1954[b]	1958[c]	1962[d]	1967[e]	1970[f]
Algeria	—	—	—	—	6.00	6.20
Egypt	42.00	40.00	50.29	25.73	23.73	15.16
Iraq	20.00	17.00	15.98	10.94	12.00	12.20
Jordan	3.00	3.00	2.82	1.93	1.93	1.50
Kuwait	—	—	—	13.00	15.50	15.00
Lebanon	6.00	6.00	5.64	3.85	3.85	3.00
Libya	—	2.00	1.88	1.29	4.24	13.30
Morocco	—	—	—	13.68	7.99	7.25
Saudi Arabia	7.00	15.50	14.57	9.97	12.47	12.47
Sudan	—	—	6.00	4.11	4.11	4.25
Syria	16.00	13.50	g	8.69	4.00	3.00
Tunisia	—	—	—	4.88	4.67	4.67
Yemen (San'a)	6.00	3.00	2.82	1.93	.50	1.00
Yemen (Aden)	—	—	—	—	—	1.00
	100.00	100.00	100.00	100.00	100.00	100.00

Sources:
a The League of Arab States, General Secretariat, *1945/1946 League Budget*.
b The League of Arab States, *Review Report of the Accounts for Fiscal Year 1954*.
c Robert W. MacDonald, *The League of Arab States*.
d The League of Arab States, General Secretariat, *Minutes of the League Council*, 38th Ordinary Session, 1962.
e The League of Arab States, General Secretariat, *1966/1967 Budget*.
f Ibid., *1971/1972 Budget*.
g After union with Egypt, Syria's share was included under the United Arab Republic.

the influence of new members on the percentages allocated to member states since 1945 and the decrease of the percentage of Egyptian contributions over the years.[37] Egyptian contribution to the budget of the Arab League continued to shrink throughout the 1970s. In 1976, for example, Cairo's contribution dwindled to 13.70 per cent of the total budget,[38] a share equal to that of Kuwait, a country of no more than one million inhabitants, yet an extremely wealthy one. It is true that increasingly new member states helped to lessen the burden of Egypt, but it is equally true that Egypt is becoming increasingly reluctant to pay the greater share and thus less interested in playing the dominant role in the League, which Cairo practised until the early 1970s.

Egypt's large share of the League's budget, and Cairo's occasional withholding of its dues in an effort to exert pressure, led to, among other factors, strengthening Cairo's grip over the League of Arab States during much of the 1950s and 1960s.

Location, Employees, Media

Any organization is bound to be affected by its immediate environment. It would have to rely on the host country to provide important facilities and services. The Arab League has been located in Egypt. Why was Cairo chosen as the headquarters of the League? One answer is that the British, who were the first to propose the idea of creating the League, were also in favour of having it located in Cairo.[39] It has been the centre for several Arab societies prior to World War I and afterwards.[40] King Abdallah wrote to Mustafa Nahas, the Egyptian leader, that 'the Arab World as fowl has two wings, Egypt is the chest of this fowl'.[41] Other reasons for selecting Cairo as the League headquarters include its population, economic achievements, domination of the Arab media, and centrality in education and Arab intellectual activities.[42] Geographic, demographic, and economic factors made it easier for Egypt to convince the Arab states, against the wishes of its rival Iraq, to have Cairo as the headquarters of the Arab League. Article 10 of the pact states in part that 'the permanent seat of the League of Arab States is established in Cairo.'[43]

The League's permanent seat in Cairo is advantageous to Egypt. The League's staff can be influenced by the fact of living in Cairo. It becomes more sympathetic to Egyptian aspirations. Furthermore, as the headquarters of the League Cairo is the permanent legal seat of the council and the secretariat-general, and as such it is the centre for their meetings.[44] Until the early 1970s Egypt also benefited financially from the League's location in Cairo. All its financial transactions were conducted in Egyptian pounds, thus strengthening the shaky currency and increasing Cairo's foreign currency earnings.[45]

The secretariat has grown from only six men in the Egyptian foreign ministry in 1945 to a complex organization with a staff of several hundred professional personnel. This growth prompted the Egyptian government in early 1954 to award the Arab League a new site, lying not surprisingly next to the Egyptian foreign ministry building, for the construction of a new building that 'matches the League's and Egypt's stature'.[46] Nasser believed that a bigger and more complex League could further his influence over other member states. He used the League, on occasions, as a forum to lecture other Arab states on pan-Arabism and Egypt's leadership. In 1963, for example, Nabih Abdel-Hamid, Cairo's chief delegate to the League's council, used the forum of the League to air Egypt's views:

> On behalf of the United Arab Republic, it is my great pride
> and pleasure to welcome your excellencies to the Arab
> League Council meeting in Cairo, your Arab [country]
> which is full of confidence [and] of pan-Arabism . . . [Egypt]
> is anxiously hopeful to reach the unity of Arab goals in order
> to regain our Arab people's greatness, and to achieve a
> better future for the Arab generations.[47]

Such speeches, beaming throughout the Arab world through the Egyptian propaganda machines, had considerable impact not only on the other Arab officials, but more importantly, on the man in the street.

Moreover, the location of the League in Cairo was used to bring foreign dignitaries to Egypt and thus increase its prestige among the Arabs. In November 1950, for example, Azzam stated: 'We shall always be glad to welcome in Cairo, which is the seat of the Arab League, the secretary-general and other officials and organs of the United Nations.'[48] During French rule in North Africa, when Arab delegations from the region visited the League, Egypt took advantage of their presence to press Egyptian views on liberation and national movements in the Arab world and elsewhere. Implicitly Boutros Boutros-Ghali has in effect recognized Egyptian influence on the

League, due in part to its location. Thus, he recommended the removal of the League's headquarters to another Arab city that 'should be far from any capital of the member states'. The country where the city was to be located 'must concede its sovereignty over that city and sovereignty to be given to the organization which represents all Arab countries.'[49]

The location of the League in Cairo influenced personnel matters as well. The Egyptian secretary-general was in charge of employment. He appoints the principal officials provided the council agrees, but he enjoys full freedom in appointing the rest of the staff which is responsible only to him.[50] The secretary-general plays a prominent role in selecting those of the highest position in the League's hierarchy. At the end of 1953 Hassouna wrote to his government asking for its approval of his choice of Abdel Muneim Mustafa as an undersecretary-general. Within 48 hours Cairo's approval was on the secretary-general's desk. Within two months the political committee and the League council had no choice but to agree to an Egyptian nominee. He remained in his position for many years.[51] The procedure for selecting the assistant secretary-general for political affairs, Sayed Nofal, another Egyptian, followed a similar course. The undersecretaries-general advise him, and they supervise the activities of the various secretariat-general departments.[52] The secretary-general selected mostly Egyptians for numerous other positions in the League. Out of 150 secretariat officers the largest number of employees were Egyptian in the 1960s.[53] When abroad they carried Egyptian passports.[54] The League's offices in foreign countries represent some of the member states which have no representatives in the capital where the League's office is located.[55] The staff of the League in foreign countries was also predominantly Egyptian.[56]

A close look at the national composition of the staff until the mid-70s indicates Egyptian predominance.[57] Besides the secretary-general, the assistant secretaries for political affairs have been mostly Egyptian. The important position of military assistant secretary was always occupied by an Egyptian general. The Egyptian predominance was even more evident in the civil servants of all ranks. The Arab League's employees in 1953 totalled 135; in 1956 they totalled 211, in 1963 233, in 1967 359, and in 1970 394.[58] Official and unofficial records indicate that the majority of them were Egyptian nationals. In 1964 the national composition of the Arab League secretariat showed that out of 150 staff members, 92 were Egyptian. This means, in percentages, that 61.3 per cent of the total staff were nationals of that country.[59] Again, the national composition of the League's secretariat in 1970 shows a similar pattern. Out of 235 staff members, 176 were Egyptian nationals. This is close to 75 per cent of the total staff,[60] a very high figure indeed.

The equitable national composition of the League in general and the secretariat in particular could be a problem. But the most serious problem is the allegiance of those employees. In theory their allegiance is to the League. But as the secretary-general was attached to his mother country, so were his employees. Even if as individuals they chose to be neutral during their tenure at the League, their government would expect otherwise. Government pressure is continuous, and nationals tend to respond positively to their government's expectations, especially because the majority of them are not permanently employed by the League.[61] Thus, as a commentator wrote, international officials hired on a 'short-term secondment are not conducive to ... international loyalty since each temporary official would naturally buy his own long-term career prospects in national service.'[62] Relations between the League's employees and the member states are good as long as League policies are in line with members' policies. However, whenever differences arise, the state that does not like an employee's behaviour will immediately stage not only a protest but also a drive to remove him.[63] To express its displeasure, a member state might also ask for the hiring of more of its nationals. An illustration of this took place during an ordinary session of the League's council in 1954, when Iraq nominated several Iraqi nationals for the general secretariat. But the council, due to Egyptian reservations, did not even discuss the matter, and when the Iraqi delegation brought up the subject, the secretary-general said that he preferred that the political committee should deal with it. Lebanon and Jordan supported the Iraqi request, and they too asked the council for more equitable representation in the general secretariat.[64]

Member states' dissatisfaction with Egyptian predominance in the League continued throughout the 1950s and 1960s, and there were no substantial changes in the 1970s. An official League document on the general secretariat, for example, reveals continuing Egyptian predominance in 1974 (see Table 2.2).

Table 2.2 indicates that Egyptian presence in the general secretariat constituted over 65 per cent of the total. Having an organization dominated by nationals of a particular state, clearly, then, would have

Table 2.2 *National composition of the Arab League secretariat, 1974*

Country	Number of permanent staff members	Number of non-permanent staff members	Total
Jordan	8	4	12
Bahrain	—	1	1
Saudi Arabia	4	1	5
Sudan	4	5	9
Syria	13	8	21
Somalia	—	1	1
Iraq	4	11	15
Lebanon	8	3	11
Libya	—	1	1
Egypt	129	37	166
Morocco	—	1	1
Yemen (Sana)	2	—	2
Palestine	5	3	8
	177	76	253

Source of data: General Secretariat, The League of Arab States, *General Secretarial Staff*, 31 July 1974.

an impact on the orientation and policies of such an organization.

A word on the role of the media in influencing the views and attitudes of the League of Arab States is appropriate. Since the headquarters of the Arab League was in Cairo, staff and employees of the League were most likely to be exposed to the influence of the Egyptian media. Perhaps because of convenience, or maybe because of country ties, the League's 'citizens' would most likely read government-controlled Egyptian newspapers, listen to Cairo radio and watch its TV stations.[65]

The League subscribed to Egyptian papers and to the Middle East News Agency and its various information services.[66] The most powerful media in the Arab world are Egyptian. In the 1950s and 1960s, as well as today, the Egyptian leadership used the media 'as a primary instrument of Egypt's foreign policy . . .'.[67] Reading papers and listening to radios in Cairo, coupled with the transmissions of the powerful 'Voice of the Arabs' (which started transmission in July 1953), have a major impact not only on the League's policies, but also on the attitudes of the illiterate Arab masses.[68]

The League includes an information organ, or a propaganda machine, for Arab as well as foreign consumption. The official supervising it is the secretary-general himself. The League's information service in the Arab countries aims to inform the public about the League's activities and obtain the support of Arab public opinion for the League.[69] The other purpose of the League's information service in Arab countries is to propagate the cause of pan-Arabism.[70] These aims were among Egyptian foreign policy goals. The League's information organs within the Arab world are closely associated with the Egyptian media establishment as well.

Nasser's Personality

Lord Acton wrote: 'For history is often made by energetic men, steadfastly following ideas, mostly wrong, that determine events.'[71] Sociologist Max Weber, seen by many as the originator of the concept of charisma, defines it as 'a certain quality of an individual personality by virtue of which he is set apart from ordinary men and treated as though endowed with supernatural, superhuman or, at least, specifically exceptional qualities . . . . These are not accessible to the ordinary person, but are regarded as divine in origin, or as exemplary, and on the basis of them the individual concerned is treated as a leader.'[72] Weber saw charisma as 'an extraordinary duality', 'a gift of grace', 'a charm' that elevates the individual above ordinary men, confers 'exceptional powers' on him, and confirms him 'as a leader'.[73] Erik Erikson notes that 'the charismatic leader is one who offers a people protection, identity, or ritual.'[74] Jacques Ellul writes that 'the leader is not solely the decision maker, the initiator . . .. He is much more: he is the incarnation of the group, its mirror, its spokeman in the mysterious domain of power.'[75]

Perhaps President Gamal Abdel-Nasser (1918–70) enjoyed such characteristics more than any other contemporary Arab leader. Nasser's charisma,[76] personality, and beliefs were frequently cited as reasons for his high popularity in the Arab world in general and in Egypt in particular.

On 23 July 1952 the Egyptian army ousted King Farouq. Initially, the new regime was headed by General Muhamad Naguib, an elderly man who was, more or less, a figurehead. Soon it became obvious that the real leader of the 1952 revolution was a young officer, Gamal Abdel-Nasser. He was an energetic and forceful figure within the revolutionary council. His compassion won him the respect of his colleagues. Even Naguib, who was removed from office at the request of Nasser, said of Nasser's objection to the trial and execution of King Farouq: 'I have never felt greater admiration for Abdel Nasser than I felt at that moment.'[77] Moreover, Naguib respected the 'young man of exceptional ability.'[78]

By 1954 Nasser had consolidated his power, and Egypt was to follow him with little opposition to his authoritative rule. This reminds us of what the great Arab philosopher and historian, Ibn Khaldun, said: 'Some countries are destined for empire. The ruler need never worry about protest movements or revolt, which are rare: such is Egypt's case . . . . There we find only one sovereign and his obedient subjects.'[79] Such was the case under Nasser where the Egyptian people tend to follow and support the policies of their president, no matter how disastrous.

President Nasser, shortly after Naguib's 'resignation', established himself as the central and dominant figure in the Egyptian decision-making process especially in the external relations sector. Since Egyptians had been subjected to foreign oppression Nasser spoke loudly against foreign oppressors, mainly Britain at the time. His charismatic appeal was so strong that mass support for his foreign policy was always forthcoming.[80]

Until 1954 Nasser's action was centred within Egypt to remove internal challenges to his control. He consolidated his power, destroyed his opponents, and secured the end of the British occupation of the Suez Canal area.[81] The following year Nasser began to devote his energy and attention to the regional environment. He advanced the myth of Egypt's greatness, and later, the 'Arab nation'. By 1955 Nasser perceived that his country's security, as well as his own prestige, required closer relations with other Arab states, and thus he adopted the symbol of Arab unity.[82] In his *Philosophy of Revolution*, Nasser discusses his quest for Arab unity which in the Arab world 'is a role, wandering aimlessly in search of a hero.'[83] Whether the hero was the Egyptian people or Nasser himself was not clear. However, no doubt it was in Nasser's mind that he at least would play the role of the leader of this unity.

Nasser became a symbol of Arab nationalism. He soon gained the position as the leader of the nationalist Arab states. Because Cairo was viewed by many Arab nationalists as their hope for achieving their goal of Arab unity, Nasser's supporters were willing to serve his interests at the expense of those of their own states.[84] To further his aims Nasser utilized his powerful propaganda machine. Cairo was the propaganda centre of the Arab world through the 'Voice of the Arabs', which was listened to throughout the Arab lands. Its superior propaganda skill made the Arabs look to Cairo for guidance and inspiration.[85]

A statement by Nasser such as 'Our Arabic policy aims to unite the Arabs, and to make them one nation. It is our hope that [a defense system] would come out from this great rich land composed of the Arabs alone, because this would definitely lead to the liberation from the domination of colonialism [Isti'mar] and foreign states whether they are big or small'[86] would be repeated until most of the Arabs heard and believed his message. Such statements made Nasser appear to many Arabs as 'the man of providence'. On many occasions he was hailed as a giant, a hero, a superman, a man who if he entered the desert would make it green (a popular Egyptian song), and if he confronted 'imperialism' would defeat it. 'He is the charismatic leader who continually explores new possibilities, who electrifies the masses and awakens their innermost hopes and expectations. He alone commands a mass following.'[87] Iraqi, Syrian, Algerian, and other nationalists saw Nasser as 'the symbol of their movement'.[88] To most Arab nationalists, President Nasser 'was like a folk hero, a mountain guerilla warrior whose fame trickled out in the form of legends which inspired like-minded people. He did not command, but he stimulated.'[89] For example, the then Syrian president, Shukri al-Quwatli, described Nasser several times as 'the correctionist revolutionary who always works for goodness', and that his character puts him in 'the rank of the greatest men in history'.[90]

Nasser's popularity can be seen in the context of the momentous events of his time. The Baghdad Pact, the Gaza raid, the Bandung Conference, the Soviet arms deal, the nationalization of the Suez Canal Company, the formation of the United Arab Republic, and a host of other events served to boost Nasser as the unchallenged leader of Arab nationalism, which because it is dear to the Arab masses allowed him to interfere in other Arab countries' affairs with little opposition. Indeed the Arab masses wanted him to interfere in their affairs, as pro-Nasser riots in Baghdad, Beirut, Amman, and Damascus demonstrated throughout the 1950s and early 1960s.

However, the major catalyst in the emergence of President Nasser's charismatic leadership in the Arab world was certainly 'the overwhelming enthusiasm with which his anti-Western policies were greeted' throughout the Arab world.[91] The observer of the past Western domination of Arab states can easily understand the reasons behind Arab alienation from the West.

Fearing that his position as well as that of Egypt would be jeopardized by a defence treaty that had been proposed by the West (the Baghdad Pact), Nasser was inflamed with rage. He unleashed his propaganda against Iraq and Britain, and he initiated active political contacts with other Arab leaders to prevent any Arab state from joining the new pact. Nasser's campaigns against the pact, combined with the already high Arab nationalist sentiments against the British, did succeed. 'Thus between the public announcement of the intention to form the Baghdad Pact and its actual signature, a space of only a few months, Egypt was able to organize a successful counterattack, preventing any other Arab state from joining Iraq.'[92] Nasser's success with his first major Arab drive prepared him for his second major foreign policy drive, the Bandung Conference.

This non-alignment conference was held in April 1955. Due to his stand against the West and the Baghdad Pact, Nasser's name became a household word to many people in the newly emerging states, better known as Third World countries. However, Nasser's high point was at the Bandung Conference itself, where he established himself as the undisputed leader of the Arab world, and where he was accorded treatment as such. On 17 April Nasser called the heads of Arab delegations to a dinner party where he asked the other Arab delegates to take one stand at the conference.[93] At the conference Nasser introduced the Palestine cause and the issue of colonialism in North Africa, winning at the end the conference's endorsement on both causes. Even on other international issues, Nasser was very active. Nehru attributed Bandung's success to the 'wisdom and personality' of Nasser.[94]

However, Nasser's responsiveness to Arab nationalist sentiments did not end at Bandung. The Communist (Czech) arms deal added to Nasser's already powerful credentials as the undisputed leader of the Arab world. Despite the rhetoric of Egyptian leaders and the media about Egypt's constant victories over their 'Zionist enemy',[95] when Israel attacked Egyptian-held territory, particularly the massive raid on Gaza on 28 February 1955, the Egyptian armed forces were in no position to defend their territories. To ameliorate the situation Nasser attempted, in vain, to purchase Western-made weapons. On 27

September 1955 Nasser spoke to his armed forces: 'I asked America, England, France, Russia and Czechoslovakia' for arms. Some of these countries replied that 'I can arm the army with weapons, but on conditions.' Nasser went on, 'but I rejected these conditions.' To 'the bursts of applause [that] sounded like static on a stormy night', as an observer noted,[96] Nasser revealed that 'Egypt has signed last week an arms contract with Czechoslovakia.'[97]

Nasser's arms deal, and his rejection of Western conditional offers, gained him great support. Throughout the Arab world, 'the reaction was hysterical. It was not only that the arms that were needed for defense, or attack, against Israel were now available, but that Nasser was able to defy the West openly and prove his independence from it as no Arab leader before Nasser had done it. This is why Nasser began to look like a "new Saladin" and "savior of the Arabs"'.[98]

Nasser's next sensational act against the West, and perhaps his most successful one, where he turned his military defeat into a great political triumph, was his nationalization of the Suez Canal Company — 'a stroke of genius', as his successor was to describe it.[99] It is widely believed that this act led 'the Arab nation to have Abdel-Nasser as its Zaim (leader).'[100] In his 26 July speech Nasser proclaimed: 'Today, citizens, the Suez Canal [Company] was nationalized, and this decision was in fact published in the official *Gazette* and this decision became a matter of fact.' He went on, 'Today, citizens, the income of the Suez Canal [is] . . . one hundred million dollars annually, five hundred million dollars in five years . . . why should we look to the seventy million dollars, the amount of the American aid?'[101] (a reference to the amount the USA initially offered for the Aswan High Dam). Nasser added that whenever talk comes out of Washington, 'I shall say: Die by your Fury [Ghaithkum].'[102] These words were sensational to people who had been subjected to foreign rule for centuries. Nasser's nationalization act sent Egyptians and other Arabs alike out onto the streets hailing his latest action. Sadat summed up Egypt's reaction:

> I did in point of fact feel proud. For there it was: Egypt, a small country, was at last capable of speaking loud and clear in defiance of the biggest power on earth. [Perhaps meaning the West in general] It was a turning point in the history of Egypt. The nationalization decision had vast repercussions both inside and outside Egypt. From that moment on Nasser turned into an Egyptian mythical hero.[103]

Indeed Nasser turned into an Arab 'mythical hero'. For the Arabs, the Western rebuff transcended Nasser's person and was directed against pan-Arab nationalism as a whole.[104] Throughout the Arab world, from Morocco to Kuwait, people's slogans included: *Ya Gamal Hat-Hat . . . Kaman Ta'minat* (O Gamal give give more nationalizations); *min al Muheet al-Hadir Ela al-Khalij al-Tha'ir, Labiek abdel-Nasser* (from the raging ocean to the revolting Gulf yes Abdel-Nasser), or *Ya Gamal la Tihtam . . . wel'arab Hawalik Teltam* (O Gamal, Don't worry . . . and the Arabs united around you).[105] Thus, Nasser's decision made Arabs hysterical with joy. 'Palestinians, Iraqis, Syrians, Lebanese, Jordanians all were wild in praise of Gamal.'[106]

Nasser's nationalization of the Suez led to the invasion of Egypt by Israel, France, and Britain. But thanks to the USA and the Soviet Union which turned Nasser's 'defeat into victory', [107] the evacuation of the invading armies, and the subsequent fall of the British prime minister made it possible for the Egyptian president to tell his people, 'You have sent Anthony Eden to his doom . . .. Once Anthony could remove any prime minister in Egypt in twenty-four hours.'[108] The Arabs loved what Nasser said and did. For to many Arabs what Nasser did was a resounding defeat of Western 'imperialism'.

Again, by the time the Suez was restored to Egyptian sovereignty, Nasser's stock in the Arab world was extremely high. It was an appropriate time for him now to start practising what he had been preaching for several years. The process of Arab unity had to show real progress to make Nasser's exhortations credible. Egypt's unity with Syria in 1958 was a first step in that direction. Arab unity seemed to be within reach after this widely acclaimed move. The formation of the United Arab Republic raised Nasser's prestige and popularity among the Arab people to its climax.

To his delight, a few months later, in July 1958, Nasser's arch-enemy in Iraq, Nuri al-Sa'id, was toppled and the monarchy was abolished, another climax in Nasser's upswing. 'Nasser seemed to be moving toward absolute domination of the Arab world and to making Iraq the eastern province' of the UAR 'just as Egypt and Syria had been made its southern and northern provinces respectively.'[109] None the less, Nasser's happiness did not last long. A few months later, Iraq and Egypt were back to their earlier quarrels and rivalry. Indeed, the UAR itself began to experience difficulties before its first anniversary. In 1961, for reasons we shall examine later, Syria seceded from the union which had 'demonstrated that Nasser's personality was not enough on which to build a union.'[110]

For a year following the secession Nasser shifted his concentration from Arab affairs to domestic problems. Nasser believed that transforming Egypt into a socialist state and a socialist revolution in the Arab world were prerequisites for Arab unity.

On 28 September 1962 the San'a imamate was toppled, but to have the new republican regime stay in power, it needed outside help. The new leader, Abdallah el-Sallal called on Nasser to send in Egyptian troops to defeat the 'reactionary' royalists. Nasser seized the opportunity to reestablish his presence in other Arab states (Yemen was one) and he was quick to dispatch his troops to San'a. 'Whatever prestige Nasser had lost because of the Syrian secession was quickly regained by his ready response "to brothers in Yemen". His stock soared high among the peoples of Iraq, Syria and Jordan.'[111] Several Saudi and Jordanian pilots defected to Cairo that year. Furthermore, in early 1963, military coups ended the anti-Nasser regimes in Iraq and Syria. After these new changes Nasser announced his identification with the 'progressive Arab states', which included Egypt, Syria, Iraq, Yemen, and Algeria, and his ambitions for Arab unity were immediately revived. For much of 1963 Syrian and Iraqi delegations were in Cairo for unity talks with Nasser; 'The weight of Nassir's prestige was the priceless asset that the Syrian and Iraqi delegations had come to Cairo to seek.'[112] Throughout the unity discussions, Nasser displayed his powerful personality. As an observer of Egyptian presidents noted:

> Nasir always supremely confident, always steering the
> discussion in the direction of his choice, always conscious of
> the substantive or psychological point at issue, blunt,
> forceful, clear and often witty in his expression, alternatively
> charming or bullying according to his purpose, not hesitating
> at times to harass, interrupt, or embarrass his visitors and
> decisively rejecting opposing claims or criticisms whenever
> he did not fancy their implications.[113]

Nasser's skills and personality influenced the formulation of the charter of the federation on 17 April 1963,[114] which was never implemented because of the mutual distrust of Nasser and the Ba'athists.

Nasser's concept of the 'unity of rank' was also attempted. For several important factors, not the least of which was Nasser's own prestige and Egypt's interests, Nasser called for an Arab summit meeting. The official reason given by Nasser for his call was Israel's diversion of the river Jordan. However, the Yemeni morass must have been a major factor in his decision too. For at this time his troops in that country were locked in a bloody and protracted war which was costing Egypt heavily in men and money.

The Arab response to Nasser's call was quick and unanimous. It was a relief for Arab leaders, at least for a while, to be on good terms with Nasser and thus escape his attacks and those of his propaganda machine. Indeed Nasser himself said later that the years of 1964, 1965, and 1966 were 'a rest period for the reactionaries', meaning conservative Arab leaders.[115]

For one thing, Nasser hoped that Arab leaders, particularly King Faisal, would help in extricating him from the Yemeni war. But that goal was not achieved. As a result of the failure of his hope, Nasser, in early 1966, abandoned the summit spirit and resumed his violent attacks on Arab 'reactionaries', especially those who supported the royalists in Yemen: Faisal and Hussein.[116] By the end of that year Nasser concluded a mutual defence pact with Syria. The 'progressive Arab states' lined up behind Nasser's policies.

Throughout 1966 and until May 1967, Nasser continued to attack Arab 'reactionaries' violently and in a hysterical way. In a speech on 22 February 1967, Nasser accused them of plotting with the Muslim Brotherhood 'to hit the revolutionary system in Egypt'.[117]

However, as often occurs in the unpredictable Arab world, Nasser was caught offguard in rapidly changing circumstances, and in a matter of only two months the enemies became friends again, a friendship that was to lead to a disaster that changed the course of the Middle East. In April Israel attacked Syria, which responded by victorious rhetoric through its radio and press, but, none the less, appealed to Egypt for help. In a matter of weeks Nasser replaced UN peacekeeping forces in the Sinai with Egyptian forces and then closed the Tiran strait which Arab leaders called on to him to close against Israeli navigation. Furthermore, to make the situation worse, Nasser held a press conference in Cairo, on 28 May in which 'he showed himself at his most defiant and violent.'[118] 'If they [the Israelis] want to try the war I say to them again today: *Ahlan Wasahlan* [welcome],' he said.[119]

Throughout the Arab world Nasser received nothing but praise. People went out onto the streets shouting his name, and Arab propaganda machines, even those of the anti-Nasser camp, repeated what Nasser was saying. Popular pressure forced King Hussein and Iraq to join the Syrian-Egyptian defence treaty. The following week was to expose the accumulated miscalculations of Nasser's presidency. On 5 June 1967 Nasser was to experience perhaps the worse moment in his life. The Israelis destroyed his army in Sinai and Gaza, and the Syrians and Jordanians were pushed out of the Golan and the West Bank. What happened to President Nasser's vociferous threats and claims of the 'biggest striking force' in the Middle East? Suddenly facing the realities of the situation, Nasser offered his resignation. 'I am ready to shoulder all the responsibility,' for the disaster, he declared in his 9 June speech, adding: 'I decided to resign completely and for good from any official position and from any political role.'[120]

Nasser's personality and charisma would play its part now. The minute he ended his speech, the streets of Cairo were filled with people. The full dimensions of the charismatic component came into clear view. The people simply said 'No' to Nasser's resignation decision. 'Men, women, and children from all classes and walks of life, united by their sense of crisis into one solid mass, moving in unison and speaking with the same tongue, calling on Nasser to stay on.'[121]

Eric Rouleau, a long-time observer of Nasser, wrote after that fateful event: 'In the morning, having learned of their defeat, they blamed Nasser alone and were ready to send him packing; that evening, the news of his retirement made them cling to him as their sole refuge, their teacher, symbol, and breath of life: "Gamal, Gamal don't desert us, we need you."'[122] None the less, June 1967 was too much for Nasser. It 'dealt him a fatal blow. It finished him off. Those who knew Nasser realized that he did not die on September 28, 1970, but on June 5, 1967, exactly one hour after the war broke out.'[123] Lord Acton's famous words had come true. President Nasser 'served the nation and did his duty the way he could believe in it, and history has to judge for or against him.'[124]

Nasser, as we have seen, was a very popular president among Arabs. His impact on the Arab masses led to a large following for his policies. Indeed, even Arab leaders could not help but accept, at least in rhetoric, Nasser as the undisputed leader of the Arab world. Such an impact definitely influenced the behaviour and views of the Arab League policy-makers as well as the organization's staffs and employees. Who dared to take a policy line contrary to Nasser's policies in his own capital?

Notes to chapter two

1 The importance of the general-secretariat is shown by the numerous important departments which fall within its arena: 1) the general secretariat; 2) the finance and personnel department; 3) the secretariat department; 4) the propaganda system; 5) the cultural departments; 6) social affairs and youth department; 7) Arab manuscript institute; 8) the general secretariat library; 9) the legal affairs department; 10) the political affairs department; 11) the economic affairs departments; 12) Israel boycotting agency; 13) Palestine affairs department; 14) the technical agency for Arab youth welfare; 15) the communication department; 16) oil affairs department; 17) the health affairs department; 18) the protocol department; 19) the regional staff for combating illiteracy; 20) the scientific and technological section.

For the Arab League systems see: Abdel-Futuh Hamed Auda, 'Arab League Systems', reprint from *Egyptian Political Science Review*, Special Issue on the Arab League, March 1972, New York, Arab Information Center (October 1972), pp. 1–39.

2 Muhammad Khalil, *The Arab States and the Arab League*, Beirut, Khayats, 1962, vol. II, p. 59.

3 Inis L. Claude, Jr., *Swords into Plowshares*, New York, Random House, 4th edn, 1971, p. 191.

4 Ibid., p. 192.

5 Judith Jackson and Stephen King-Hall (eds), *The League Yearbook, 1932*, New York, Macmillan, 1932, pp. 153, 156, quoted in Claude, p. 199.

6 *The International Secretariat of the Future*, London, Royal Institute of International Affairs, 1944, pp. 19–20.

7 Claude, p. 205.

8 Sayed Nofal, *al-'Amal al-Arabi al-Mushtarak*, book II, Cairo, Institute of Arab Studies and Research, 1971, p. 144; Ahmad Musa, *Mithaq Jam'iat al-Dowal al-Arabiyyeh*, (The Pact of the League of Arab States), Cairo, Matba'at Misr, 1948, p. 192; Muhamad Abdel-Wahab el-Sakit, *al-Amin al-'Aam Le-Jammi'at al-Dowal al-Arabiyyeh*, (The Secretary-General of the League of Arab States), Cairo, Dar al-Fikr al-Arabi, 1974, pp. 271-73.

9 The first secretary-general of the Arab League (1945–53), Abdel-Rahman Azzam, was the Egyptian minister plenipotentiary in 1936 in Iran, Iraq, Saudi Arabia, and Afghanistan, and the minister plenipotentiary for Arabic affairs in the Egyptian foreign ministry in 1944. He was also an ambassador in the foreign ministry and a member

of the Egyptian delegation to the political subcommittee in the Cairo Arab conference. The second secretary-general (1953–72), Abdel-Khaliq Hassouna, worked in Egyptian embassies in Berlin, Prague, Brussels, and Rome; he was minister plenipotentiary in the foreign ministry until 1939, deputy minister in the social affairs ministry, Alexandria governor, 1942; deputy foreign minister in 1948, social affairs minister in 1949, education minister; and foreign minister in 1952. The last Egyptian secretary-general, Mahmoud Riad (1972–78) held similar jobs and was Egyptian foreign minister before he was appointed secretary-general.

10   el-Sakit, p. 109.

11   Ibid., p. 139.

12   Ibid., pp. 140–43.

13   Ibid., p. 151.

14   Ibid., pp. 152–55.

15   *King Abdallah's Memoire*, (*Muthakarat al-Malik Abdallah*), Beirut, n.p., 1965, p. 253.

16   Sati al-Husri, *al-'urubah awwalan*, Beirut, 1956, pp. 116ff. Quoted in Anwar Chejne, 'Egyptian Attitudes toward Pan-Arabism', *Middle East Journal*, vol. 11, no. 3 (summer 1957), p. 260.

17   See el-Sakit, p. 156.

18   '*Muthakarat Mass'ool Arabi Muttali*' (Memoire of an Informed Arab Official), (Anonymous), *al-Ahram*, 5 February 1978, p. 7.

19   Sir Alec Kirkbride, *From the Wings: Amman Memoirs 1947–1951*, London, Frank Cass, 1976, p. 51.

20   Ibid., pp. 24–25.

21   Khalil, vol. II, pp. 62–63.

22   *Egyptian Gazette*, 4 May 1944, quoted in Paul Seabury, 'The League of Arab States', *International Organization*, vol. 3, no. 4 (November 1949), p. 641. The secretary-general defended himself. He replied to the Iraqi criticisms by stating: 'These accusations constitute a transgression unacceptable to reason and unsupported by facts. The function of the Secretary-General in any international institution is not restricted to the supervision of the keeping of records and the communication of the decisions.' Khalil, vol. II, p. 65. Egyptian delegates to the League supported Azzam's views. See el-Sakit, pp. 276–80.

23   el-Sakit, p. 164.

24   *The Memoirs of Abdel-Rahman Azzam*, (*Muthakarat Abdel-Rahman Azzam*), Cairo, Matb'a't al-Ahram al-Tijariyyeh, 1977, p. 324.

25   Ibid., p. 325.

26   Ibid., p. 327. Azzam said that by the end of 1954, Gamal Abdel-Nasser, the new Egyptian leader, visited him several times, asking him

to go back to the League saying: 'Tomorrow you go to your office in the League, and Egypt will mail all the communications to re-elect you as Secretary-General.' Azzam, according to him, refused to accept Nasser's offer. However, he did not mention why Nasser wanted him back and failed to make clear if this new approach to him came as a result of the revolutionary council's dislike of the way Hassouna, the second secretary-general was handling matters. Ibid., pp. 332–34.

27   el-Sakit, p. 369.

28   Robert MacDonald, *The League of Arab States*, Princeton, N. J., Princeton University Press, 1965, pp. 113–14.

29   See Hussein Hassouna, *The League of Arab States and Regional Disputes*, Dobbs Ferry, N. Y., Oceana, 1975, pp. 365, 378.

30   *Washington Post*, 7 September 1958, p. A7, quoted in MacDonald, p. 156.

31   Ibid.

32   In 1977 Jordan, Syria, and Lebanon nominated the former Jordanian prime minister, Abdel-Mun'im al-Rifai, as a candidate for that job. But Egypt rejected this selection, because Cairo considered this as intruding on 'Egyptian rights'. Thus Egypt rejected this nomination as if it were rivalry for Egypt's position and rights. Jordan was forced to withdraw its nomination. Abdel-Mun'im al-Rifai to the author, Amman, 12 August 1978.

33   Boutros Y. Boutros-Ghali, '*al-'Amal al-Arabi al-Mushtarak fi al-Jamá h al-Arabiyyeh*', (The Joint Arab Activities in the Arab League) Al-Siyyassah al-Dawliyyah (Cairo), no. 20, April 1970, p. 288.

34   In 1948/1949, Egypt's population was 19 million and its budget was 133 million Egyptian pounds, while Jordan's population was ½ million and its budget was equal to 3 million Egyptian pounds. Kamal Ghali, *Mithaq Jamiá t al-Dowal al-Arabiyyeh*, (The Pact of the League of the Arab States), Cairo, Matba'at Nahdat Misr, 1948, p. 94.

35   Ibid., p. 95.

36   el-Sakit, pp. 310–11.

37   It should be noted that member states at various stages used to withhold their dues in an effort to exert pressure (e.g. Iraq after the signing of the Baghdad Pact, Syria in 1961, Egypt in 1962, and a host of others).

38   League of Arab States, the General-Secretariat, *Budget of 1976*.

39   Abdel-Mun'im al-Rifai to the author, Amman, 12 August 1978.

40   See Mahmoud Kamel, '*al-Dawlah al-Arabiyyeh al-Kubra*' (*The Great Arab State*), Cairo: Matba'at Dar al-Ma'arif, 1967, pp. 424–26.

41   Abdel Mun'im al-Rifai to the author, Amman, 12 August 1978.

42   See Ralph Magnus in Kenneth Thompson, James Rosenau, and Gavin Boyed (eds), *World Politics*, New York, The Free Press, 1976, p. 229.

43   Khalil, vol. II, p. 50.

44   Ahmad Musa, '*Mithaq Jamiá t al-Dowal al-Arabiyyeh*', (*The Pact of the Arab League*), Cairo, Matba'at Misr, 1948, p. 203. Beside the

League council, the general-secretariat departments and other organizations instituted within the League framework, the League's systems include the influential Arab unions, many of which have their permanent seats in Cairo. These include the Arab postal union, the Arab scientific union, the Arab union for telecommunications, the Arab union for car and tourism clubs, the Arab veterinary union, and the Arab agricultural union. For further information on this matter, see Abdul-Futuh Hamed Suda, 'Arab League Systems', New York, Arab Information Center, October, 1972. However, after Egypt and Israel signed the Camp David agreements in 1979 many of these organizations were moved to other Arab capitals.

45 See el-Sakit, p. 174.

46 Abdel-Kahliq Hassouna, in a letter to Abdel-Latif Baghdadi, member of the revolutionary council, dated 15 June 1954. *Minutes of the League Council Meetings*, 21st ordinary session, 31 March 1954–9 September 1954.

47 *Minutes of the League's Council*, 40th ordinary session, first meeting, September 1963, p. 12.

48 Khalil, vol. II, p. 82.

49 Boutros-Ghali, *op. cit.*, p. 288.

50 *al-Musawar*, March 1964, p. 124.

51 el-Sakit, pp. 224–25.

52 See ibid., pp. 228–45.

53 MacDonald, p. 129.

54 Nofal, book II, pp. 112–124.

55 Ibid.

56 Boutros Y. Boutros-Ghali, 'The Arab League 1945–1970', *Revue Egyptienne de Droit International*, vol. 25 (1969), p. 80.

57 See, for example, *Middle East, 1956–1970*, Europa Publications, London.

58 General Secretariat, *Budgets of 1953, 1956, 1963, 1967*, and *1970*.

59 MacDonald, p. 130.

60 el-Sakit, pp. 252–53.

61 Robert W. Cox, 'The Executive Head, An Essay on Leadership', *International Organization*, vol. 23, no. 2, (spring, 1969), pp. 214–16.

62 Ibid., p. 215.

63 See Nofal, book II, p. 116.

64 *Minutes of the League Council*, 22nd ordinary session, sixth meeting, 11 December 1954, pp. 51–55.

65 During my frequent visits to the League's headquarters in the summer of 1978, the only papers I noticed employees and staff reading were *al-Akhbar, al Goumhuriah*, and *al-Ahram*, all of which are Egyptian. Also I saw several reporters there, on several occasions, interviewing various League officials, and all of the reporters were Egyptians.

66 See Financial Allocation for Media Services, General Secretariat, *Budget of the League*, 1953.

67 A. I. Dawisha, *Egypt in the Arab World*, London, Macmillan, 1976, p. 163.

68 Ibid., p. 164.

69 el-Sakit, p. 337.

70 Ibid., p. 140.

71 Lord Acton, *Lectures on Modern History*, London, Fontana, 1960, p. 77, quoted in Hans E. Tütsch, *Facets of Arab Nationalism*, Detroit, Wayne State University Press, 1965, p. 98.

72 Max Weber, *The Theory of Social and Economic Organization*, transl. by A. M. Henderson and Talcott Parsons, London, Oxford University Press, 1947, pp. 358–59. Quoted in Dawisha, p. 102.

73 Max Weber, *The Theory of Social and Economic Organization* (New York: Glencoe Free Press, 1957). Quoted in Jean Lacouture, *The Demigods: Charismatic Leadership in the Third World*, New York, Knopf, 1970, p. 15.

74 Erik Erikson, 'The Leader as a Child', *The American Scholar* (Autumn, 1968). Quoted in Jean Lacouture, *The Demigods*, p. 17.

75 Ibid., p. 3.

76 For an interesting debate on whether or not President Nasser was a charismatic leader see Leland Bowie and R. Hrair DeKmejian, 'Nasir's Role and Legacy I and II', *The Middle East Journal*, vol. 30, no. 2 (spring, 1976), pp. 142–72.

77 Muhamad Naguib, *Egypt's Destiny*, New York, Doubleday, 1955, p. 120.

78 Ibid., p. 10.

79 Quoted in Jean Lacouture, *The Demigods*, p. 82.

80 R. Hrair DeKmejian, *Egypt under Nasser*, Albany, N. Y., State University of New York Press, 1971, p. 250.

81 George M. Haddad, *Revolutions and Military Rule in the Middle East: The Arab States, Part II: Egypt, the Sudan, Yemen, and Libya*, vol. III, New York, Robert Speller, 1973, p. 82.

82 DeKmejian, p. 56.

83 Gamal Abdel-Nasser, *The Philosophy of Revolution*, Washington, D.C., Public Affairs Press, 1955, p. 87.

84 Magnus in Thompson *et al*, p. 231.

85 See Wilton Wynn, *Nasser of Egypt: The Search for Dignity*, Cambridge, Mass., Arlington Books, 1959, pp. 134–49.

86 *al-Ahram*, 8 September 1955, p. 6.

87 Tütsch, p. 95; see also p. 91.

88 Wynn, p. 140.

89 Ibid.

90 *al-Ahram*, 8 September 1955, p. 6.

91 Dawisha, p. 103; see also Charles Issawi, 'Negotiation from Strength?

A Reappraisal of Western-Arab Relations', *International Affairs*, vol. 35, no. 1 (1959).

92 Magnus in Thompson *et al*, p. 237.

93 *al-Ahram*, 18 April 1955, p. 1

94 *al-Ahram*, 29 April 1955, p. 1.

95 See *al-Ahram*, January–August 1955.

96 Jean Lacouture, *Nasser*, New York, Knopf, 1973, p. 161.

97 United Arab Republic, Information Bureau, *Majmu'at Khutab al-Rais Abdel-Nasser* (Collection of President Abdel-Nasser's Speeches), part I, 23 July 1952–1958, p. 409. In his 26 July 1956 speech Nasser said: 'We were able to get the arms from Russia. From Russia and not from Czechoslovakia.' Ibid., pp. 551–52.

98 George M. Haddad, *Revolutions and Military Rule in the Middle East: The Arab States*, New York, R. Speller, 1971, vol. II, p. 84.

99 Anwar el-Sadat, *In Search of Identity*, New York, Hagerstown, San Francisco, London, Harper and Row, 1978, p. 145.

100 *October* (Cairo), 10 April 1977, p. 21.

101 *Majmu'at Khutab al-Rais Gamal Abdel-Nasser*, part I, 23 July 1952–1958, p. 563.

102 Ibid.

103 el-Sadat, *op. cit.*, p. 143.

104 DeKmejian, *op. cit.*, p. 46.

105 Mohamed Amarah, '*al-Aummah al-Arabiyyeh wa-Quaddiatt al-Tawhid*' (*The Arab Nation and the Unity Issue*) Cairo, Dar al-'Ahd al-Jadid, 1966, pp. 43–44.

106 Wynn, p. 162.

107 el-Sadat, *op. cit.* p. 147.

108 Quoted in George M. Haddad, *Revolutions and Military Rule in the Middle East*, vol. II, p. 87.

109 Ibid., p. 90.

110 Malcolm Kerr, *The Arab Cold War, 1958–1964: A Study of Ideology and Politics*, London, Oxford University Press, 1965, p. 62.

111 Shirley Graham DuBois, *Gamal Abdel-Nasser: Son of the Nile*, New York, The Third Press, 1972, p. 196.

112 Kerr, pp. 73–74.

113 Ibid., p. 76.

114 Haddad, p. 92.

115 al-Ahram's Center for Strategic and Political Studies, *Watha'iq Abdel-Nasser* (Abdel-Nasser's Documents), January 1967–December 1968, p. 62.

116 Ibid., p. 93.

117 Ibid., p. 62.

118 el-Sadat, *op. cit.* p. 173.

119 *Watha'iq Abdel-Nasser*, p. 191.

120 Ibid., p. 228.

121   el-Sadat, *op. cit.* p. 179.
122   Eric Rouleau, *Israël et les Arabes, le troisième combat*, Paris, Ed. du Sevil, 1967, p. 135. Quoted in Jean Lacouture, *The Demigods*, p. 130. It could be argued that since Nasser understood the emotional responses of the Egyptian people, his resignation was no more than a theatrical act.
123   el-Sadat, *op. cit.* pp. 179–80.
124   Anwar el-Sadat in a speech to the Third Army, *al-Ahram*, 7 June 1977 p. 9. Nasser's long-time loyal servant, Mohamed Heikal wrote: 'It has to be admitted that in 1967 Nasser failed in one of the fundamental duties of any ruler — he failed to defend the borders of his country. By that failure the legitimacy of his régime was flawed.' *Autumn of Fury*, London, André Deutsch, 1983, p. 114.

Chapter Three

Egyptian Foreign Policy Under President Gamal Abdel-Nasser

In order to understand why Nasser used the Arab League, it is necessary to discuss briefly Egyptian foreign policy goals during his presidency. When President Nasser came to power after the 23 July 1952 revolution, his foreign policy goals were several. Most importantly he sought autonomy at home (ending the British presence in Egypt), and autonomy abroad, which included maximization of Egypt's position in the Arab world and pursuing pan-Arab policy.

Autonomy at Home as Policy Goal

Achieving Nasser's goals in the Arab world depended largely on the situation inside Egypt, for 'the concept of autonomy involves the construction or restoration of self-respect abroad [and] is inextricably interrelated to redefinition of self at home.'[1] Thus, in order to achieve his foreign policy goals, Nasser first had to ameliorate the domestic situation, which he and his colleagues claimed to be the major purpose of their revolution. Domestic ills, they thought, could be traced to corruption, feudal land practices, the hated monarchy, and above all, the British presence in Egypt. The last was particularly offensive, since it wounded Egyptian pride and self-respect.

From the Persian conquest of 525 BC until the middle of the twentieth century, Egypt lacked genuine independence. Muhamad

Naguib wrote: 'After having been Iranized, Hellenized, Romanized, and Byzantinized, we were Arabized in the seventh century only to be Ottamanized in the thirteenth. Six centuries later we were Gallicized by Napoleon and Anglicized by a succession of British proconsuls, including Cromer, Kitchener, and Allenby.'[2] It was the presence of the proconsuls that helped to stimulate an Egyptian nationalist movement. The 'Urabi revolt against the Ottomans, ironically, encouraged British imperial interests in the area and thereby set the stage for local agitation against the new, Western rulers of Egypt. A nationalist party, the Wafd, emerged to press, first, for the end of the British protectorate and, then, for a new treaty of alliance that gave Egypt greater freedom. The treaty of 1936, however, also sanctioned the stationing of 10,000 British troops in the Suez Canal Zone.[3]

It was against this background that the Free Officers' movement emerged as a nationalist force within the army. It, like the general populace, was discontented with the continuing British presence in Egypt. In October 1951 Mustafa Nahas did abrogate the Anglo-Egyptian treaty of 1936, but that only signalled the beginning of intense Egyptian-British hostility. Capitalizing on this turmoil, the Free Officers gained a majority of the seats of the Officers' Club Board in early 1952. The king, however, cancelled the election, and this along with the infamous Cairo fire prompted the young revolutionaries to move their target date from November 1955 to 23 July 1952.[4]

The real leader to emerge from the Free Officers was Gamal Abdel-Nasser. Nasser as a proud Egyptian had detested the British occupation of his country since high school days. He recalled that, 'I so often shouted in my childhood, whenever I saw an airplane in the sky: "Ya 'Azeez, Ya 'Azeez. Dahiya takhud al-Ingleez."' (O Almighty God, may a calamity take the English.)[5]

He also said: 'I led demonstrations in the Nahda Secondary School, and I shouted from my heart for complete independence.'[6] His resentment against the British was even stronger when he was a member of the Free Officers. He would tell his colleagues: 'It is the English who are the sources of all our miseries.'[7] Following his lead, the young officers 'wanted to get rid of this dishonor, the expulsion of the English.'[8]

Negotiations dragged on until July 1954 when an agreement was finally reached.[9] According to the Anglo-Egyptian evacuation agreement, the British agreed to leave the base in the Canal Zone in twenty months. However, the British 'would retain some of their stores and some 1,200 civilian experts for a period of seven years, after which the stores and everything else in the old base would be given to Egypt in full'.[10] Nasser praised the agreement:

> The British forces will evacuate our country after twenty months. After twenty months, for the first time, we will feel we are living in a country where there is no occupation which hurts *al-Izzah* (strength or pride). Thus the internal freedom has been completed by the Republic, and the external freedom has been completed by the Agreement. And after twenty months, there will be no English soldier in this country.[11]

The goal of achieving internal autonomy was achieved by June 1956 when the last British soldier left the country.

Autonomy Abroad as Policy Goal: Maximization of Egypt's Position in the Arab World

President Nasser's tactical skill in diplomatic bargaining, which led to the Anglo-Egyptian agreement of 1954, was a turning point in Egyptian foreign policy. For the first time in twenty-five centuries a native Egyptian was in charge of Egypt's destiny. Internally, Nasser became the 'undisputed master of Egypt'. Externally, Nasser became the sole formulator of Egyptian foreign policy. As Boutros Boutros-Ghali explained,

> the formulation of foreign policy . . . is strictly the prerogative and sole responsibility of the Chief Executive. The extent to which the executive is guided by the counsel of his principal associates, including the Minister of Foreign Affairs, is a matter of his personal choice, made in the light of the interest of the state.[12]

Freedom of action was clearly what Nasser needed to enhance his prestige and to 'restore' Egypt's self-respect and to secure its national interest.

It was no secret that Egypt was first in Nasser's mind. His famous formulation of the three circles at whose centre lay Egypt was an obvious indicator of what Nasser thought. The Arab circle was the most important. 'When the struggle was over in Palestine and the seige lifted [where Nasser was caught], and I had returned to Egypt,' Nasser wrote, 'the Arab Circle in my eyes had become a single entity. The events that have taken place since have confirmed my belief.' He went on to say that 'what happened in Cairo had its counterpart in Damascus the next day, and in Beirut, in Amman, in Baghdad and elsewhere.'[13] The homogeneity, history, strategic location, and oil of the Arab world seem to have been the main reasons for Nasser's emphasis on the Arab circle as the most important, which would serve Egypt's prestige, security, and economic interests.[14] To him these great sources of strength called for a hero as leader. 'Here is the role. Here are the lines, and here is the stage. We alone, by virtue of our place, can perform the role,'[15] Nasser wrote.

During Nasser's first few years in power, Egypt and the Arab world were to experience important events, largely due to Nasser's own policies and initiatives. He supported Arab liberation movements, opposed the Baghdad Pact, refused to recognize Israel, attended the Bandung Conference, opened Egypt for Soviet arms, nationalized the Suez Canal Company, attempted to create favourable revolutionary environments in other Arab states, and achieved unity with Syria. In these years Nasser seemed to enjoy his greatest success which, undoubtedly, established Egypt in a unique position in the Arab world. Nasser's quest for autonomy abroad led to the Egyptian drive for hegemony in the Arab countries.

One of Nasser's earliest policies designed to achieve this was the combination of strong anti-colonialism with neutralism. He began to support first the Algerian Liberation Movement which turned to open rebellion in November 1954,[16] one month after the signing of the Anglo-Egyptian treaty. He had reportedly told the French foreign minister, Christian Pineau, that Egypt was training Algerians because 'It is our responsibility to help our Arab brothers everywhere.'[17] Nasser's support for the Algerian nationalist and other North African liberation movements did not cease until the countries concerned gained their independence.

In the Arab Middle East, particularly in the Arabian Peninsula, Nasser also was morally and materially supportive of the national liberation movements against British rule. Egypt openly aided the liberation movement in Aden and said repeatedly that Britain must grant independence to its various colonies in the Arabian peninsula.

His support for liberation groups continued throughout the 1960s. For example, on the occasion of his visit to Yemen, Nasser spoke on 23 April 1964 in San'a, saying that 'Britain must evacuate Aden. Aden and the Arab south are Arab land, and it is impossible for Britain to separate Arabs from Arabs or Yemenis from Yemenis . . .. We will not allow colonialism to remain in any part of the Arab nation.' He added that Britain 'must carry its stick on its shoulders and move out of Aden and the Arab south.'[18]

The Arab masses and leaders admired Nasser for his open opposition to the British and French and for his support for Arab liberation movements. The Arab League also, on the initiative and urging of Egypt, discussed British imperialism in the Arabian Peninsula. On 11 May 1964, the Egyptian foreign ministry asked the League for 'positive Arab support' for national liberation movements in Aden and the Arab south against the British.[19] On 18 and 19 May the political committee of the League discussed Egypt's requests. The committee strongly denounced 'British imperialism in Aden' and called for the member states to 'extend all kinds of aid . . . to liberate the occupied Southern Yemeni.'[20]

Egypt's support for liberation movements was repeatedly pronounced with pride throughout its participation in the non-alignment (or neutralist) conferences of which Egypt was one of the most active members. Nasser's policy was to lead the Arab states under the banner of non-alignment. According to Nasser, his Arab policy 'aims at uniting the Arabs, and making them one nation, and our hope is that a special defence (alliance) would come out from this great rich area, for its inhabitants, carried out by the Arabs alone. Because this definitely will lead to the liberation from colonialism and the foreign powers whether they are big or small.'[21]

Nasser raised this banner at the first major non-alignment conference which was held in Bandung in April 1955. At Bandung he succeeded in forming a united Arab bloc under his leadership.[22] To the delight of many Arabs, he succeeded at this conference in securing the participants' support of his stand on the Palestine problem and on the issue of colonialism in Algeria, Tunisia, and Morocco. The conference called for their independence and the right of self-determination.[23] Nasser also vigorously participated in the Brioni Conference with Tito and Nehru and in the African Conference in Casablanca and the Belgrade Conference in 1961, the Addis Ababa Conference of 1963, the Non-alignment Conference of 1964 which was held in Cairo, and the Lusaka Conference of 1970.[24]

Undoubtedly, Nasser's championing of the 'Arab cause' and his success and prominent role in the international arena were major achievements, inspiring the admiration of the Arab people and strengthening Egypt's position in the Arab world. The Syrian president, Shukri al-Quwatli, for example, saw Nasser in the ranks 'of the greatest men in history', and said that Egypt was the 'hope of the Arabs'.[25]

It is not surprising, therefore, that the Arab League followed Nasser's policy of non-alignment. On the suggestion of Egypt, the League and its members participated in the Bandung Conference.[26] The League's secretary-general, Abdel-Khaliq Hassouna, who attended the conference, summarized his impressions of Arab participation.

> many believed that the Arab States will be disunited inside the conference, and this will hurt the position of the League of Arab States. But I thank God, the participating Arab members were contrary to what people believed, because his Excellency President Gamal Abdel-Nasser made sure in inviting them [Arab delegations] before the Conference started its business and exchanged views with them in all the conference affairs. Agreement was achieved in this meeting to follow a united plan, particularly in relation to the Arab causes submitted to the conference. These are the Palestine, Arab Maghrib and the Trucial issues . . .. It is the honor of every Egyptian, and the honor of every Arab to see the prestigious status of President Gamal Abdel-Nasser bestowed on him by participating representatives of the countries in Bandung, and to the respect, appreciation and admiration which he won for his country and the Arab world.[27]

The political committee of the League met in September and adopted President Nasser's non-alignment policy. Even the cautious Lebanon 'emphasized Lebanon positive responsiveness with the Egyptian President.'[28]

Some observers see that Egyptian-led neutralism is intertwined with a second policy — Arab nationalism. In the words of Boutros-Ghali, 'Arab unity has not yet been achieved in the Middle East; thus, neutralism is a tool for achieving unity, rather than a tool for achieving conciliation outside the Arab world . . .. It is a partial and subjective neutralism rather than an objective neutralism. It will remain so until Arab states pass from the confederation to the federal stage.'[29] This took the form of pan-Arabism which was so badly desired by the Arabs.

This drive for pan-Arabism (al-Qawmiyyah al-Arabiyyeh) preceded President Nasser by many years. The high level of Arab homogeneity (culture, history, language, religion, among other factors) made Arabism emotionally and sentimentally closely linked with what we know as 'the Arab nation'. It is often used interchangeably with 'Arab nationalism'.[30] Al-Qawmiyyah, as a political scientist noted, is an 'expression of values in which a particular nation (*ummah*) attached to them, feels them, and is part of them.'[31] Ibn Khaldun commented that Arab nationalism, in the words of Majid Khadduri, is 'an attachment to the ethnic structure of the group'.[32] An Arab intellectual wrote that pan-Arabism is composed of those who 'spoke Arabic and who wanted to be an Arab, regardless of his religion or origin.'[33]

Until the early 1950s several Arab nationalist movements championed pan-Arabism and Arab unity. However, it was during the presidency of Nasser that pan-Arabism experienced perhaps its most dynamic phase in recent history. For it was Nasser who captured the imagination and admiration of Arab nationalists. In return, Nasser capitalized on this concept to further his own and Egypt's interests in the Arab world. It was he who stood up and spoke openly against Western 'imperialism', and he who called explicitly for fighting foreign rule in the Arab world. Nasser championed Arab causes and preached Arab unity as a means to defeat 'imperialism' and create a strong, prosperous Arab nation. He saw pan-Arabism as strength, independence, the end of foreign domination and exploitation, dignity, construction, the end of the traitors' era, and as unity and power.[34] Pan-Arabism commanded wide popular support among the Arab masses and became a source of popular and elite expectations that made Nasser attempt to live up to it. To achieve pan-Arabism, Nasser was aided by Egypt's population, its relatively high level of economic development, its role as the centre of Arab educational and intellectual activities and, above all, by his own charisma and personality. Furthermore, one year after the revolution, the powerful 'Voice of the Arabs' was established and rapidly became the most popular radio station in the Arab world. The 'Voice of the Arabs' not only beamed Nasser's views but also said what the Arabs wanted to hear. Since the majority of the Arabs rely on the transistor for information, Nasser's speeches and views drew him strong support from all segments of Arab society. According to John C. Campbell, a sound observer of the Middle East, Nasser won Arab support 'because his successes correspond to the profound emotional desires of so many Arabs: to assert their pride in themselves, their feeling of unity, their right of equality, their sovereignty, their place in the sun; to humiliate those who so often had humiliated them; to gain revenge for the disaster of Palestine.'[35]

Several issues gave rise to a prounounced pan-Arab sentiment, which Nasser manipulated to maximize Egypt's role in the Arab world. One was the Arab response to Western-inspired military pacts. The Western powers, to 'contain' Communism, introduced the Middle East defence system. The USA and Britain urged the Arab states to join in an alliance with Turkey, Iran, and Pakistan. In reaction to this system, Nasser attempted to form his own 'Arab System'. Heikal said that 'Nasser felt that the answer to communist infiltration did not lie in joining Western-sponsored alliances with their 'imperialist' overtones, but rather in prompting internal economic and social development and in affirming the spirit of nationalism and independence.'[36] This, perhaps, explains why Egypt began to emphasize the 1950 Arab collective security pact one month after the revolution.

The council of this pact met for the first time in 1953 and again in 1954. In August 1953 Nasser spoke to the chiefs-of-staff of the Arab Armies Conference in Cairo. He said, in part, 'The Collective Security Pact between the states of the Arab League was as a matter of fact only a natural result of the principles' of the collective desire for security and co-operation.[37] This concern of Nasser was a natural result of geopolitics, for Egypt's national security was, and still is, a matter of priority. This 'is partly a reflection of Egypt's historic vulnerability: in modern as well as earlier times she has been invaded and occupied on repeated occasions — by France, Britain, the Ottoman Turks, Italy, Germany, again France and Britain, and Israel,' Middle Eastern expert, Malcolm Kerr, wrote.[38]

After Egypt concluded the Anglo-Egyptian agreement of 1954, Nasser, henceforth, pursued a vigorous pan-Arab policy. The revolution's spokesman, Major Salah Salem, began to make references to 'some sort of Arab unity' and 'simultaneous federation of Arab states.'[39] Nasser himself used this theme more explicitly to advance his quest for pan-Arabism. For example, when the Baghdad

Pact became known, Nasser exhorted the Arab masses and leaders to oppose the pact as an 'imperialist' pact that sought to serve Western interests against Arab wishes. He asked the Arabs to steer clear of any Western pact and propounded the view that 'pan-Arabism is the real threat to colonialism.'[40] Due in part to Egyptian use of public pressure, demonstrations swept Arab countries, praising Nasser and opposing the pact. In Jordan King Hussein not only changed his view about joining the pact, but also dismissed the British General Glubb, who until then was the Jordanian army chief-of-staff.

A second issue which prompted pan-Arabist feeling, and accrued to Nasser's benefit was the reaction to Israel's manœuvres in the mid-1950s. For strategic and other reasons (to weaken American-Egyptian relations), Israel carried out continuous attacks on Egyptian territories in this period. The Egyptian troops were no match for the Israelis and the Egyptian leaders knew it. However, Nasser, rhetorically, claimed that Egypt was teaching Israel unforgettable lessons. His information minister, Salah Salem, said that the Egyptian army (in July 1955) was stronger 'seven times more than all the other Arab armies put together'.[41] Salem claimed that the revolution in Egypt 'achieved a miracle in three years which made it possible to create an army . . . which, alone, can win over Israel.'[42] Salem's president told the visiting Syrian chief-of-staff, Shawkat Shuqair, that 'Israel today thinks ten times before it attacks Egypt because of its knowledge of (our) army's strength and readiness.'[43] Despite all these assertions and exaggerations, Israel inflicted considerable losses on the Egyptian army, which exposed Egyptian weakness.

Jordanians, Syrians, Lebanese, Saudis, and even Egypt's Iraqi rivals proclaimed their 'readiness' to come to the aid of Egypt.[44] Arab radios and papers (mostly government controlled) praised the Egyptian army's 'victorious' and 'heroic' stand against the Israeli aggression.[45] Abdel-Khaliq Hassouna, the secretary-general of the Arab League, called on all the Arab countries and the whole world to support Egypt in its stand against Israel. He said that the 'stand of Egypt's army is a pride to every Arab.'[46] Nasser responded to the emotional Arab reaction by saying that

> Egypt appreciates the high spirit, which the Arab States'
> peoples and governments, expressed in their support of
> Egypt in its struggle with Israel. Israel's aggression on Egypt
> proved to the whole world that the Arabs are one nation and

that foreign conspiracies and colonialist attempts will never divide them (the Arabs) . . .. *I promise all the Arabs that I will be always the faithful soldier to Arabism, who works for its strength and unity.* [47] (author's emphasis)

The above events and statements by various Arab leaders had great psychological impact on the Arab masses. Indeed, the reaction to Nasser's moves was hysterical and he 'began to look like a "new Saladin" and to be called savior of the Arabs.'[48] The pan-Arabist Ba'ath leaders Aflaq, Hurani, Bitar, and Rimawi were immensely impressed by Nasser's stand. 'From early 1955, the Ba'athists hitched their ideological wagon to the Nasser star' and 'he was made the symbol of Arab unity.'[49]

Support for Nasser's policy came also from the Arab League. During the October 1955 Council meeting, the president of the Council, Muhammad al'-Amri of Yemen, endorsed by other members, supported Nasser's foreign policy stance. The council, unanimously, sent the Egyptian president a telegram in which the League's members 'express to your excellency its appreciation for the Egyptian government's stand and its solidarity with the vigilant policy that Egypt [was] pursuing which aims to strengthen its powers which in turn [was] the strength of the Arabs and their power.'[50]

A third issue stimulating pan-Arabism was Nasser's nationalization of the Suez Canal Company. The nationalization of the Suez Canal Company was the retaliation to John Foster Dulles, the US secretary of state, who on 19 July 1956 announced American withdrawal of his government's offer to help in building the Aswan High Dam. Nasser's blunt act was seen in the Arab world as a resounding defeat of Western 'imperialism'. Egyptians and other Arabs were jubilant over Nasser's nationalization of the Suez Company. They shouted the canal is an 'Arab canal'. 'Arab nationalism began to appear in its best form and clearest meaning,' wrote political scientist Leonard Binder.[34]

The nationalization led to the invasion of Egypt by Britain, France, and Israel. For a variety of reasons, Nasser was able to turn his military defeat into a political triumph. The tripartite open aggression aroused the Soviet Union, the USA, and the UN to support Egypt, resulting in the withdrawal of the invading forces. Nasser's stand in the Suez episode gained him far-reaching support throughout the Arab world. Nasser was careful to express his appreciation for the Arab stand and the support of pan-Arabism's strength.

Support for Nasser against the foreign invasion came not only from the masses, who reacted by violent demonstrations and destruction of oil pipelines, but from Arab leaders as well. Even arch-rival Iraq, which disliked Nasser's foreign policies, was compelled, by Nasser's soaring popularity in the Arab world to support him against the West. Hussein of Jordan, al-Quwatli of Syria, Saud of Arabia, al-Mughrabi of Sudan, Faisal of Iraq, Sham'oun of Lebanon, Ben-Halim of Libya, and al-Badr of Yemen, met in Lebanon on 13–15 November 1956 and discussed the invasion of Egypt. Their attitudes were expressed through President al-Quwatli: 'We hope to meet next time and the man who defends Pan-Arabism, in all these states and the dear part of the Arab world, Egypt, will be among us. We hope the national defence leader of all the Arab States will be with us.'[52]

The secretary-general of the Arab League also denounced the Western threat after the nationalization of the Suez Company and spoke as if Egypt were the Arab nation.

> All the sons of the Arab nation agreed on total unity to
> defend their nation's sovereignty and promised to stand as
> one rank in the face of danger which surrounds the national
> independence, and to oppose imperialism who try through
> violence and aggression to regain its lost authority and to
> defeat the Arab people . . .

Furthermore the Arab League unanimously supported Egypt's stand on complete sovereignty over the Suez Canal.[53]

Another issue of importance to pan-Arabism was Arab unity. The slogan of Arab unity was of paramount importance in Nasser's speeches and statements on his pan-Arabist policy. The Egyptian president had to take drastic action in the name of this policy, before another Arab leader, for example King Saud, could preempt his leadership of the Arab world. That action was union with Syria.

Before the end of 1957 an Egyptian parliamentary delegation visited Syria and discussed union between the two countries.[54] On 12 January 1958 the Syrian chief-of-staff and other Syrian officers who went to Cairo, were joined by the Ba'athist foreign minister, Salah al-Bitar, and the subject was unity. The discussion was followed by a visit of the Syrian president, Shukri al-Quwatli, who along with Nasser, announced the birth of the United Arab Republic on 1 February 1958. The two leaders proclaimed that this unity was a 'fruit of pan-Arabism'.[55] Yemen signed a pact of confederation with the

UAR a month later. This was indeed the climax of Nasser's pan-Arabism. The Arab people went wild and hysterical about the new unity, which brought back to them 'the memory of the earlier union' between the two states under Saladin.[56] The scene in Syria, Egypt, and other Arab states was one of hysterical joy. Sadat describes the scene in Syria right after the official announcement of the union:

> We [Nasser, Sadat and Quwatli] arrived in Damascus and spent a whole week in the Presidential Guesthouse . . . It was like a constant delirium — a stream of talk that followed day and night, Nasser making a speech, followed by al-Kuwatli, then by me, then by Nasser again, *ad infinitum*! We were joined in that speechmaking marathon by some Syrian leaders and we simply couldn't stop, for our Syrian audiences wanted more. The crowds couldn't get enough and seemed to grow increasingly frenzied. All that was said was hailed, applauded, celebrated. People chanted and screamed and called for more. For a week the crowds besieged the Guesthouse. They camped outside in the wide square, eating, drinking, and sleeping in the open air.[57]

Pan-Arabism under the leadership of Nasser was enthusiastically revived after the new pro-Cairo Ba'athist leaderships in Damascus and Baghdad came to power in 1963. The Ba'athists initiated proposals for a possible tripartite union between Egypt, Syria, and Iraq. However, the unity discussions, which were held in Cairo in March and April 1963, did not go well. For Nasser was still bitter over the Ba'athist role in the secession and never trusted their 'unethical methods'. He insisted that 'If the Ba'ath party is ruling Syria and unity is to be with the party, then I definitely am not prepared to hold any discussion.'[58] The Ba'ath party was indeed ruling Syria and they did insist on a central role in any form of unity. Thus, after long days and nights of discussions, the three countries agreed on an ambiguous form of union for the future, which was announced in April. The unity talks were 'based on very little substance' and 'little had really been decided.'[59] Shortly afterwards differences between Baghdad, Damascus, and Cairo made their relations worse, and the unity plan was never carried out.

While Egypt was engaged in bitter disputes with several League members, Israel was about to complete its project to divert the waters of the river Jordan to the Negev desert. At the same time Egypt was suffering heavy losses in Yemen and no end to that conflict seemed on the horizon. Suddenly Nasser changed his tactics from violent attacks on his Arab adversaries to conciliation, inviting Arab leaders to come to Cairo to deal with the crisis of the Israeli diversion of the Jordan waters. Nasser was sensitive to Arab criticism that he was unable to do anything about the Israeli problem. He countered in these terms:

> Who is naturally and understandingly calling for Pan-Arabism? We called for Pan-Arabism and when called upon us we sent 40 thousand soldiers to Yemen . . . And when Ben-Bella sent a letter asking for troops to help him to stop the aggression we answered him 24 hours later . . .. We don't say Pan-Arabism by tongue and then practice it through conspiracies and the ancient political methods . . .. I suggest a meeting of the Arab kings and presidents and I will notify the Arab League to call for this meeting, as soon as possible.[60]

The first Arab summit meeting took place less than a month after Nasser called for it. In his reaction to the achievements of this summit he said: 'We attempted to create a united Arab front and I think we stepped into success.' He said that to achieve Arab unity was 'to stop our internal differences and to settle our disputes and to resume our friendly relations, and this was among what the summit had achieved.'[61] The 'friendly relations' did indeed prevail throughout 1964 and 1965. The summit meetings were supposed to solve the Yemen war, but the conflict in Yemen was not settled and Egyptian losses were becoming unbearable. Throughout 1966 and until May 1967 Nasser was engaged in bitter disputes with the Arab 'reactionaries' led by the Saudi king who, to the dismay of Nasser, advocated an Islamic conference following his visits to the conservative states of Iran, Jordan, Morocco, and Turkey. Undoubtedly, until then Nasser was considered as the natural leader of Arab unity.[62] Nasser ended the era of Arab summits and on 22 July vowed not to meet Arab 'reactionaries' until they mended their ways.

Nasser's success, particularly in the Suez crisis, brought his popularity to a climax in the Arab countries, and Cairo became the Mecca of Arab nationalism. By now the 'new Saladin' unquestionably was the leader of pan-Arabism and the champion of Arab unity. But from this pinnacle, he began to interfere in the internal affairs of other Arab countries with little, if any, opposition. He encouraged the opponents of Arab regimes at odds with Egypt in the name of pan-Arabism.[63] In a speech to his general staff, Nasser dropped some hints:

> Those who think unity of the Arabs will come as a result of speeches should open their eyes and look at our army. But the Army is not the only means. There are special political means. We must work to strengthen opposition groups . . . you officers should know that the work of military attachés is very dangerous, but we cannot do without it . . . Army officers must be able not only to use guns, but to pursue a war of nerves and to direct commandos.[64]

Shortly after the 1957 heads of state conference in Cairo (in which Egypt, Syria, and Saudi Arabia agreed to replace British subsidies to Jordan), the military attachés in Lebanon, Libya, and Tunisia were implicated in plots against these countries' governments. Less than two months after Nasser had kissed King Saud at Cairo airport, a plot to kill the king was discovered in which the Egyptian military attaché was implicated. In Jordan a coup d'état against the king was foiled, and Hussein bluntly accused Nasser of trying to bring about his downfall.[65]

King Saud, King Hussein, and King Faisal of Iraq patched up their differences and vowed to come to each other's aid in the event of a threat to their thrones. Nasser was angered by the new alignment of the three kings and unleashed his propaganda machine against them. In response to the formation of the UAR and due, in part, to Nasser's own agitations, unrest broke out in Lebanon and Jordan and the Iraqi monarchy was overthrown. Popular demand nearly toppled the regimes in Lebanon and Jordan, and American marines and British troops were sent to Beirut and Amman respectively, to bolster the two regimes.

In 1958 the news of the new republican regime in Baghdad was welcomed by Nasser, but his satisfaction with the new regime did not last long. The new Iraqi leader, Abdel-Karim Qassim, was no less an arch-rival to Nasser than his predecessor, Nuri al-Sa'id. Egyptian media soon began to call him the 'red butcher'. On 8 December 1958 Qassim said that a conspiracy aimed at overthrowing his regime had been discovered. He said the plot 'was the work of some corrupt elements with the help of foreigners outside Iraq.' Although he did not specifically say who the 'foreigners' were, it was widely believed that he was pointing the finger at Cairo.[66] In early 1959 Colonel Abdel-Wahab el-Shawaf, commander of the local garrison, and a group of pro-Cairo officers, seized power in the city of Mosul and denounced Qassim. The rebellion was brief, however, and Egypt was implicated in this short-lived revolt.[67] These events exacerbated the already bad relations between Iraq and Egypt. Indeed, the UAR itself was soon to experience major difficulties which led to the Syrian secession in 1961.

The policy of destabilization adopted new ideological terms after the breakup of the UAR. The new term of Nasser's pan-Arabism was 'unity of goal' instead of the old slogan, 'unity of rank'. On the occasion of the fourth anniversary of the union, Nasser asked: 'Do we want unity of the Arab rank? I am for unity of the Arab goal to be reached before talking about the unity of the Arab rank.'[68] Mohamed H. Heikal explained this new strategy in an editorial in *al-Ahram*. He argued that the UAR's new Arab policy distinguished between 'Egypt as a state' and 'Egypt as a revolution'.

> As a state, Egypt deals with all Arab governments, whatever their forms or systems ... As a revolution, Egypt should deal only with the people. We should do our utmost to co-operate with governments, but we should not extend such co-operation to the point where popular movements are affected. If the Arab League were to be used to paralyze our movement, *we should even be prepared to freeze the operation of that body.*[69]
> (author's emphasis)

This attitude perhaps stimulated a new round of destabilizing tactics. The new Syrian regime, for example, called for a meeting of the Arab League to stop Egyptian 'subversive' activities in Syria. The League met at Shtoura, Lebanon, and discussed the Syrian complaints. Egypt threatened to walk out of the meeting if Syria did not withdraw its complaint. Damascus pressed for the League's condemnation instead. Egypt angrily walked out and for a while withheld its share of the League's finances.

Another example of Egyptian destabilizing tactics in keeping with the new revolutionary line was the Yemeni case. An Egyptian-inspired coup d'état overthrew the royalists in San'a, and the new revolutionary leader, Abdallah al-Sallal, immediately called on Nasser for help to sustain his movement. Nasser was quick to dispatch Egyptian troops to that unfamiliar land. Nasser's military intervention was highly praised by revolutionary pan-Arabists, but it was denounced by Arab royalists, particularly by King Saud whose country was subjected to periodic Egyptian bombing from Yemen. Nasser said that Egyptian troops in Yemen were fighting 'the noblest battle; for the battle of Pan-Arabism and Arab Unity'.[70] None the less, Egyptian involvement in Yemen led to a protracted war, and, thus, to unhappy consequences for Egypt.

On other fronts, Nasser found himself drawn into the conflict between Algeria and Morocco. He called the Moroccans the 'aggressors', and, he asked the Arab League to mediate between the two countries. He then went further and sent troops to aid the Algerians. In response to Nasser's actions the Moroccan king recalled his ambassador from Cairo, expelled hundreds of Egyptians from Morocco, and accused the League of Arab States of being under the domination of Egypt.[71]

Conclusion

Egyptian foreign policy under Nasser was designed principally to increase the freedom of action of the country. This search for autonomy led to Nasser's expulsions of the British from Egyptian soil, and it gradually, in the external realm, generated a search for hegemony in the Arab world. Nasser's ambitions were to make Egypt central and to have the other Arab states follow its lead. The defeat of 1967, however, dashed these ambitions. From then until his death in September 1970, Nasser had no choice but co-operate with other Arab leaders. He was no longer the undisputed leader of the Arab world.

Notes to chapter three

1   R. K. Ramazani, *Iran's Foreign Policy, 1941–1973: A Study of Foreign Policy in Modernizing Nations*, Charlottesville, University Press of Virginia, 1975, p. 15.

2   Muhamad Naguib, *Egypt's Destiny*, New York, Doubleday, 1955, p. 168. See also Robert Stephens, *Nasser: A Political Biography*, New York, Simon and Schuster, 1971, p. 11.

3   See Muhamad Sbaih, *Days and Days* (in Arabic), Cairo, Matba'at al-'Alam al-Arabi, 1967, p. 420; Anthony Nutting, *No End of a Lesson: The Story of Suez*, New York, Clarkson N. Potter, 1967, p. 8; Mahmoud Kamel, *Islam and Arabism*, (in Arabic), Cairo, Al-Haiy'ah al-Misriyyah al-'Amah lil-Kitab, 1976, pp. 199–201; 'Min Awraq al-Rais el-Sadat' (from the papers of President Sadat), *October* (Cairo), 23 October 1977, p. 16; Kamel, p. 174; Stephens, p. 36.

4   Anwar el-Sadat, *In Search of Identity*, New York, Harper and Row, 1978, pp. 103–06; Sbaih, p. 422; Muhamad Naguib contends that out of 19 officers who won seats on the Officers' Club Board only five were from the Free Officers' group. *Rose el-Youssef* (Cairo), 29 August 1977, p. 10.

5   Gamal Abdel-Nasser, *Egypt's Liberation: The Philosophy of the Revolution*, Washington, D. C., Public Affairs Press, 1955, p. 55.

6   Ibid., p. 50.

7   Anwar el-Sadat, *Secrets of the Egyptian Revolution* (in Arabic), Cairo, al-Dar al-Qawmiyyah lil-Tiba'ah wal-Nashr, 1965, p. 34.

8   'Min Awraq al-Rais el-Sadat', *October*, 4 December 1977, p. 20.

9   *Abdel-Latif al-Baghdadi Memoire*, part I, Cairo, Alexandria al-Maktab al-Misri al-Hadith, 1977, p. 77.

10 el-Sadat, *op. cit.* p. 133.

11 United Arab Republic. Information Bureau, *Majmu'at Khutab Watasrihat Wabianat al-Rais Gamal Abdel-Nasser* (President Gamal Abdel-Nasser Speeches), part I (23 July 1952–1958), p. 227.

12 Boutros Boutros-Ghali, 'The Foreign Policy of Egypt', in Joseph E. Black and Kenneth W. Thompson (eds) *Foreign Policy in a World of Change*, New York, Harper and Row, 1963, p. 320.

13 Gamal Abdel-Nasser, *op. cit.* p. 98.

14 Ibid., p. 106.

15 Ibid., p. 114.

16 Stephens, p. 157.

17 Ibid., p. 182. For Egyptian support for Moroccan and Tunisian nationalists, see Kennett Love, *Suez: The Twice-Fought War*, New York, Toronto, McGraw-Hill, 1969, pp. 134–35.

18 *President Gamal Abdel-Nasser Speeches*, part IV (February 1962–June 1964), pp. 551–52.

19 *Minutes of the League Council*, 41st ordinary session, 21 March 1964–21 May 1964, pp. 342–44.

20 Ibid., pp. 35–36.

21 *al-Ahram*, 8 September 1955, p. 6.

22 Ibid., 18 April 1955, p. 1.

23 Ibid., 22 April 1955, p. 1.

24 See Boutros Boutros-Ghali, '*al-Nasseriyyeh wal-Siyyaseh al-Misriyyeh al-Kharijiyyeh*', (Nasserism and Egyptian Foreign Policy), *al-Siyyassah al-Dawliyyah* (Cairo), no. 23 (January 1971).

25 *al-Ahram*, 8 September 1955, p. 6.

26 '*Muthakarat Masśo ol Arabi Muttali*', (Memoire of an Informed Arab Official), (Anonymous), *al-Ahram*, 23 March 1978, p. 5.

27 *al-Ahram*, 5 May 1955, p. 6.

28 Ibid., 4 September 1955, p. 9.

29 Boutros Boutros-Ghali, 'The Foreign Policy of Egypt', p. 347.

30 A. I. Dawisha, *Egypt in the Arab World*, London, Macmillan, 1976, p. 129.

31 William Griffith, *al-Siyyassah al-Dawliyyah* (Cairo), no. 52 (April, 1978), p. 242.

32 Majid Khadduri, 'The Problem of Regional Security in the Middle East: An Appraisal', *Middle East Journal*, vol. 11, no. 1 (winter, 1957), p. 14.

33 al-Mussawar (Cairo), March 1964, p. 17.

34 Ahmad Farid Ali, *The Arab League Between the Reactionary Forces and the Popular Forces* (in Arabic), Cairo, al-Mo'assasah al-Misriyyah al-'Amah, 1972, p. 76.

35 John C. Campbell, *Defense of the Middle East: Problems of American Policy*, New York, F. A. Praeger, 1960, p. 77.

36 Muhamed H. Heikal, 'Egyptian Foreign Policy', *Foreign Affairs*, vol. 56, no. 4 (July 1978), pp. 719–20.

37 Boutros Boutros-Ghali, 'Nasserism and Egyptian Foreign Policy', p. 12.

38 Malcolm H. Kerr, 'Regional Arab Politics and the Conflict with Israel', in Paul Y. Hammond and Sidney S. Alexander (eds), *Political Dynamics in the Middle East*, New York, American Elsevier Publishing Company, 1972, p. 39.

39 *al-Ahram*, 17 January 1954 and 18 April 1954, quoted in R. Hrair DeKmejian, *Egypt under Nasser*, p. 38.

40 Ahmad Shafiq Abu-'Ouf '*al-Ma'thuratt al-Khalidah le-Mabadi wa-Ta'aleem al-Zaim Gamal Abdel-Nasir*', (*The Eternal Principles and Teachings of Gamal Abdel-Nasser* Cairo, Matba'at al-Amin, 1970, p. 50.

41 *al-Ahram*, 5 July 1955, p. 6.

42   Ibid., 8 July 1955, p. 8.
43   Abdel-Latif al-Baghdadi in *Rose el-Youssef* (Cairo) 22 August 1977, p. 24.
44   *al-Ahram*, 3 September 1955, p. 1.
45   Ibid., 4 September 1955, p. 1.
46   Ibid., 26 August 1955, p. 6; 2 September, 1955, p. 6.
47   Ibid., 6 September 1955, p. 1.
48   George M. Haddad, *Revolutions and Military Rule in the Middle East: The Arab States, Part II: Egypt, the Sudan, Yemen, and Libya*, vol. 3, New York, Robert Speller 1973, p. 84.
49   Wilton Wynn, *Nasser of Egypt*, Cambridge, Mass., Arlington Books, 1959, pp. 141–42.
50   *Minutes of the League Council*, 24th ordinary session, 1 October 1955–19 January 1956, p. 507.
51   Leonard Binder, *The Ideological Revolution in the Middle East*, New York, John Wiley and Sons, 1964, p. 211.
52   Mitri Matta, *'Mo'tamar Ashab al-Jalalah wal-Fakhamah Milook wa-Roa'sa' al-Dowal al-Arabiyyeh fi Lubnan'* (*Conference of their Majesties and Excellencies Kings and Presidents of the Arab States in Lebanon, 1956*), Beirut, Jaridatt al-Balagh, 1956.
53   Muhamad Ali al-Rifa'i, The Arab League and the Liberation Causes (in Arabic), Cairo, al-Sharikah al-Misriyyah lil-Tiba'ah wal-Nashr, first edn 1971, pp. 188–89.
54   Muhamad Tal'at al-Ghuneimi, *The League of Arab States* (in Arabic), Alexandria, Minsha'at al-Ma'arif, 1974, p. 262.
55   Mahmoud Kamel, *Arab International Law* (in Arabic), Beirut, Dar-al'ilm lil-Malayeen, 1965, p. 402.
56   Dawisha, *Egypt in the Arab World*, p. 106.
57   el-Sadat, *In Search of Identity*, p. 152.
58   *United Arab Republic, Mahadar Jalsat Mubahathat al-Wuhda*, Cairo, National Printing and Publishing House, 1963, p. 574, p. 7. Quoted in Dawisha, *op. cit.*, p. 41.
59   For lucid and detailed discussion of the unity talks of March and April 1963, see Malcolm H. Kerr, *The Arab Cold War: Gamal Abdel-Nasser and His Rivals, 1958–1970*, London, New York, Oxford University Press, third edn, 1971, pp. 48–95.
60   *'Khutab Wa-Tasrihatt wa-Baianatt al-Rais Gamal Abdel-Nasser'*, (President Gamal Abdel-Nasser Speeches) part IV (February 1962–June 1964), pp. 492–93.
61   Ibid., p. 497.
62   P. J. Vatikiotis, *The Modern History of Egypt*, New York, Washington, Praeger, 1969, p. 407.
63   Nasser once said, 'I tell my intelligence service that the only revolutions which succeed in the Middle East are those we don't make.'

Humphrey Trevelyan, *Diplomatic Channels*, London, Macmillan, 1973, p. 118.

64 Quoted in Robert St. John, *The Boss: The Story of Gamal Abdel-Nasser*, New York, Toronto, London, McGraw-Hill, 1960, p. 275.

65 Ibid.

66 George Lenczowski, *The Middle East in World Affairs*, Ithaca and London, Cornell University Press, third edn, 1962, p. 301.

67 Ibid., p. 303. See also Boutros Boutros-Ghali, 'The Foreign Policy of Egypt', in Joseph E. Black and Kenneth W. Thompson (eds) *Foreign Policies in a World of Change*, New York, Harper and Row, 1963, p. 340.

68 *Address by President Gamal Abdel-Nasser on the Occasion of the Fourth Anniversary of the Union, February 22nd, 1962*, Cairo, Information Department, 1962, p. 27.

69 Malcolm H. Kerr, *The Arab Cold War, 1958–1964: A Study of Ideology in Politics*, London, Oxford University Press, 1965, pp. 38–39.

70 *President Gamal Abdel-Nasser Speeches*, part IV (February 1962–June 1964), p. 384.

71 Dawisha, *op. cit.*, p. 42.

Chapter Four

The Baghdad Pact: 1955

The 1955 Iraq case was the first important situation where President Gamal Abdel-Nasser utilized the Arab League to serve his ambitions and Egypt's interests in the Arab world. Here Nasser attempted, and, by and large, succeeded in manipulating the League's collective security arrangement. The League's secretary-general and its council supported Nasser's foreign policy in the case of Iraq in 1955.

When Iraq concluded with Turkey the Western-inspired Turco-Iraqi treaty (henceforth the Baghdad Pact), Nasser was enraged. He opposed the Baghdad Pact for several reasons. He argued that foreign-inspired pacts were a threat to the Arab League and to the security of the Arab states. They were mainly to serve Western interests in the region (i.e. containment of Communism, oil). But underlying these contentions were more important concerns:
1 Nasser saw agreements inspired by the West were likely to isolate Egypt from the rest of the Arab countries;
2 he perceived such treaties would strengthen his Arab rivals such as Nuri al-Sa'id of Iraq;
3 therefore, Nasser concluded, such pacts would severely undermine his aspirations and ambitions in the Arab world.

It followed that Nasser was determined to prevent such a thing from happening. To stop Iraq from joining a non-Arab pact, Nasser invoked the sanction of two Arab pacts. This did not work effectively and the Iraqi prime minister, Nuri al-Sa'id, signed the Baghdad Pact anyway. This challenge to Nasser's position in the Arab world led to the Arab League leaders' conference in Cairo, called by Nasser. Nasser, through the conference, tried to pressure Nuri al-Sa'id to abide by the Arab League and the collective security pacts. When this failed, Nasser launched a vigorous campaign against Iraq and its leader. His campaign discouraged any other Arab League member from joining the pact and resulted ultimately in the downfall of the Iraqi monarchy. A brief comment on the Arab collective security pact and the Baghdad Pact is important in order to understand why Nasser used the former against the latter.

The Arab Collective Security Pact

The idea of an Arab collective security scheme goes back many years. The turning point was the Palestine tragedy which alerted Arab leaders to the external threat to their countries. Because of this, Syria suggested to the League council that members conclude a political and military alliance. The council submitted the Syrian suggestion to the political committee, which created a committee comprised of one representative from each member state to study and formulate a plan form. A collective security committee was established and discussed the subject of Arab collective defence. This committee commenced meeting in early November 1949. The committee discussed Syrian, Lebanese, Iraqi, and Egyptian proposals. By the end of November, the committee reached an agreement on the collective defence treaty plan[1]. Egypt worked vigorously to help the Arab collective pact come into existence. The pact appeared to combat foreign threats, but it was quite conceivable that the Arab security pact 'was designed by Egypt not merely against Israel, but also against any such initiatives on the part of one or more member states.'[2]

The League council met on 25 March 1950 and sent the collective security committee's suggestions to the political committee which discussed them in seven meetings held between 1 and 11 April. To improve their military situation and to strengthen economic co-operation, the League council met on 13 April and studied and approved the proposed treaty of collective security and economic co-operation.

Before it was signed, Britain, France, and the USA issued a tripartite declaration on 25 May 1950 envisaging maintenance of armed balance and the status quo in the Middle East. The Arab League met on 12 June 1950, studied the tripartite declaration, and reacted promptly to it. The council passed a resolution prepared by the political committee which stated that 'the primary responsibility in keeping stability and peace in the region falls on the Arab countries individually and collectively (the Arab League) as a regional organization under Article 52 of the United Nations Charter. The governments of the Arab States cannot grant the right to another country or several ones who work outside the United Nations as international police in this region.'[3] The Arab countries through the Arab League opposed any foreign country's right of interference in the affairs of the Arab countries.

On 17 June 1950 the Arab collective security pact was completed, and Egypt, Lebanon, Saudi Arabia, Syria, and Yemen signed the pact that day. Iraq and Jordan appended their signatures on 2 February 1951 and 16 February 1952 respectively, and it came into force on 23 August 1952 when the requisite formalities of ratification were completed. Iraq and Yemen made certain reservations.[4]

The main aims of the pact were defined as 'realizing the common defence of their existence and maintaining security and peace.'[5] It called for a collective security system to repel any aggression. The pact also provided for the establishment of a joint defence council, composed of the foreign and defence ministers of the contracting states, and a permanent military commission, representing the general staffs of the armies of the participating states. The treaty limited the freedom of the member states by stating that the members could not conclude treaties that contradict the provisions of the Arab collective security pact. Decisions of the defence council by a two-thirds majority vote of the members were binding upon all.[6] Thus the Arab collective security pact can be seen as an attempt to discourage Arab countries from joining foreign, primarily Western, alliances and to tighten the loose alliance stipulated by the Arab League pact.

The Baghdad Pact

Six months after Iraq ratified the Arab collective security pact (25 March 1953), Nuri al-Sa'id sent a letter to King Faisal of Iraq suggesting that countries within, and outside, the Middle East the active participation of which would bring great benefits (i.e., arms) 'could join in the Arab defence'. Or, as an alternative if it was not possible to consider this suggestion, it was plausible to establish some sort of co-operation between 'the Collective Security bloc and another group which has relations [interests] with the Middle East region'.[7] On 10 January 1954 Iraq submitted to the political committee of the Arab League a proposal for a federation of the Arab countries. The Iraqi delegation, led by Fadil al-Jamali, requested that the League recommend to its members a federation on a piecemeal basis. Al-Jamali accused some Arabs (alluding to Egypt) of being obstacles to the achievement of Arab unity because they insisted on total unity. 'Why shouldn't two or more Arab states unite or federate forthwith and wait for other states to join them when their domestic circumstances and international commitments permit?' al-Jamali asked.[8]

A few months later Iraqi intentions became more explicit. Nuri communicated with Arab states on the possibility of having close relations with the West. In August 1954 he suggested the enlargement of the Arab collective security pact to a regional alliance in which Iran, Pakistan, and Turkey would be included. This new alliance would receive military aid from Britain and the USA. Such a regional framework, however, would only be a cover for Nuri's old ambition, the Fertile Crescent scheme, to unite Syria, Lebanon, and Jordan under Iraqi leadership.[9] Nuri visited Turkey in October and talked with Turkish Prime Minister Adnan Menderes about the possibility of 'gathering' the Arab countries with Iran, Pakistan, and Turkey in order to co-operate on matters of mutual concern. Both men seemed to agree on the need for some kind of Iraqi-Turco alliance. Discussion and conclusion of this plan were left for the Menderes visit to Baghdad which took place in early January 1955.

The joint communiqué of 12 January stated that Iraq would conclude a military alliance with Turkey. The alliance, the communiqué said, would be for co-operation between the two countries in preserving stability and peace in the region and for repulsing any aggression that comes from any quarter.[10] Other Middle Eastern countries were invited to join the Iraqi-Turco pact (the Baghdad Pact). Soon after the conclusion of the Menderes-Nuri pact, Fadil al-Jamali visited Syria, Jordan, and Lebanon. He explained the purpose of the new pact and tried to induce these countries to join it.[11] Eventually, Great Britain, Pakistan, and Iran, with American blessing, joined the pact.

The pact's purpose was 'the maintenance of peace and security in the Middle East region'.[12] It called for the contracting parties to 'cooperate for their security and defence'[13] and to 'refrain from any interference whatsoever in each other's internal affairs'.[14] The pact also stated that it was 'open for accession to any member of the Arab League or any other state actively concerned with the security and peace in this region'.[15]

The conclusion and signing of the Baghdad Pact were to lead to a furious reaction from President Nasser who, at first, through the members of the Arab League meeting in Cairo, attempted to dissuade Nuri from concluding such a pact. Egypt's opposition to Iraq was pursued through several tactics.

Egypt's First Tactic in the Arab League Against Iraq

Anthony Eden's remark that 'Jealousy plays a part in this [Egyptian opposition to the Baghdad Pact] and a frustrated desire to lead the Arab world'[16] has at least some truth in it. Nasser feared that the pact might attract Syria, Lebanon, and Jordan (thus achieving the Fertile Crescent scheme) and so take over the Arab leadership and isolate Egypt from the Arab countries that were confronting Israel. Moreover, Nasser believed that the pact would weaken and divide the Arab League at a time when Egypt was attempting to dominate that organization. The Egyptian president sought, by using the Arab collective security pact, to dissuade Baghdad from joining the pact.[17]

Egyptian opposition to foreign pacts goes back some years. As noted in an earlier part of this chapter, the Arab League was designed to co-ordinate the relations among the Arab countries, and the collective security pact was designed to implement the League's pact for defence against outside aggression. But when Baghdad proposed to associate this pact with a broad defence arrangement with the West, particularly with Britain, Egypt opposed the Iraqi intentions on the grounds that the Arab security pact was designed to protect the collective interests of the Arabs. Under Cairo's influence the Arab League 'tended to oppose the policy of cooperation with the West' and supported Egypt's objection to any Arab-Western alliance.[18] However, as mentioned before, the real reason behind Egypt's opposition was Nasser's drive for domination of the Arab League and the Arab collective security pact to serve Egypt's interests. In July 1952 Egypt, in a memo to the League's council, suggested the activation of the Arab security pact. The council, in its meeting on 30 September, agreed with the Egyptian memorandum, and said it was necessary for the security pact council to meet as soon as possible to activate the pact. Soon after that memo the political committee met and appointed Egyptian General Muhamad Ibrahim as a military under-secretary-general of the Arab League. On 4 September 1953 the security defence council held its first session. The resolutions of that meeting called for co-ordination of collective Arab defence matters.[19] The security defence council met again in January 1954, but it faced difficulties in creating and equipping an army under the command of the permanent military commission. At this time Iraq was interested in joining the agreement for friendly co-operation between Pakistan and Turkey of 2 April 1954. The Arab League under the pressure from Egypt strongly opposed the Iraqi intentions. In early April the political committee issued an Egyptian-inspired communiqué stating:

> Every member [of the League] declared that his government
> had not been invited to adhere to this Pact and had never
> thought of joining it. [They] also declared in this connection,
> that their Governments were anxious to respect their
> obligations, exacted by the Pact of the League of Arab
> States and by the Treaty of Joint Defence and Economic
> Co-operation between the States of the League.[20]

Iraq, however, did not retreat from its interest in concluding a pact with non-Arab countries, despite Egypt's opposition 'both inside and outside the League'.[21] This was to lead to a very heated debate in the meeting of the foreign ministers of the Arab League council at the end of 1954.

The foreign ministers met at the Egyptian foreign ministry on 30 November and the meeting was opened by the Egyptian foreign minister, Dr Mahmoud Fawzi. Abdel-Khaliq Hassouna, secretary-general of the Arab League, spoke first. He emphasized the nature of Arab-West relations, noting in particular the West's pro-Israel policy due to 'the Zionist pressure on America and the Western countries'.

The Iraqi foreign minister, Musa el-Shabinder, talked about the importance of an Arab military alliance with the Western countries and Turkey and called on the Arabs 'to unite against Communism'. Co-operation with the West was important for supplying the Arab armies with heavy weapons, and he pointed out further that Egypt itself called for this kind of co-operation after it concluded the evacuation agreement with London. 'The Arabs have two arenas: to struggle against Communism from the East and to struggle against Zionism from the West,' el-Shabinder concluded.[22]

Mahmoud Fawzi realized what the Iraqi minister had in mind and, in an unusual manner, he used strong language in responding to el-Shabinder's speech. He spoke of the Arab interests, from the Egyptian point of view, of course. He said that it was not the Arab responsibility to serve as a bulwark against Communism in the East. With increasing anger, Fawzi said, 'If the purpose [of el-Shabinder's speech] is to conclude international military pacts, I would like to hear this in frankness. Do we want to go back to what we rejected in 1950? Do we want to sell ourselves without a price!!' Fawzi concluded his speech by emphasizing that Arab alliances with foreign pacts 'hurt our interests', and that 'we are not Communist, and we welcome Arab co-operation in the struggle against Communism.'[23] This Arab policy of anti-Communism was however, to be led by Cairo.

The Second Tactic: The Meeting of the Arab League Members in Cairo

Fawzi's strong words against Iraq and the Egyptian effort to pressure other League members to oppose the Iraqi policy only accelerated the concluding of the Turco-Iraqi pact. The Arab foreign ministers were supposed to attend the joint defence council on 10 January, which was to be preceded by the permanent military commission. But Iraq declined to attend the meeting and thus delayed the commission meeting till 17 January, which did not take place.[24] On 12 January 1955 a joint communiqué issued at Baghdad announced the conclusion of an alliance with Turkey — the Baghdad Pact. This infuriated President Nasser who promptly called for an extraordinary meeting of the Arab League prime ministers in Cairo to be held on 22 January, in an attempt to dissuade Iraq from ratifying the pact. Egypt also threatened to withdraw from the Arab collective security pact. Nasser's national guidance minister, Salah Salem, spoke against the pact and said that Egypt believed in strengthening the Arab League and wanted to implement the Arab security pact. Salem claimed that Egypt was 'surprised' by the announcement of the Baghdad Pact. He observed that Nasser told Nuri al-Sa'id that Egypt rejected any alliance outside the League and was opposed to any non-Arab states' joining the Arab collective security pact. 'What is the usefulness of all these efforts utilized under this great name "the League of Arab states"?' Salem asked.[25] Obviously he wanted inter-Arab politics to remain within the framework of the League so that Egypt could deal with the Arabs as it pleased.

In preparation for the Arab prime ministers' meeting, there were meetings in the League's secretariat between Egyptians, Abdel-Khaliq Hassouna, and other League officials. They examined the pacts of the League and of collective security, after which they prepared a memorandum for the general secretariat about the Baghdad Pact. Hassouna also met other Arab officials at the League to express his unhappiness about the Iraqi move and urged Arab governments to refrain from joining foreign pacts. Half-heartedly they expressed their understanding and assured him of their countries' support of Egypt.[26] A close observer of the League noted that Hassouna was very active during the Arab conference meetings in Cairo. He attempted to rally an Arab consensus against the Baghdad Pact because, in his view, the pact was contrary to the pacts of the League and of collective security. But Nasser's vigorous role at the conference overshadowed Hassouna's.[27]

The conference of the Arab prime ministers was held in Cairo at the foreign ministry on 22 January. All the participants, due to Nasser's urging, supported the Egyptian position against Iraq. Nasser's persistence led the Arab officials to accept the Egyptian view that Iraq had violated the League's pact.[28] Iraq at first did not attend this conference. Arab leaders agreed with Nasser's view that the collective security pact stipulated that 'the contracting parties bind themselves not to sign any international agreement which would constitute a derogation to the provisions of this treaty and not to adopt, in their dealings with other powers, an attitude which may be inconsistent with the aims of the present treaty.'[29] Egypt argued forcefully that the Baghdad Pact was clearly inconsistent with the League since Iraq, like the other members, had agreed from the start not to enter into any foreign alliances. Moreover, in the League's response to the tripartite declaration on security in the Arab-Israel crisis in 1950, Iraq supported the 'deep sense of responsibility' of Arab states for protecting 'the internal security of their countries as well as the international security in the region which is primarily the obligation of the Arab League as a regional organization under Article 52 of the United Nations Charter'.[30] Iraq, therefore, in the view of Arab leaders led by Nasser, defied the League by concluding an alliance with a non-Arab country.

Nasser, who chaired the meetings, lectured the assembled Arabs on their duty not only to reject but also to condemn the Baghdad Pact. In his view Iraq had become 'the ally of the ally of Israel'.[31] Nasser wanted the prime ministers to declare that any military pacts concluded by League members with foreign countries were inconsistent with the League's charter and the joint defence pact.[32] The Arab leaders were hesitant in submitting to all his demands, but, by and large, they bowed to Nasser's pressure and they decided on 24

January to:
1   confirm the Arab ministers' decisions (noted above);
2   refuse to join the Baghdad Pact.
The next day, on Nasser's urging, they agreed to establish a joint command in peacetime, which would be enlarged in wartime, made permanent, and charged with co-ordinating training, arming, planning, and communication. It would also be in charge of specifying how many troops each country would contribute within the general policy of the League members who signed the collective defence pact.[33]

On 26 January an Iraqi delegation, led by the former prime minister, Fadil al-Jamali, arrived in Cairo and joined the conference's ninth session in which al-Jamali explained to the conferees the Turco-Iraqi pact. He also told them that 'although Iraq emphasizes its obligations toward the Arab League pact and the joint defence pact, Iraq has the right to take additional steps to ensure its security.'[34] Egypt, after the Iraqis had explained their position, requested, first, the withdrawal of the special decision to establish a joint Arab command in peacetime; second, the end of the collective defence treaty in the event of Iraq's signing the pact with Turkey; and, third, the immediate announcement of this.

Egypt insisted that no Arab country bound by the defence treaty had the right to join any pact other than the Arab pact, except in an unanimous decision by all member states. Egypt, to win the other League members to its side against Iraq, based its position on the argument that it was bound by the Arab pact to help Iraq and that it was not its policy to extend its obligations to include non-Arab countries or to join alliances with the West. Egypt also contended, to stir Arab nationalist sentiments to its advantage, that these kinds of pacts confirm forever the existence of Israel. According to Sayed Nofal, the other Arab countries agreed with Egypt's point of view.[35] But without any doubt, their agreement came as a result of the pressure exerted by Nasser on the premiers. Iraq persisted in its position and when al-Jamali was asked if Iraq was still determined to sign an alliance with Turkey, his answer was 'definitely'.[36] Nasser, strengthened by his success with the Arab leaders, threatened to withdraw from the Arab collective security (or defence) pact. Egyptians now were accusing Nuri of going it alone 'without giving the Arab League the right to discuss with him his policies'.[37] Nuri, according to *al-Ahram*, and in defiance of Nasser's usage of the League meeting, informed the conference that 'I am an independent country and I refuse to let the Arabs govern me', adding that he was the father of the realist school of the Arab world and that the Arabs would realize his value in the future.[38]

The League's prime ministers, although they were, by and large, in support of Egypt's position, were alarmed by the inflexibility of both Cairo and Baghdad. Jordan suggested, and the conference approved, sending a delegation to Iraq to see Nuri in order to work out a compromise. On 31 January the Lebanese prime minister, Sami al-Sulh, the Egyptian minister of national guidance, Salah Salem, the Syrian foreign minister, Faydi al-Atasi, and the Jordanian foreign minister, Walid Salah, arrived in Baghdad.

While the Arab delegation was meeting Nuri in Baghdad, Egypt once again threatened that if Iraq signed the proposed pact with Turkey, Cairo would have no other choice but to withdraw from the Arab collective security pact and to create a new Arab defence pact that would include the Arab states that declined to join foreign alliances.[39] Lebanon's president, Camille Sham'oun, appealed to the Iraqi prime minister to defer signing the Baghdad Pact for four months and to accept an invitation to meet Nasser in Lebanon. Nuri's answer was negative, stating merely that Iraq would not submit to Nasser's 'dictation in the Arab League'.[40] The Arab high-level mission to Baghdad was to be a futile final appeal to Nuri, who reportedly told Salem, at the end of the Arab mission that 'I am not a soldier in Abdel-Nasser's army. Please tell him that I will never obey his orders.'[41]

The emergency Arab League conference resumed its sessions in Cairo on 3 February, chaired by Nasser. The special delegation explained the results of its negotiations with Nuri and revealed that there had been no change in the Iraqi position. Furthermore, the Iraqis told the Arab mission that Baghdad would like to continue as a member of the Arab League and the collective security pact. Again, Lebanon suggested that Nasser and Nuri meet, but before Nasser would accept Sham'oun's suggestion, he asked Lebanon to send two questions to Nuri:

1   Was he ready to discuss the basics of his agreement with Turkey or was he still determined to sign it?

2   Was he ready to accept the consensus of the majority of the Arab states that the pact with Turkey was illegal?[42]

Nuri's answers were that Iraq considered the Ankara-Baghdad agreement consistent with the Arab League pact, and that submission to majority vote was contrary to the sovereignty principle on which the League's pact is based.[43]

During the last session Jordan, to escape Nasser's pressure, suggested that they revert to the decisions which the conference already had approved, namely, the rejection of joining the proposed pact between Turkey and Iraq, and the strengthening and enforcement of the collective defence pact. But the Lebanese and Syrian representatives stated that they would have to consult with their governments first, an indication of their dissatisfaction with Nasser's pressures and tactics. Iraq went along with the other Arab countries, but said it had the right to take additional steps to ensure its safety. Despite its apparent failure to bring Iraq back to the Arab fold, Amir Faisal, then prime minister of Saudi Arabia, and a supporter of Nasser against their common arch-rivals, the Hashemites, said the conference was 'successful' and that 'the policy of Egypt is the policy of Saudi Arabia.'[44] Yemen and Libya, under Egyptian pressure and supported by the Saudis, were in agreement with Egypt. Cairo explained that the purpose of the meeting was to discuss with the other Arab countries their foreign policy, and to explain its point of view in regard to the proposed pact.[45] After fifteen sessions, the Arab prime ministers' conference came to an end on 7 February without reaching any firm decision on how to stop Iraq from ratifying the Baghdad Pact. After a month of Nasser's manœuvring inside and outside the Arab League to prevent the signing of the Turco-Iraqi alliance, the pact was signed in Baghdad on 24 February.

Nasser's Third Tactic: The Isolation of Iraq

President Nasser's success in preventing any of the Arab League conference from joining the pact did not stop there. In fact the end of the conference marked the beginning of a violent Egyptian campaign against arch-rival Iraq and its leader Nuri in an attempt to isolate Baghdad and to bring about the downfall of its leadership. To have a free hand in this matter, and after it became clear that Iraq was in the process of signing the pact with Turkey, Nasser requested that the Egyptian cabinet approve his determination to isolate Iraq; this they did.[46] Nasser then launched a vigorous and violent policy against the Baghdad Pact. This policy included the unleashing of the Cairo propaganda machine, particularly the 'Voice of the Arabs' radio which sent its top propagandist, Ahmad Sa'id, and others to Arab capitals, including Baghdad, from which they reported back to Cairo allegations of unrest and demonstrations against the pact.[47] This amounted to a Cairo propaganda campaign agitating for upheaval in the Arab world against Iraq and those who were inclined toward joining the pact, particularly Jordan. Egyptian high officials also were active in visiting Damascus, Riyadh, Beirut, Amman, San'a, and even Baghdad to persuade Arab leaders not to join the pact and to rally behind Nasser's policies; to urge Arab countries to form Arab defence pacts; and to incite popular uprisings against Baghdad in order to isolate Iraq and to encourage the overthrow of the monarchy.[48]

To inflame the Arab masses, Egypt's relentless campaign was aimed not only against Iraq, but also against the Western powers. The threat of the Baghdad Pact to Egypt's leading position in the Arab world led to Nasser's more definitive, pronounced, and perhaps, genuine commitment to the policy of pan-Arabism which generated Arab sentiments in favour of Nasser's policy. In doing so, Nasser came into immediate collision with his arch-rival, Nuri al-Sa'id. Because of dynastic and strategic reasons, as well as Nasser's pressure, Saudi Arabia and Yemen were on Nasser's side. In Syria, Lebanon, and Jordan, the Egyptian campaign was successful and popular opinion was strongly in favour of Nasser's independent, pan-Arabist policy.

Nasser convinced the Arabs that an agreement such as the Baghdad Pact would serve the Western countries. In his view the pact was detrimental to the cause of Arab unity since it caused the weakening of and divisions in the Arab League.[49] But actually he felt the pact would undermine his drive for leadership of the Arab world. Nasser conceived that the Arab countries, individually and collectively as a regional organization, under his leadership, were responsible for the preservation of peace and stability in the Middle East. He believed that the Arab countries, within the framework of the Arab League, opposed any foreign power interfering in Arab affairs. 'The Arab League is real power and the collective security pact is the basis for our defence co-ordination in the Middle East,' Nasser told a French journalist on 19 December 1954.[50] However, arguing in this way would be in his interests. At first Nasser wanted Iraq to be in line with the Arab League policies which, by and large, was the Egyptian policy. He believed that the League should be the guide to Arab foreign policies. 'Today I feel that the League does not need a written pact... It is there among yourselves and among all the Arabs,' Nasser said to a group of Lebanese in Cairo on 2 February 1955.[51] In the Egyptian view, the Baghdad Pact 'deeply hurt the League of Arab States and its pact' and the only course for Arab unity was to stay away from foreign pacts.[52] But such a contention was largely to sell his own foreign policy line.

In his first major speech against the pact, Nasser ridiculed those who insisted that the pact was for defence against the threat of Communism to the area. He believed that colonialism was no less dangerous to the Arabs than Communism. Nasser's emphasis on anti-colonialism was mainly to win support of the Arab masses. 'All that matters to them [the West] is to fill the vacuum, the vacuum between Pakistan and Turkey. Basically it is Afghanistan and Iran. But they consider Iran not strategic enough if Iraq does not join in. Thus they are concerned about defence and we are concerned about our freedom,' said Nasser bitterly of the Iraqi move.[53] When Eden attempted to dissuade Nasser from attacking the pact and to persuade him that the pact was mainly against Communism, Nasser retorted: 'Where is Russia? Russia is three thousand miles away from us ... Britain was the one who colonized us, Britain occupied Egypt, and still occupies Jordan, Iraq and Libya. Do you really want us to forget the continuing danger on our land and look at a possible danger that lies three thousand miles away?'[54] Nasser, unquestionably was against British colonialism, but he also feared that with the help of the British, Nuri might be able to achieve his dream of the unification of the Fertile Crescent and thus become the leader of the Arab world. Nasser, therefore, was determined to see such a thing did not take place.

Nasser's vigorous campaign against Western pacts did accomplish what he hoped for. Even King Hussein, a cousin of the king of Iraq, was forced, by popular demand and the Egyptian leaders' pressure, to hold back from the pact. Before the end of February Hussein was in Cairo to reassure Nasser that he would not join the Baghdad Pact. Syria too supported Nasser's opposition to the pact.[55] Amir Faisal (later king) of Saudi Arabia and Saif al-Islam Hassan, prime minister of Yemen, also objected to the pact and they strongly endorsed the Egyptian policy.[56] To please Nasser the Saudis and Yemenis even went further and said that their governments were in complete agreement with the Egyptian government on all matters of Arab and foreign policy. The Arab countries' support of Nasser's policy against the Baghdad Pact was reaffirmed throughout 1955. For example, the Saudi prime minister said on 12 August 1955 that 'If it was not for Egyptian steadfastness, along with Saudi Arabia, against the Western (activities), the Arab countries today would be a tail of the colonialist tails and client to it.'[57] Indeed what Faisal was saying was in line with Egyptian foreign policy.

The Arab League also expressed to Nasser 'its appreciation for the Egyptian government's stand and its solidarity with the vigilant policy that Egypt [was] pursuing which aims to strengthen its power which in turn [was] the strength of the Arabs and their power.'[58] In effect the League was following the Egyptian foreign ministry directions.

To ensure the success of his drive against Nuri al-Sa'id and the pact, and thus secure Egypt's dominant position in the Arab world, Nasser, after many months of continuous Egyptian persistence, in October 1955 concluded a joint Saudi-Syrian-Egyptian command under Egyptian leadership. Yemen, to escape Egyptian threats, joined this command in April 1956. This command was viewed as a replacement to the by now moribund Arab collective security pact. The new joint command was basically based on the provisions of the 1950 collective security pact. Its purpose was to 'safeguard peace and security [of the participants] in accordance with the principles of the Arab League Charter.'[59] However, this pact was viewed as an Egyptian ploy against Baghdad.

Nasser's Success and Nuri's Demise

From early 1955 until 1958, when the Iraqi monarchy was toppled and the Baghdad Pact collapsed, Nasser took successive actions which made his policies of opposition to foreign-inspired pacts irresistible to the Arab masses. In April 1955 he travelled abroad and was received as a hero wherever he went, including Pakistan and India. At the Bandung Conference he was riding very high. In September he concluded the Soviet arms deal, thus freeing himself from a Western monopoly of the supply of arms to his country. He nationalized the Suez Canal Company in 1956 and concluded an agreement with the Russians to build the Aswan High Dam. By 1957, with the exception of Iraq, he had concluded solidarity pacts with the independent Arab countries; it climaxed with his union with Syria in early 1958. All these actions brought Nasser great admiration from the Arab populace. It became common to have pro-Nasser demonstrations in the streets of Beirut, Amman, Damascus, and other Arab cities whenever Nasser or his 'Voice of the Arabs' demanded. For example, Syria and Jordan lost high officials who did not toe Nasser's line in assassinations attributed to Egyptian agents. In addition, at least because of popular demands inspired by Cairo, King Hussein dismissed his army's British commander, Glubb Pasha.

In December 1955 the British government sent Field Marshal of the Imperial General Staff, Sir Gerald Templer, to Amman to try to persuade Jordan to join the Baghdad Pact. Egypt, unleashing a violent propaganda campaign against the Templer mission, called on its loyal supporters in Jordan to resist his efforts.

Not only did riots and widespread strikes bring upheaval to the country, but two Jordanian cabinets were also brought down. Templer returned to London empty-handed and a new pro-Cairo government vowed not to join the pact.[60] Furthermore, to end any hope of Jordan's joining the pact, Nasser was instrumental in 1957 in persuading Riyadh and Damascus, along with Egypt, to agree on replacing British subsidies to Jordan, thus freeing Amman from British pressure. Like Jordan, Lebanon too was subject to Cairo's destabilization efforts, which often led to trouble and civil disturbances in that country. Egyptian military attachés smuggled in bombs which were often thrown at various pro-Western and Western institutions, including the British embassy.[61] Nasser, believing that the British with the help of Nuri were pursuing a hostile policy towards him by trying to isolate Egypt, intensified his drive against Nuri and British 'imperialism'.

On the whole, Nasser succeeded brilliantly in arousing public and official opinion in the Arab world against the Western-inspired pact. This success made it very difficult for any other Arab state to join it. However, it is a mistake to think that Egyptian efforts were the sole cause of the isolation of the pact. Arab intellectuals and nationalists opposed the pact from its inception, for, in their eyes, it was tied to the Western countries that caused the Palestine tragedy; it was thus traitorous of Arabs to support such a Western-designed pact. It was natural that Nasser first concentrated his efforts on Syria, since it was a base for Arab nationalists. Supported by the Saudis, traditional adversaries of the Hashemite dynasty, he soon brought Syria to his side. It then became extremely difficult for both Jordan and Lebanon to go along with Nuri's plans.[62] All the Iraqi, Turkish, and Western efforts, incentives, and pressures on various Arab countries to join the pact failed. In contrast, by the time of the nationalization of the Suez Canal Company, Nasser succeeded in establishing a dominant position in the Arab world. Syria, Saudi Arabia, and Yemen were allies; Jordan and Lebanon stayed out of the Baghdad Pact; Nuri al Sa'id was isolated from the mainstream of Arab politics, and in 1958 a republican coup replaced the monarchy, Nuri was killed, the Baghdad Pact came to an end, and the Egyptian pan-Arabist policies became dominant in Arab League orientations.

The Baghdad Pact, the Arab League, and Nasser: An Assessment

In this chapter we have seen the first case where Nasser manipulated, not necessarily the Arab League machinery itself (as the following chapters show he did on other occasions) but rather the interpretation of the League pact and its follow-up, the Arab collective security pact. He did so to constrain the policies of Egypt's traditional rival, Iraq. He believed that the success of Iraq under the leadership of Nuri al-Sa'id simply would work to the disadvantage of Egypt under his leadership and to the enhancement of the leadership of Nuri in the Arab world. Thus when Nuri was about to conclude a British-inspired defence treaty with Turkey, Nasser was enraged, especially when it became known that the Iraqi leader was actively soliciting other Arab countries' membership in the new pact.

Nasser used several tactics to frustrate the Iraqi policy. First, besides the foreign ministers' meeting of 30 November, 1954, he sent emissaries to Iraq itself and to other Arab countries to persuade Nuri not to conclude the proposed pact, because, in the Egyptian view, such a pact was a threat to Arab security and it would undermine Arab solidarity. Moreover, his contacts with other Arab leaders were intended to discourage them from joining the pact. He concentrated on the three countries which were initially inclined to join the Iraqi move: Jordan, Lebanon, and Syria. Furthermore, Nasser, claiming that the Baghdad Pact was to serve Western 'imperialism' in the Arab world, appealed to the Arab masses to oppose their governments if they attempted to go along with the Iraqi leaders. This tactic of Egyptian 'shuttle diplomacy' failed to dissuade Iraq from concluding the pact. This infuriated Nasser who became increasingly apprehensive about the prospect of seeing Egypt isolated, and thus, undermining his foreign policy goals in the Arab world.

After his initial failure, Nasser resorted to his second tactic, 'conference diplomacy'. He invited, in a sense requested, Arab leaders of his rank (at the time, premier) to come to Cairo to discuss Iraq's situation within the framework of the Arab League. The League's leaders met at the Egyptian foreign ministry under his chairmanship. Here the Arab League secretary-general and other League officials confirmed Nasser's interpretations of the Arab pacts, after which he effectively lectured the Arab leaders that the proposed Baghdad Pact was a violation of the two Arab pacts and that therefore

Iraq was acting contrary to Arab interests. He asked the League leaders not only to oppose Nuri's behaviour, but to condemn him and bring him back to the Arab ranks before he concluded that treaty. He forcefully convinced Arab leaders that what he was trying to do was to 'preserve' and 'strengthen' the Arab League and to implement the collective security pact. The Arab delegates most likely were aware of Nasser's real aims and probably did not believe his contentions about Arab solidarity. But, aided by the League's secretary, Nasser's interpretations of the two pacts were actually accurate and the collective security arrangement did call specifically on the contracting states not to conclude treaties with foreign powers. The conference, however, met Nasser's demand halfway: they refused to condemn Iraq but those who were inclined earlier to join Baghdad now submitted to Nasser's arguments and were effectively discouraged from joining the Turco-Iraqi pact.

Before Iraq ratified the Baghdad Pact, Nasser tried one more tactic: launching a vigorous campaign against Nuri and Iraq. This included the unleashing of Egyptian propaganda instruments and Nasser's direct appeal to the Arab people to demonstrate their opposition to Iraq and to reject any inclination by their governments to soften their opposition to Baghdad. Moreover, Nasser invited Arab leaders, particularly those who were close to Iraq, to visit him in Cairo. King Hussein of Jordan, the Syrian leader, Shukri al-Quwatli, the king of Libya, in addition to Saudi and Yemeni leaders, all visited Cairo, some of them several times, and reassured Nasser that they would remain faithful to the Arab pacts and that they would continue to reject Nuri's policy. Furthermore, Nasser persuaded Saudi Arabia, Syria, and Yemen to join Egypt in the defence pact which was mainly to counter the Iraqi leaders and to isolate them. This tactic, enforced by the second tactic, was extremely effective: Nasser became more popular in the Arab world. No Arab countries joined the pact and Iraq was politically completely isolated from the rest of the Arab world. This ultimately, to the pleasure of Nasser, brought about the fall of the Iraqi monarchy and the collapse of the Baghdad Pact.

The significance of Nasser's use of the Arab League and the collective security pacts was very considerable. Without invoking those two pacts Nasser would likely not have succeeded in bringing Arab leaders to Cairo. Furthermore, using the interpretations of the Arab pacts rather than the League's machinery itself proved a successful ploy. The Arab premiers accepted Nasser's arguments that the Iraqi action was in violation of these pacts and as they were in favour of preserving them they submitted to Nasser's pressure not to join the pact. It is true that Saudi Arabia at that time was an ally of Egypt largely because of its distrust of its traditional rivals, the Hashemite kings of Iraq and Jordan. But it is also true that the Hashemite kings of Jordan, Syria, and Lebanon, before Nasser's campaign, were inclined to join the Baghdad Pact. But Nasser's tactics foiled their inclination. In short, the utilization of the two Arab pacts worked for the advantage of Egypt which thereafter enhanced its position in the Arab world.

Notes to chapter four

1 Arwa Radwan, *The Political Committee of the League of Arab States* (in Arabic), Beirut: Dar al-Nahar lil-Nashr, 1973, p. 136.

2 G.E.K., 'Iraq, Egypt and the Arab League', *World Today*, vol. 11, no. 4 (April 1955), p. 146.

3 Sayed Nofal, '*Al-'Amal al-Arabi al-Mushtarek*' (The Joint Arab Activities) book II, Cairo, Ma'had al-Buhuth Wal-Dirasat al-Arabiyyeh, 1971, p. 62. See also, Mohammad Iqbal Ansari, *The Arab League, 1945–1955*, Aligarch Muslim University, Institute of Islamic Studies, 1968, p. 98.

4 Ratifications of or accessions to the Arab collective security treaty occurred on the following dates: Syria, 31 October 1951; Egypt, 22 November 1951; Jordan, 31 March 1952; Iraq, 7 August 1952; Saudi Arabia, 19 August 1952; Lebanon, 24 December 1952; Yemen (San'a), 11 October 1953; Morocco, 13 June 1961; Kuwait, 12 August 1961; Tunisia, 11 September 1964; Algeria, 11 September 1964; Sudan, 11 September 1964; Libya, 11 September 1964; Bahrain, 14 November 1971; Qatar, 14 November 1971; and Yemen (Aden), 23 November 1971. See Hussein A. Hassouna, *The League of Arab States* and *Regional Disputes: A Study of Middle East Conflicts*, Dobbs Ferry, New York, Oceana, 1975, p. 13; Ansari, p. 98. The Yemeni reservation centred on its intentions to apply the new system only in the event of an aggression directed against its own

territory. Yemen also accepts as binding only the decisions made by the council of common defence to which it has given its formal consent. Iraq's reservations concerned the application of the provisions of Article 6, concerning the two-thirds majority, to certain special plans which may be executed for the defence of each Arab state. See Muhammad Khalil, *The Arab States and the Arab League*, vol. II, Beirut, Khayats, 1962, pp. 101-02.

5   Khalil, preamble, vol. II, p. 102.

6   Boutros Boutros-Ghali, 'The Arab League: 1945–1955', *International Conciliation*, no. 498 (May 1954), p. 390. See also Ansari, p. 99; Muhamad Hafiz Ghanim, *Lectures on the League of Arab States* (in Arabic) Cairo, Institute of Higher Arabic Studies, 1965, pp. 70–75.

7   Sayed Nofal, *The Joint Arab Activities*, Book I, Cairo, Ma'had al-Bohuth wal-Dirasat al-Arabiyyeh, 1968, Book I, p. 141.

8   Ansari, p. 97; also see Muhamad Tal'at al-Ghuneimi, (*The League of Arab States*) Alexandria, Minsha'at al-Ma'arif, 1974, p. 260.

9   Kennett Love, *Suez: The Twice-Fought War*, New York, Toronto, McGraw-Hill, 1969, p. 196.

10   *al-Ahram*, 13 January 1955, p. 1 and 14 January 1955, p. 3. Unless otherwise noted, all the information quoted from *al-Ahram* for this chapter was from the year 1955; thus the year will be disregarded in the notes.

11   Ibid., 20 January, p. 1.

12   Preamble.

13   Article 1.

14   Article 3.

15   Article 5.

16   Quoted in Love, p. 199.

17   Sayed Nofal to the author, Cairo, 19 June 1978.

18   Majid Khadduri, 'The Problem of Regional Security in the Middle East: An Appraisal', *The Middle East Journal*, vol. 11, no. 1 (winter, 1957), pp. 21–22.

19   Nofal, book I, pp. 139–40.

20   Boutros Boutros-Ghali, *op. cit.*, pp. 392–93.

21   Ibid.

22   '*Muthakarat Massó ol Arabi Muttali*', (Memoire of an Informed Arab Official) (Anonymous), *al-Ahram*, 16 February 1978, p. 5.

23   Ibid.

24   *al-Ahram*, 15 January, p. 1.

25   Ibid., 17 January, pp. 1, 4.

26   Ibid., 18 January, p. 1.

27   Zakaria Niel to the author, 10 July 1978.

28   See *al-Ahram*, 19 January–24 January.

29   *The Arab Collective Security Pact*, article 10.

30   Ansari, p. 101.

31   G.E.K., *op. cit.*, p. 148.

32   George Lenczowski, *The Middle East in World Affairs*, Ithaca and London, Cornell University Press, 3rd edn, 1962, p. 292.

33   Nofal, book I, pp. 145–46.

34   Ibid.

35   Ibid., pp. 146–47.

36   *al-Ahram*, 28 January, p. 6.

37   Ibid., 30 January, p. 11.

38   Ibid.

39   Ibid., 3 February, p. 1. Note that under article 12 of the Arab collective security pact between the states of the Arab League of 1950, a party cannot withdraw before a lapse of ten years from the date of the ratification of the treaty. See Boutros Boutros-Ghali, *'Fuqdan al-'Oudwiyyeh fi Jamiá t al-Dowal al-Arabiyyeh'*, (Loss of Membership in the League of Arab States), *Revue Egyptienne de Droit International*, vol. 11 (1955) pp. 123–32.

40   G.E.K., *op. cit.*, p. 149.

41   Robert Stephens, *Nasser: A Political Biography*, New York, Simon and Schuster, 1972, p. 150.

42   *al-Ahram*, 5 February, p. 1.

43   See Nofal, book I, pp. 148–49.

44   *al-Ahram*, 9 February, p. 5; see also ibid., 7 February, p. 11.

45   Nofal, book I, pp. 148–50.

46   *al-Ahram*, 3 February, p. 6.

47   Ibid., 22 January, p. 1. See also ibid., 28 January, p. 1.

48   President Anwar el-Sadat, for example, was one of the high officials who participated in the campaign against the Baghdad Pact. He wrote: 'I played an important part in the frustration of the Baghdad Pact. In Jordan, for instance, although the King belonged to the same ruling family that ruled in Iraq, I was able to persuade him not to join the Pact. One important consequence of this was the dismissal of Glubb Pasha, the British commander-in-chief of the Jordanian Army. It was the decision of King Hussein. In Lebanon I met President Camille Sham'oun and his family on the one hand and the Turks on the other. In Baghdad I met Nuri al-Sa'id to try to persuade him not to join.' *In Search of Identity*, p. 136.

49   Wilton Wynn, *Nasser of Egypt*, Cambridge, Mass., Arlington Books, 1959, p. 115.

50   *President Gamal Abdel-Nasser Speeches*, part I (23 July 1952–1958), p. 269.

51   Ibid., p. 272.

52   *al-Ahram*, 20 June, pp. 1, 13.

53   *President Gamal Abdel-Nasser Speeches*, part I, p. 290.

54   Ibid., p. 276.

55 See *al-Ahram*, 28 February, p. 1; 3 March, p. 1; 8 September, p. 6.

56 Ibid., 6, 8, 9 February; 7 February, p. 5.

57 Ibid., 12 August. See also ibid., 5 May, 24 June, 9 July, and 5 August.

58 *Minutes of the League Council*, 24th ordinary session, 1 October 1955–19 January 1956, p. 507.

59 For the text of the Egyptian, Saudi, and Syrian mutual defence pact see Khalil, vol. II, pp. 242–45. For more details see: Mahmoud Kamel, '*Al-Dawlah al-Arabiyyeh al-Kubra*' (The Great Arab State) Cairo, Dar al-Ma'arif, 1967, pp. 435–36; ibid., *Al-Qanoon al-Dawli al-Arabi* (The Arab International Law) Beirut, 'Dar al-Malayyeen, 1965, pp. 398–401; Muhamad Tal'at al-Ghuneimi *Jamiá t al-Dowal al-Arabiyyeh*, (The League of Arab States), Alexandria, Minsha'at al-Ma'arif, 1974, pp. 260–61. Nofal, book I, pp. 151–52; Boutros Boutros-Ghali, '*Al-Nasseriyyah wa Siyyassitt Misr al-Kharijiyyah*' (Nasserism and Egyptian Foreign Policy), *al-Siyyassah al-Dawliyyah* (Cairo), no. 23 (January 1971), p. 14; Ghanim, p. 77.

60 Randolph S. Churchill, *The Rise and Fall of Sir Anthony Eden*, New York, Putnam's, 1959, p. 223.

61 Anthony Nutting, *I Saw for Myself: The Aftermath of Suez*, New York, Doubleday, 1958, p. 35.

62 See *al-Ahram*, 4 May, p. 1.

Chapter Five

Lebanon: 1958

The Lebanese civil war of 1958 sparked an international crisis that involved regional powers as well as world major powers. Lebanon accused the United Arab Republic (UAR) of being the cause of its internal civil disorders. The Lebanese government resorted first to the Arab League to settle the crisis. But when the League passed an Egyptian-inspired resolution, Lebanon rejected it, reasoning that it failed to address the substance of the complaint — UAR intervention in Lebanon. Lebanon then resorted to the UN Security Council which failed to reach a unanimous resolution. The Lebanese matter was shifted to the UN General Assembly where the Arab League secretary-general succeeded in persuading Lebanon and other Arab states to consider a League resolution which was broad and acceptable to the UAR. Lebanon, reaching a point of frustration, accepted the League's resolution. The UAR claimed the final outcome of this crisis was a victory for itself and its allies.

The Internal Crisis

The Lebanese-Egyptian crisis came during the presidency (1952–58) of Camille Sham'oun, which was to witness a chain of serious events that swept the Middle East and had an impact on the Lebanese domestic situation as well as on its foreign relations, particularly with the Arab countries. Internally, until 1957, relative calm prevailed in

Lebanon. However, under the surface of this situation strong undercurrents of hostility between Christians and Muslims, rich and poor, left and right, Palestinians and Lebanese, were discernible. The fact that the capitalist Christians were predominant in practically every area, with the possible exception of numerical superiority, underlay the basic problems of the Lebanese situation. Muslims wanted a fairer say in the running of the affairs of their country.

On the external level, Lebanon during Sham'oun's presidency was to cause an international crisis that involved regional powers as well as major powers with an interest in the Middle East area. None the less, its proximity and its significant role in Arab commercial and political arenas made Lebanon of crucial importance to the Arab states. Indeed Lebanon is a mirror which reflects Arab rivalries and activities. When the Arabs were at peace with each other, generally Lebanon too would be at peace with itself and with its neighbours. But when the Arab countries were engaged in intrigue and plotting against each other, Lebanon, because of its circumstances, was bound to be involved. This was well illustrated during Gamal Abdel-Nasser's championing of pan-Arabism and Arab unity.

Sham'oun was pro-Western and, in the view of some Lebanese leaders, such as Kamal Junblatt, he was 'an agent of the British intelligence service'.[1] This became evident after the Suez crisis, when all the Arab countries but Lebanon broke off relations with Britain and France. This failure on the part of Sham'oun angered Arab nationalists, including many Lebanese who openly criticized his action. Obviously Nasser, who was riding high in the Arab world under the banner of pan-Arabism, did not like it at all. How, in Nasser's perception, could an Arab leader defy the rest of the Arab countries and continue his normal relations with the aggressors? As if to strengthen Nasser's case against him, the Lebanese president subscribed to the Eisenhower doctrine in 1957. Nasser was the first Arab leader to reject the doctrine, and he was soon joined by the pan-Arabist press and radio in Damascus which violently attacked the Sham'oun government for accepting it.[2] An Egyptian official spokesman said that Cairo would not allow any power, eastern or western, to fill the previously British and French imperialist role in that area. The spokesman described the Eisenhower plan as 'the replacement of the British and French aggression'.[3]

These external pressures on Lebanon affected its internal political life. Nasser's pan-Arabism had a profound impact on Lebanon which led to the polarization of forces between rightist Lebanese nationalists and Lebanese pan-Arabists. To make the situation worse, in the 1957 Parliamentary election the pro-Sham'oun candidates won and the pro-Nasser candidates suffered a setback; they accused the president of interfering in the election.[4] The Lebanese pan-Arabists did not like losing and they argued that Sham'oun engineered the election so that the winners would approve his wish to amend *al-Mithaq al-Watani* (the National pact) which outlaws a president from succeeding himself, so as to allow him to run for re-election. Pro-Nasser Lebanese, Christians, and Muslims strongly objected to Sham'oun's ambitions. Saib Salam, Kamal Junblatt, Hamid Franjiyyeh, and other Lebanese leaders called on Sham'oun not to violate *al-Mithaq*:

> There is no doubt at all about the fact that one of the principal causes of the critical situation in which the country has been plunged lies in the equivocation with regard to the renewal of the presidential term.
>
> A renewal shall be an attack on the constitution itself and will go against the very aims which its framers had laid down.[5]

Sham'oun did not yield to the opposition.

In February 1958 Egypt and Syria announced the formation of the UAR. This union was welcomed enthusiastically by the anti-Sham'oun pan-Arabists in Lebanon. Despite the government's censorship and bans, schools were closed down for celebrations and pro-Cairo demonstrations were held throughout the country. For example, Lebanese politician Rashid Karami told Nasser on February 27: 'The Lebanese people, O President, believe in your principles and mission, and are following your footsteps and example... You can rest assured, O President, that when the hour strikes we will all leap up as one man to hoist the banner to which all the Arabs will rally.'[6] A few days later President Nasser repeated Karami's comment and hinted to a Lebanese delegation his wish to see Lebanon join the UAR: 'we feel that this unity which springs from the heart of the Arab nation and from its will is the strength we aim at achieving and the nucleus of the all-embracing unity we hope to see accomplished soon in every Arab country.'[7] The opposition forces were obtaining moral and material support from the UAR. Egypt's man in Damascus, Abdel-Hamid al-Sarraj, chief of intelligence and security in Syria, was organizing the UAR to help the pro-Nasser groups, and bloody clashes and press attacks on Sham'oun intensified.

On 8 May Nasib Metni, editor of the pan-Arabist *al-Telegraf*, was assassinated, igniting the Lebanese civil war. Lebanese leaders such as Rashid Karami and Junblatt asked for and received from the UAR arms, men, and financial support to defend their position. Egyptian media encouraged the opposition, called for the overthrow of Sham'oun, and hoped for his replacement by a pro-Cairo president. To make things more difficult for Sham'oun, the Lebanese army commander, General Fu'ad Shihab, refused to back the president and his supporters and remained neutral.[8]

To calm the situation, the Lebanese government declared in May that it would not support a second term for Sham'oun. But the anti-Sham'oun forces demanded the resignation of the president. For Nasser's pan-Arabism and his call for Arab unity had profoundly affected the pro-Cairo groups, and their enmity toward the pro-Western Sham'oun was gaining more support than had been expected from the Lebanese masses and leaders, including the influential family of Franjiyyeh and the patriarch of the Maronite Church, Paul Ma'ushi.[9]

On 13 May the pro-Western Dr Charles Malik, foreign minister of Lebanon, accused the UAR of interfering in the internal affairs of his country. A week later the Lebanese government lodged two complaints against the UAR: the first submitted to the Arab League on 21 May and the second submitted to the UN Security Council on 22 May 1958.

Lebanon's Complaint to the Arab League

Although internal opposition to the Sham'oun regime was the strongest factor in the internal Lebanese conflict, as we have seen, evidence showed that the UAR, morally and materially, was aiding the opposition. On 16 May the government of Lebanon asserted 'that investigations have shown beyond any doubt that a large number of Syrian mutineers and subversive elements had infiltrated into Lebanon.' The statement said that on 13 May an Egyptian boat was captured by the Lebanese coast guard. Aboard the boat 'were 11 Egyptian and Palestinian agents of destruction and crime, as well as a large sum of money and arms and ammunition to be used by them and their colleagues in Lebanon for subversion, destruction and assassination.' The Lebanese government statement also noted that on 11 May Lebanese custom officials seized on the Syrian border 'a large quantity of arms and ammunition' sent from Damascus 'to the agents in Beirut'. Lebanese security, according to Lebanon, also 'confiscated about 100 rifles with Egyptian army markings which had been sent to mutineers in Tripoli.' The statement also charged the UAR with responsibility for 'official broadcasts and press campaigns against the regime in Lebanon' calling on the Lebanese people to 'revolt against the government.'[10]

On the basis of these Lebanese allegations and evidence, on 21 May Lebanon requested an urgent meeting of the Arab League council 'to be convened either in the Sudan or in Libya to consider its complaint against the United Arab Republic in accordance with article 6 of the Pact, for the unfriendly acts of intervention in the internal affairs of Lebanon, which constitute a threat to its independence, territorial integrity and consitutional forms of government'.[11]

One day after its complaint to the League, Lebanon requested an urgent meeting of the UN Security Council to consider 'a situation and a dispute the continuance of which is likely to endanger the maintenance of international peace and security' as a result of 'the intervention of the United Arab Republic in the affairs of Lebanon'.[12]

The secretary-general of the League, strongly supported by Egypt, intervened and requested the Security Council to postpone consideration of the Lebanese question, in accordance with article 52 of the UN charter, to allow the Arab League to settle the regional dispute between Lebanon and UAR, since the League was the regional organization that supervised the security of the region where the two disputing states were located.[13] The Security Council met on 27 May and Fadil al-Jamali of Iraq informed it that the League was expected to meet on 31 May to discuss the Lebanese situation and asked that the council 'adjourn the discussion' of Lebanon until 2 June.[14]

The Arab League council agreed to meet in Benghazi, Libya, on 31 May and hold six sessions to consider the Lebanese government complaint. The Lebanese representative, Bashir al-A'war, explained to the council that Lebanon stood for Arab solidarity, that his country was attached to the League's pact, and that its resort to the council was based on its belief in the settlement of the dispute by Arabs.[15] Al-A'war accused the UAR of interference in the internal affairs of Lebanon.

The Lebanese chief delegate to the council went on at length explaining the alleged UAR intervention. He listed three kinds of provocation:

1 Provocation of the army against the civilian authorities and picturing these authorities in an ugly light.

2 Provocation of the Arab states against Lebanon. The UAR press often said 'The revolting people in Lebanon calls on the Arab people to supply it with volunteers and arms to confront the foreign troops.'

3 Provocation of the population against its government through the waging in the UAR of a media campaign. For example the UAR press would write: 'Lebanon's population is ready to carry arms and create a bloody revolution' against the established authorities in Lebanon.[16]

Al-A'war enumerated other methods, such as the exploding of bombs in various parts of the country by UAR agents. He then asked the League council to take the measures necessary to put an immediate end to such interference by stopping Cairo's provocative propaganda and preventing arms and terrorists (*Mukharibeen*) from infiltrating Lebanon. The Lebanese delegate noted that his government's desire was to settle the crisis within the framework of the League and not outside it.[17]

Sayed Fahmi, UAR chief delegate, rejected the Lebanese charges and restated what President Nasser had said on 16 May: that the UAR 'supports Lebanon's independence and respects its sovereignty.' Fahmi tried to convince the council that Cairo had nothing to do with Lebanon and that the Lebanese situation was an internal matter. However, Fahmi's major criticism was focused on Lebanon's request for a UN Security Council meeting, since such action would limit Egypt's freedom to deal with Lebanon. The Egyptian delegate raised the banner of pan-Arabism and deplored Lebanon's act, asking 'What is the objective behind this decision? The Arab League gathers all of us, the brotherly Arab states, in a holy organization that deals with our affairs as brothers united by suffering and hope.' He argued that by going to the Security Council, Lebanon was weakening the League, and he attempted to solicit the other Arab delegates' support against Lebanon's resort to the UN.

We [the UAR], feeling the meaning of this action as an
Arab state, leave it up to the Arab sister states, the League
members, evaluation of the impact of this decision on the
League. The Lebanese government's resort to the Security
Council was a matter that shook the feeling of many in the

Arab world, which led them to protest this dangerous decision.[18]

In the face of UAR manœuvring and influence, the council asked, and Lebanon agreed, to postpone further Security Council consideration of its complaint.[19]

In the third meeting, the League council heard the UAR and Lebanon trade charges against each other.[20] After a short discussion outside the council meeting, which led to the adjourning of the fourth meeting, the council held its fifth meeting on the evening of 4 June. At this meeting, Muhamad Ahmad Mahjoub, Sudan's foreign minister and chief delegate to the meeting, and a close ally of Egypt during the council meeting, with the help of the League secretary-general, submitted a draft resolution which he said was accepted by the member states with the exception of the UAR and Lebanon. The draft resolution stated that the League council, after hearing the UAR's and Lebanon's statements, has '. . . . felt the desire of each of the two parties to settle the dispute by peaceful means, within the Arab League, and, in pursuance of the letter and spirit of the Pact of the League of Arab States.' The council resolved:

> First: All [activities] likely to disturb, in any way, the cordial atmosphere among States members [of the League] should cease;
> Second: The Government of the Republic of Lebanon should withdraw its complaint from the Security Council;
> Third: An appeal should be addressed to the various Lebanese factions for stopping disturbances and disorders and for working towards the settlement of [their] internal conflicts by constitutional peaceful means;
> Fourth: The dispatch of a commission to be appointed by the Council of the League of Arab States from amongst its own members; in order to appease sentiments and to implement the resolution of the Council.[21]

Mahjoub claimed that this resolution would show that the Arab League was able to solve disputes among its members without recourse to external international organizations.

The draft resolution, acording to the League and Sudanese

officials, was unanimously approved by the council. However, the UAR and Lebanon delegations reserved final approval until they had referred the matter to their respective governments in Cairo and Beirut.[22] In effect Cairo was in favour of the resolution but it attempted to outmanoeuvre Lebanon, which was disappointed by the council's inability to address the heart of its complaint.

On 6 June the League council held its last meeting. At this meeting the Lebanese representative told the council that his government rejected the council's resolution for several reasons. The resolution, according to the Lebanese government, was very broad and did not address the substance of the crisis. The resolution was, in Lebanon's view, only a recommendation or mediation. Furthermore, Lebanon argued that 'The Arab League [was] evading the insuring of a resolution concerning interference and contents itself with substituting for such a resolution the calling for reaching an understanding, although the Lebanese Government and its delegation insist on a resolution on the substance of the complaint.'[23] The Lebanese delegate to the council meeting told the Arab delegates that Lebanon now would not withdraw its complaint from the Security Council. This, of course, drew fire from the UAR representative who argued that Lebanon, by going to the Security Council, was attempting to undermine the effectiveness of the Arab League.[24] But by going to the Security Council, Lebanon was really trying to escape Egypt's domination and dictation in the League. The other Arab delegates expressed their regrets at the outcome of this extraordinary session. The League council called on the Lebanese factions to stop the violence and work toward re-establishing peace and harmony in Lebanon.[25]

The Security Council Meeting

Lebanon was disappointed about the Arab League council's failure to call explicitly for an end to UAR interference. The UN Security Council began its discussion of the Lebanese crisis on the day the League's council meeting was ended, 6 June 1958. The Lebanese foreign minister, Charles Malik, spoke to the Security Council in a characteristically lengthy speech in which he reiterated his government's charges against the UAR. 'The case which we have brought to the attention of the Security Council consists of three claims,' said Malik.

> The first is that there has been, and there still is, massive, illegal and unprovoked intervention in the affairs of Lebanon by the United Arab Republic. The second is that this intervention aims at undermining, and does in fact threaten, the independence of Lebanon. The third is that the situation created by this intervention which threatens the independence of Lebanon is likely, if continued, to endanger the maintenance of international peace and security.[26]

Malik elaborated on the evidence against the UAR. Then he emphasized his belief in the UN Charter as a protection for small states and concluded, 'We ask this Council . . . to bring its wisdom into play, to the end that the unprovoked massive intervention stop, that our independence, to which we have every right, be preserved and indeed strengthened, and that as a result the threat to international peace and security inherent in this situation be removed.'[27]

Omar Loutfi, the UAR representative at the UN rejected Malik's accusations and accused Lebanon of acting in bad faith during the Arab League meetings at Benghazi. 'It appears that the Lebanese Government was not very serious in submitting the complaint to the Arab League and that this was merely a device to show that, before submitting its case to the Council, it has exhausted local remedies,'[28] Loutfi said, referring to his government's preference for the League over the Security Council. He argued that the Lebanese internal conflict was due mainly to President Sham'oun's intentions to amend *al-Mithaq* so he could run for re-election. He accused Lebanon of trying to internationalize 'a problem which is exclusively one of Lebanese domestic policy,'[29] and thus the problem was 'not and could not be a threat to international peace.'[30]

The views expressed at the Council showed that it was merely cold-war politics. The USA failed to see that the Lebanese crisis was largely a domestic product. Washington was convinced that the Communists and the pro-Soviets (Nasser) were the main trouble-makers in Lebanon, intent on undermining Western interests in the area. Thus the USA was in strong support of the Sham'oun regime policies. On the other hand, the Soviet Union strongly supported Cairo's views and accused the Western powers, primarily the USA, of interference in the internal affairs of Lebanon. But, none the less, the majority of the Security Council expressed their concern about the Lebanese conflict. The Council meeting was adjourned and met again on 10 June.

The Security Council meeting on 10 June witnessed similar trading of accusations between the Lebanese and UAR representatives. Malik appealed to the Security Council for help and argued that the situation had 'become exceedingly serious.'[31] In this meeting, Iraq came out strongly on the side of Lebanon and vehemently criticized the Soviet Union as troublemaker in the area. The Iraqi delegate insisted that the situation in Lebanon was 'a struggle between the West and the East, between freedom and subjugation, between the forces of democracy and dictatorship, between evolution and revolution, between peaceful and educational methods and the use of force and revolution in achieving change and progress.'[32] It was indeed a cold-war confrontation in which each bloc tried to show its sympathy and support for the countries which were unfriendly to their adversaries. For Lebanon was an international base for forces operating in contrary directions and each bloc was hoping to win a friendly government in Beirut.[33]

Moreover, during this meeting Iraq distributed two documents on the Arab League meeting in Benghazi. The Lebanese delegate told the Council that the Arab League meeting in Benghazi failed because of UAR tactics and not because of Lebanon. He argued that when the UAR attempted to amend the draft resolution at Benghazi, in which it would be stated that there was no Egyptian intervention in Lebanon, the other Arab delegations 'completely rejected it.'[34] Al-Jamali of Iraq was even harsher than the Lebanese delegate in criticizing the UAR when he stated that the League council meeting at Benghazi failed because of Egyptian domination of that organization: 'The Arab League has been paralysed; it has not been meeting (since June 6). Why? Because it did not serve Egyptian purposes. After all, those who know the internal story of the Arab League know that it is more or less one department of the Egyptian Foreign Office — no more, no less.'[35]

None the less, at the meeting next day, 11 June, the Council voted and passed a Swedish draft resolution which had been submitted on the preceding day. The draft resolution stated that the Security Council:

Having heard the charges of the representative of Lebanon concerning interference by the United Arab Republic in the

internal affairs of Lebanon and the reply of the
representative of the United Arab Republic,
1   *Decides* to dispatch urgently an observation group to
proceed to Lebanon so as to ensure that there is no illegal
infiltration of personnel or supply of arms or other *matériel*
across the Lebanese borders;
2   *Authorizes* the Secretary-General to take the necessary
steps to that end;
3   *Requests* the observation group to keep the Security
Council currently informed through the Secretary-General.[36]

The draft resolution was adopted by ten votes to none, with one
abstention (the Soviet Union).[37]

The secretary-general moved quickly and in three days he was able
to form the United Nations Observation Group in Lebanon (UNOGIL)
which held its first meeting in Beirut on 19 June. On 3 July UNOGIL
submitted its first report to the Security Council through the secretary-
general. The report noted that instability prevailed in much of the
country and that 'throughout the country the possession of arms is
common practice.' Furthermore the report stated that inspecting
frontier areas, controlled by opposition forces, required free passage
from particular opposition leaders which 'has so far not been
forthcoming.' The report concluded that there were 'substantial
movements of armed men within the country and concentrations at
various places'.[38] The report, however, did not confirm Lebanon's
assertion that there was UAR 'mass infiltration' into Lebanon.
Lebanon reacted to the report with disappointment and criticism that
the report was premature. The UAR considered the report as a
vindication of its position that the upheaval in Lebanon was primarily
an internal affair.[39]

The crisis in Lebanon certainly was not ameliorated after the
arrival of UNOGIL. On 8 July Sham'oun again tried to calm the
opposition and restated that he would not seek re-election. But the
opposition, led by Salam, Karami, Franjiyyeh, and others, demanded
the president's immediate resignation in order to end the crisis.
Sham'oun vowed not to resign until his term expired in September
1958.[40]

On 14 July the pro-West monarchy in Iraq was toppled and Cairo
was the first to recognize the new leaders in Baghdad. The next day
American marines landed in Lebanon, at the request of Sham'oun,
thus giving the Lebanese crisis a still wider international dimension.

Two days later, 17 July, Jordan requested the Security Council's urgent consideration of its complaint 'of interference in its domestic affairs by the United Arab Republic.'[41] At the same time King Hussein's government asked for help from London, which dispatched British troops to Jordan the same day.

The Security Council agreed to discuss the complaints from Lebanon and Jordan concurrently. The Jordanian representative spoke to the Council meeting on 17 July, charging the UAR with 'continuous attempts to overthrow [his] Government by subversive elements employed from the outside'.[42] The USA and Britain supported Jordan's claims. The Soviet Union accused the two Western powers of military 'invasion' of Lebanon and Jordan.[43] The UAR delegate rejected the Jordanian charges as 'a pretext . . . for the dispatch of British troops to re-occupy Jordan'.[44]

Several resolutions were considered in the Security Council. Sweden's draft resolution considered that the American intervention had 'substantially altered the conditions' that prevailed in June and thus '*requests* the Secretary-General to suspend the activities of the observers to Lebanon until further notice.'[45] However, Japan submitted a draft resolution which 'invites the United Nations Observation Group in Lebanon to continue' its efforts in Lebanon,[46] while the secretary-general should take the necessary measures 'to fulfill the general purposes established in [resolution S/4022], and which will, in accordance with the Charter, serve to ensure the territorial integrity and political independence of Lebanon, so as to make possible the withdrawal of U.S. forces from Lebanon.'[47] A US draft resolution called for an end to outside intervention and asked the secretary-general to take the necessary steps to ensure Lebanon's integrity and independence.[48] A Soviet draft resolution called for the withdrawal of American and British forces from Lebanon and Jordan respectively.[49]

Because of the veto power, the draft resolutions failed to obtain the required votes for adoption.[50] On 6 August the Soviet Union revised its earlier draft resolution and called for a special session of the General Assembly to consider the situation in the Middle East.[51] The following day the USA took a similar step and called for a special session of the General Assembly.[52] The Security Council met on 7 August and adopted unanimously the amended US draft resolution (S/4056/Rev./) which called for a General Assembly special session.[53] Consequently, the Soviet representative asked for no vote on its own draft resolution S/4057/Rev./.[54]

The election on 31 July of General Fu'ad Shihab as the new president to succeed Sham'oun did not end the crisis in Lebanon. The country was still strewn with unrest, barricades, and armed fighters. Sham'oun would not bow to the opposition demand for his resignation and he insisted on holding his job until his term expired on 23 September 1958. Thus the special session of the General Assembly was needed and it convened on 8 August in an attempt to find a solution to that crisis.

The Arab League Initiative

The special session of the General Assembly witnessed intensive deliberations by several different powers especially the USA and the Soviet Union. On 13 August President Eisenhower addressed the General Assembly. He emphasized that American military intervention in Lebanon had 'one single purpose — that is the purpose of the [UN] Charter.' He assured the Assembly that the American forces 'will be totally withdrawn whenever this is requested by the duly constituted Government of Lebanon or whenever, through action by the United Nations or otherwise, Lebanon is no longer exposed to the original danger.' President Eisenhower also called for an end to 'armed pressure and infiltration'. He called for the establishment of 'an Arab development institution' to work toward the development of the Middle East (in the fields of industry, agriculture, and education, among others).[55]

The Soviet foreign minister, Andre Gromyko, spoke to the Assembly following the American president. He called American and British troops in Lebanon and Jordan, respectively, forces of 'occupation' and 'aggression' and called for the 'immediate withdrawal' of these troops from the Middle East. Gromyko then submitted for consideration at the emergency session of the General Assembly a Soviet draft resolution calling on Washington and London 'to withdraw their troops from the territories of Lebanon and Jordan without delay'.[56]

A few days later seven countries — Canada, Columbia, Denmark, Liberia, Norway, Panama, and Paraguay — submitted a draft resolution to the General Assembly. The resolution '*reaffirms* that all Member States should refrain from any threats or acts, direct or indirect, aimed at impairing the freedom, independence or integrity of any State, or at fomenting civil strife and subverting the will of the people of any state.' The resolution requested the secretary-general to make the necessary arrangements to 'help in upholding the purposes and principles of the Charter in relation to Lebanon and Jordan in present circumstances.' Furthermore the resolution invited the secretary-general to consult with the Arab states about the American suggestion of establishing an Arab development institution.[57]

The seven-power resolution was supported by the majority of the Assembly. However, several delegates criticized it because it failed to ask of the USA and Britain the immediate withdrawal of their forces from Lebanon and Jordan. Lack of consensus in the General Assembly led to intensive discussions among the members in an attempt to reach a resolution acceptable to all concerned parties. These intensive discussions and deliberations were led by the Arab League. Abdel-Khaliq Hassouna, seceretary-general of the League, took the initiative without prior authorization by the League member states.

Secretary-General Hassouna succeeded in influencing the Arab delegations to follow the League's conciliatory path.[58] Hassouna held several meetings of the Arab delegations, including the UAR and the Lebanese, in the League's office in New York, during which they discussed the Lebanese crisis. Furthermore the secretary-general of the League succeeded in forming a sub-committee, chaired by Sudan and including representatives of Saudi Arabia, the UAR, Iraq, and the secretary-general himself. The sub-committee was to prepare the text of a draft for final Arab settlement of the dispute.[59] On 20 August the sub-committee met at the UN headquarters during which it finalized the draft resolution which was then submitted by Hassouna to the Arab representatives. The text of the draft resolution, at the urging of the secretary-general, was unanimously approved by all the Arab delegations, including Lebanon and the UAR.[60] Furthermore, the League's secretary held meetings with the various bloc powers at the UN. He contacted the members of the Afro-Asian bloc, the delegates of the two superpowers, the president of the General Assembly, the seven countries which submitted the seven-power resolution, the Latin American group, and others, and informed them of the text of the Arab draft resolution and asked their support for it. The next day, 21 August, the Arab delegations received their governments' approval of their draft resolution, with certain Lebanese reservations; none the less, the Lebanese delegate pledged to vote for it.[61] Hence, the Arab League members decided:

(1) to present the draft resolution to the Assembly jointly by all ten Arab member states of the United Nations; (2) that the Sudanese Foreign Minister, Muhamad Mahjoub, would submit the draft resolution to the Assembly and speak on behalf of the sponsors of the draft; (3) to convene the Afro-Asian group to a meeting at which the League's Secretary-General, Hassouna, would present the draft resolution and explain the common Arab policy.[62]

The secretary-general of the Arab League spoke to the Afro-Asian bloc at a meeting during which he explained to them the Arab draft resolution. The Afro-Asian group unanimously endorsed the League's resolution. In the last meeting of the Assembly's emergency session, which was held on the afternoon of 21 August, Mahjoub of the Sudan spoke 'in the name of all the Arab states represented in the General Assembly'. He pointed out that the draft resolution was 'co-sponsored by all the ten Arab states' which acted as 'members of one family'. Mahjoub then, reiterating the Egyptian view, emphasized the importance of the Arab League as a regional organization which can settle regional disputes and can serve as an example to others to save international peace and security. He asked the Assembly members 'to put their approval on [the League resolution] and give it the unanimous support of the Assembly.'[63] The League's draft was unanimously adopted by the General Assembly, which in part requested

> the Secretary-General to make forthwith, in consultation
> with the Government concerned and in accordance with the
> Charter, and having in mind section one of this resolution
> [see Appendix C for full text], such practical arrangements
> as would adequately help in upholding the purposes and
> principles of the Charter in relation to Lebanon and Jordan
> in the present circumstances, and thereby facilitate the early
> withdrawal of the foreign troops from the two countries.[64]

The resolution called for the observance of article 8 of the Arab League pact which calls for member states' respect for each other's sovereignty and independence and for the abstention of interference in other League members' internal affairs.

Muhamad Mahjoub commented on the adoption of this resolution by saying, 'This resolution is a new dawn for a great future. It opens the way to the Arab countries for mutual co-operation and forgiveness.'[65] Since the parties concerned accepted it, superpowers had but to praise the Arab resolution. Overall, the General Assembly participants expressed their satisfaction at the adoption of the Arab resolution. A UN representative was posted in Jordan and by 2 November British troops completed their withdrawal. In Lebanon UNOGIL was strengthened and the American marines left Lebanon before the end of October. Furthermore, UNOGIL, after it reported that disorders in Lebanon had come to an end, withdrew from Lebanon on 9 December 1958.[66] On 23 September Sham'oun's term as president expired and the commander-in-chief of the Lebanese army, General Fu'ad Shihab, was installed as president. Rashid Karami, a strong opponent of Sham'oun, was selected as the new prime minister. On 16 November the Lebanese foreign minister had requested the Security Council 'to delete from the list of matters [its agenda] . . . the Lebanese complaint submitted to it on May 22, 1958,'[67] and he announced that Lebanon was resuming its 'brotherly' relations with the UAR based on the respect for the provisions of the Arab League pact and the UN Charter. That marked the end of the Lebanese upheaval for a few years; it had claimed the lives of about 3000 Lebanese, greatly impaired the economy, gravely damaged the country's political infrastructure, and created a serious international crisis.

Observations

The Lebanese crisis was a very complex one. It was a conflict between those who supported Arab unity and the pro-Sham'oun group. Many Muslims were spiritually attached to Syria, while Lebanese Christian capitalists were opposed to unity with the UAR. Moreover, Lebanese socialists wanted close ties with the UAR, but the rightists — pro West — were against such ties. Furthermore, the Lebanese crisis had a worldwide dimension. Those who were pro-non-alignment were calling for pro-Cairo policies, while those who were pro-West were against that. The conflict between Lebanon and the UAR changed from a local dispute to an international one when the USA and Britain sent troops to the area.

The Lebanese complaint against the alleged Cairo interference in its internal affairs was a valid one. Despite its continued denials, the UAR did in fact, as the close associate of Nasser at that time, Abdel-

Latif al-Baghdadi admitted, send 'money and arms' to the opposition groups in Lebanon.[68] Lebanese complaints of the alleged UAR violent campaign against the Sham'oun regime were justified. Studies of UAR propaganda instruments, such as 'Radio Cairo', 'the Voice of the Arabs' and 'Radio Damascus' 'fully support the Lebanese acusations'.[69] Thus, the Lebanese complaint and request that the Arab League should stop this UAR intervention seemed to be justified. But was the League able at Benghazi to do that?

The Lebanese complaint to the League was based on article 6 of the pact, which states: 'In case of aggression or threat of aggression by one state against a member state, the state which has been attacked or threatened with aggression may demand the *immediate convocation of the Council*' (emphasis added). Because Lebanon thought the UAR had committed aggression against it, it invoked article 5 of the pact which prohibited the use of force to resolve disputes and relied on the League for peaceful settlement. The League received Lebanon's complaint on 21 May 1958, but it *did not* meet until 31 May, ten days after the complaint. When the League council met, however, the UAR severely criticized Lebanon for sending a complaint to the UN Security Council and it requested that Lebanon resort only to the Arab League. Cairo also rejected the Lebanese charges against the UAR. The UAR delegate attempted to corner the Lebanese delegate by appealing to the other Arab delegations, under the slogan of pan-Arabism, to support the UAR and by accusing Lebanon, in going to the Security Council, of not being serious about its participation in the 'holy organization'. The government of Lebanon, by going to the Security Council, 'shook the feeling of many people in the Arab world,' the UAR representative said.[70]

The Egyptian representative also asked the council to postpone its meeting for a few days — a request which the Lebanese representative at first refused but soon had to accept. The Egyptian delegation succeeded in securing the Sudanese delegate's active co-operation in this and other matters. For example, in the fourth meeting Cairo asked for another postponement of the meetings. Muhamad Mahjoub, the Sudanese foreign minister and its chief delegate at the council meeting, agreed with the Egyptian request, saying '*we* agree on that.' Though Mahjoub was only one delegate, he tried to speak in the name of all participants in support of Cairo. The UAR representative complimented Mahjoub and said: 'I thank Mr Minister, because he reduced a heavy load and removed a responsibility.' What he meant by that was unclear except that he was delighted by Sudanese co-operation with Cairo in isolating Lebanon. To escape Egypt's attacks and intrigues, other Arab delegates submitted to Nasser's emphasis on pan-Arabism. But the Lebanese delegate protested: 'It is the right and duty of Lebanon's delegation to reject any more postponements, and to see that you [the council] move on immediately to discuss the case.'[71]

Again when in the fifth meeting, Mahjoub introduced a very broad resolution, which did not call for an end to the UAR intervention in Lebanon as Beirut demanded, the UAR requested the amendments to the resolution at the expense of Lebanon. The UAR amendment would read 'And after having felt in the two parties to the dispute the spirit of mutual respect and certain desire not to intervene in each other's internal affairs . . .'.[72] The Lebanese delegate wanted the text to read 'The League Council calls on member states to abstain from interfering in the internal affairs of the other states.'[73] Only Yemen supported the UAR. What was even more perplexing was the Sudanese representative who attempted to make it appear that the resolution was 'accepted by all of us'. Not surprisingly, the Sudanese resolution, which did not say anything about the UAR intervention in Lebanon, the heart of the Lebanese complaint, was rejected by Lebanon. The Sham'oun regime considered that the League resolution was a kind of 'recommendation' or 'mediation'.

Indeed, the measures adopted by the League did not explicitly refer to the substance of the complaint and the League council 'abstained from pronouncing itself upon the issue as to whether interference had occurred.'[74] Thus the broad terms of the Egyptian-inspired resolution, which called for an end to disturbance of peaceful relations between member states, were not accepted by the Lebanese government. 'There is no doubt,' as a close observer of the Arab League noted, 'that the League of Arab States failed to settle the conflict [at Benghazi], because the primary revolutionary state, Egypt, was a party to it. Thus Lebanon did not trust the Arab League allegiance since [Lebanon] was totally convinced that it was a regional organization, which is totally subjected to the influence and pressure of the UAR.'[75] Furthermore, the staff of the Arab League, including Secretary-General Hassouna and his assistant, Sayed Nofal, both of whom are Egyptian, did not move positively to settle this dispute. The League council's procrastination over meeting immediately to consider the Lebanese complaint was an indication of the Egyptian desire to thwart the League's dealing with the real issues.

By contrast the Security Council met within twenty-four hours to consider the same complaint. When the League council failed, Lebanon requested a meeting of the UN Security Council which met promptly. Within three days the Security Council formed and dispatched UNOGIL. Beyond that, however, the veto power in the Security Council made it impossible for it to reach a unanimous resolution. Thereupon a special session of the UN General Assembly was called for, met, and discussed the Lebanese crisis (concurrently with the Jordanian complaint of 17 July). But where the Arab League's diplomacy failed at Benghazi, it succeeded in the UN. The role played by Abdel-Khaliq Hassouna, secretary-general of the Arab League, was very crucial and significant, as it was he who took the initiative.

We have seen that the UAR was against the Lebanese resort to the Security Council. It preferred the League where it could manœuvre more freely, but since Lebanon rejected the League's resolution and had come to the UN, the UAR had to confront it. At the Security Council Cairo relied on Moscow's veto power. But in the special session of the General Assembly, Cairo relied again on the faithful Arab League and the closer co-operation of the foreign minister of Sudan, Muhamad Mahjoub, who followed the Lebanese complaint to New York. Under the influence and guidance of Hassouna, Mahjoub played a vigorous role, similar to that at Benghazi, which ultimately triumphed through unprecedented 'Arab unity' in the passage in the UN of a joint resolution calling on the area's countries to abstain from interfering in each other's affairs and requesting the early departure from Lebanon of American troops (and from Jordan of British troops). At President Nasser's direction, UAR newspapers headlined the UN story: 'We have Won.'[76] How?

At the Security Council meetings the Arab countries revealed that they did not reach consensus at Benghazi because several League member states did not trust the Arab League on account of its domination by Cairo. An illustration of that was Iraq's placing at the disposal of the Security Council the supposedly secret documents of the Arab League meetings at Benghazi. Despite the League's and UAR's contentions that only Lebanon had dissented, Iraq revealed that the countries represented there were not in agreement and the League was not able to reach an agreed solution. Furthermore, Iraq made it known that at least three League members (Lebanon, Iraq, and Jordan) did not support the League's draft resolution. Therefore, no resolution in fact was adopted unanimously, for Iraq and Jordan took the side of Lebanon.[77] This view was in contrast to that of the

UAR representative at the UN, who insisted that, apart from Lebanon, there had been unanimous approval of the League's draft resolution by Sudan, Saudi Arabia, Iraq, Jordan, Libya, and Yemen.[78]

Why did the League fail to act unanimously at Benghazi? In the Iraqi view, which was shared by Lebanon and Jordan, the Arab League had been paralysed 'because it did not serve Egyptian purposes.' The League, moreover, was 'more or less one department of the Egyptian foreign office'.[79] Iraq argued that the Arab League would have functioned much better if it was not for Nasser's will to dominate. Thus, I believe that the League failed at Benghazi because of UAR manœuvrings which were facilitated by the mechanism of the Arab League — led by Hassouna and Nofal — and the co-operation of Sudan on its side.

But whereas this combination of co-operation failed at Benghazi (actually it succeeded in preventing the council from adopting any resolution that was unacceptable to Egypt) it succeeded in New York. Secretary-General Hassouna took the initiative, undoubtedly with Cairo's blessing but without prior authorization by the League member states, and held a series of meetings of Arab representatives at the UN, including that of Lebanon. In the light of the Security Council's failure to reach a settlement to the crisis, Lebanon's acceptance of Hassouna's attempt might have stemmed from the situation (similar to the situation which existed prior to the Benghazi League meeting) 'of a *fait accompli* in which she found herself as a result of the initiative taken by the Secretary-General' with the implied consent of other League member states.[80] Furthermore, Lebanon went along with the League's draft resolution even though the resolution abstained from pronouncing upon the issue of whether UAR interference had occurred. Rather, the tone of the resolution was conciliatory in character, as the UAR wanted. The aim of the resolution was to underline the prevalence of the Egyptian view of the spirit of Arab unity and co-operation, as reflected by the various provisions of the League's pact. Since the parties to the dispute agreed to the Arab League resolution, a unanimous vote of the Assembly, including the votes of the USA and the Soviet Union, was achieved. After all, the Soviet Union would not act against the wishes of the UAR nor would the USA follow a path different from that which Lebanon had already accepted. Thus, the Arab League, through its Secretary-General, acted in line with the views expressed by the UAR throughout the Lebanese crisis and, for this reason, Cairo did 'win'.

Notes to chapter five

1 See Malcolm H. Kerr, 'Lebanese Views on the 1958 Crisis' (book reviews), *Middle East Journal* (spring, 1961), vol. 15, no. 2, pp. 211–17.

2 Joseph J. Malone, *The Arab Lands of Western Asia*, Englewood Cliffs, N. J., Prentice-Hall, 1973, p. 169.

3 *al-Ahram*, 10 January 1957. Quoted in Boutros Boutros-Ghali, *League of Arab States and the Settlement of Local Disputes* (in Arabic), Cairo, Dar al-Tiba'ah al-Hadithah, 1977, p. 68.

4 In a policy statement made by the United National Front, 3 July 1957. M. S. Agwani, *The Lebanese Crisis, 1958: A Documentary Study*, Bombay, Asia Publishing House, 1965, p. 36. Miles Copeland observed that the US embassy and the CIA contributed to the pro-Sham'oun forces, also, according to Copeland, British, French, Soviet, and Egyptian embassies were contributing to their respective candidates; see *The Game of Nations: The Amorality of Power Politics*, London, Weidenfeld and Nicholson, 1969, pp. 192–93.

5 Agwani, p. 37.

6 Ibid., pp. 44–45.

7 Ibid., p. 45.

8 Copeland, p. 197; Malone, p. 24; John Marlowe, *Arab Nationalism and British Imperialism: A Study in Power Politics*, New York, Praeger, 1961, p. 171; Maurice Harari, *Government and Politics of the Middle East*, Englewood Cliffs, N. J., Prentice-Hall, 1962, p. 117; George Lenczowski, *The Middle East in World Affairs*, Ithaca and London, Cornell University Press, 3rd edn, 1962, p. 338; J.C. Hurewitz, in Leonard Binder (ed.) *Politics in Lebanon*, p. 233. Abdel-Latif al-Baghdadi contends that the UAR sent arms and money to the opposition, led by Saib Salam, because it considered US support to Sham'oun was a new conspiracy against the northern region of UAR (Syria). See *Abdel-Latif al-Baghdadi Memoire*, part II, Cairo, Alexandria, al-Maktab al-Misri al-Hadith, 1977, pp. 50–51.

9 See Harari, p. 118, and Lenczowski, p. 337.

10 See Agwani, pp. 65–70.

11 Memorandum of 21 May 1958, from the Lebanese embassy in Cairo addressed to the League secretariat-general, Cairo. Quoted in Hussein A. Hassouna, *The League of Arab States and Regional Disputes*, Dobbs Ferry, N. Y., Oceana, 1975, p. 62. Article 6 of the pact reads in part: 'In case of aggression or threat of aggression by one state against a member state, the state which has been attacked or threatened with aggression may demand the immediate convocation of the Council.'

12 Muhammad Khalil, *The Arab States and the Arab League*, Beirut, Khayats, 1962, vol. II, p. 190.
13 Boutros-Ghali, *op. cit.*, p. 70.
14 *Security Council Official Records (S.C.O.R.)*, 13th year, 818th meeting, 27 May 1958, pp. 1–8.
15 *Minutes of League Council, Extraordinary Session at Benghazi*, 2nd meeting, 1 June 1958, p. 15.
16 Ibid., p. 16.
17 Ibid., p. 19.
18 Ibid., p. 20.
19 Ibid., p. 25.
20 Ibid., 3rd meeting, 3 June 1958, pp. 31–86.
21 Arab League Draft Resolution concerning Lebanon's Complaint against the United Arab Republic, in Khalil, vol. II, p. 191; for the Arabic transcript see *Minutes of League Council Extraordinary Session at Benghazi*, 5th meeting, 4 June 1958, pp. 93–94.
22 Ibid., p. 101.
23 Lebanese Government's Response to the Arab League Draft Resolution Concerning its Complaint against the United Arab Republic, in Khalil, vol. II, p. 191.
24 *Minutes of League Council Extraordinary Session at Benghazi*, 6th meeting, 6 June 1958, p. 108.
25 Ibid., pp. 109–14.
26 *S.C.O.R.*, 13th year, 823rd meeting, 6 June 1958, pp. 3-4.
27 Ibid., p. 21.
28 Ibid., p. 23.
29 Ibid., p. 28.
30 Ibid., p. 32.
31 Ibid., 824th meeting, 10 June 1958, p. 13.
32 Ibid., p. 39.
33 See Copeland, pp. 192–98.
34 *S.C.O.R.*, 824th meeting, 10 June 1958, p. 19.
35 Ibid., p. 43.
36 Ibid., p. 23; S/4022.
37 *S.C.O.R.*, 825th meeting, 10 June 1958, p. 17.
38 *U.N. Doc.* S/4040; see also Muhamad Tal'at al-Ghuneimi, *Jamiá t al-Dowal al-Arabiyyeh*, (The League of Arab States), Alexandria, Minsha'at al-Ma'arif, 1974, pp. 107–08.
39 Hassouna, p. 67.
40 Ibid., p. 68.
41 *U.N. Doc.* S/4053; *S.C.O.R.*, 13th year, 831st meeting, 17 July 1958. p. 1.
42 Ibid., p. 4.
43 Ibid., p. 14.
44 Ibid., p. 19.

45 *U.N. Doc.* S/4054.
46 *U.N. Doc.* S/4055; S/4055/Rev.1./.
47 Ibid.
48 *U.N. Doc.* S/4056.
49 *U.N. Doc.* S/4057.
50 *S.C.O.R.*, 13th year, 834th meeting, 18 July 1958, p. 11.
51 *U.N. Doc.* S/4057/Rev. 1.
52 *U.N. Doc.* S/4056/Rev. 1.
53 *S.C.O.R.*, 13th year, 838th meeting, 7 August 1958, p. 45.
54 Ibid.
55 *GAOR*, third emergency special session, 733rd plenary meeting, pp. 7–10.
56 See ibid., pp. 14–16.
57 Draft resolution submitted by seven powers, 18 August 1958, in Agwani, pp. 365–66.
58 Sayed Nofal, *al-'Amal al-Arabi al-Mushtarak*, (The Joint Arab Activities) book I, Cairo, Ma'had al-Bahuth Wal-Dirasat al-Arabiyyeh, 1968, p. 97.
59 Boutros-Ghali, *op. cit.* p. 75.
60 Hassouna, pp. 72–73.
61 Ibid.; Boutros-Ghali, *op. cit.* p. 75.
62 *Report of Secretary-General to League Council*, 30th ordinary session, 1958 October, p. 35; quoted in Hassouna, p. 73.
63 *GAOR*, third emergency special session, 746th plenary meeting, pp. 169–70.
64 Quoted in Agwani, p. 372.
65 Quoted in Boutros-Ghali, *op. cit.* p. 76.
66 al-Ghuneimi, p. 110.
67 *S.C.O.R.*, 13th year, 840th meeting, 25 November 1958, p. 5.
68 *Abdel-Latif al-Baghdadi Memoire*, part II, p. 51.
69 A. I. Dawisha, *Egypt in the Arab World: The Elements of Foreign Policy*, London, Macmillan, 1976, p. 23.
70 *Minutes of League Council Extraordinary Session at Benghazi*, 2nd meeting, 1 June 1958, p. 20.
71 Ibid., 4th meeting, 4 June 1958, pp. 89–90.
72 Ibid., 5th meeting, 4 June 1958, p. 94.
73 Ibid., p. 100.
74 Hassouna, p. 79.
75 Boutros-Ghali, op. cit. pp. 79–80.
76 Robert St. John, *The Boss: The Story of Gamal Abdel-Nasser*, New York, Toronto, London, McGraw-Hill, 1960, p. 296.
77 See *S.C.O.R.*, 13th year, 823rd meeting, 6 June 1958, p. 38.
78 Ibid., 13th year, 823rd meeting, 10 June 1958, pp. 18–19.
79 Ibid., p. 43.
80 Hassouna, pp. 78–79.

Chapter Six

Syria: 1958–62

It is well known that Syria has been an important centre for Arab nationalists for centuries. The Syrians see themselves as the natural leaders of Arab nationalism since many of the Arab activities for Arab liberation came from there. By the time Syria gained its independence from the French in 1943, Syrian leaders were divided on how to pursue their goal of Arab 'unity'. The country was full of political parties; the army was indoctrinated and politicized; social cleavages were extreme; the rich and influential Syrian families were opposed to any change in the *status quo*; the Communists wanted a revolutionary Syria. Externally, Syria was the subject of constant outside intrigues: the West wanted to see a pro-Western Syria; the East worked hard to win Syrian friendship; for decades the Hashemite kings of Iraq and Jordan had wanted to bring Syria under their control. Israel was not in favour of a stable Syria; Egypt, under Nasser, wanted to see the two countries form a unit. By 1958 internal and external factors convinced Syrian leaders that the cure for their ills was the union with Egypt. Nasser, although he wanted a merger on a slower footing, was none the less looking for such unity with eagerness. The union, which took place in February 1958, did not however last long.[1] The Syrians began to feel frustrated by the way Nasser was ruling their country. Instead of progress, Syria experienced regression during the life of the UAR. Besides, the Syrian army was accustomed to intervention in Syria's politics. In September 1961 the Syrian army announced the secession of Syria from the UAR. A serious blow to Nasser's position and his dream of

Arab unity, this move precipitated a crisis of Egyptian-Syrian rivalry in the Arab League.

The Formation of the United Arab Republic

The UAR was born largely because of the popularity and personality of Nasser. Before the end of January 1958 the Syrian president, Shukri al-Quwatli and his cabinet met with the Egyptian government led by Nasser. On 1 February, at a session between the Syrian and Egyptian governments, the UAR was proclaimed. Upon signing the unity agreement, Quwatli seemed to be relieved. According to Egyptian journalist, Mohamed Heikal, Quwatli told Nasser:

> Ah . . . Mr. President, you don't know what you have
> taken on!! You have taken on people of whom every one
> believes he is a politician; 50 per cent of them consider
> themselves national leaders; 25 per cent of them think they
> are prophets; and at least 10 per cent believe they are gods.
> You have taken on people of which there are those who
> worship God; and there are those who adore fire; and there
> are those who idolize the devil.[2]

On 21 February, in a general plebiscite held in the two countries, Egyptians and Syrians overwhelmingly approved the formation of the UAR. Nasser was named as president and Cairo as the capital of the UAR. On the following day, Nasser, who had never seen Syria before, was welcomed in Damascus by Syrians, 'drunk with enthusiasm'. With the exception of Yemen, the Arab League members, such as Saudi Arabia, Iraq, Jordan, and Lebanon, were, at least tacitly, against the formation of the UAR, for Nasser's claim to Arab leadership would now be undisputed and the leaders of these countries feared that they might lose their positions to him. However, the Arab League itself, through its secretary-general, welcomed the new republic. It was a 'great gain' to the League, the secretary-general said in his report to the League council in March 1958: 'The unity of the two countries would increase their power and thus increase their ability to fulfill their obligations toward the League and to work toward achieving all its goals.'[3]

The provisional constitution of the UAR (see Appendix E) vested the executive power solely in the president of the republic. The president was authorized to appoint and determine the number of members of the national assembly. The president was also granted the right to initiate, oppose, and promulgate laws. Furthermore, the president could dissolve the national assembly at will. He appointed the ministers and relieved them of their posts. He was the supreme commander of the armed forces. He also appointed one or more vice-presidents, and could dismiss them at will. In short, the constitution centralized the authority in the hands of the president, thus granting Nasser the right to behave as he pleased, without constitutional restraints.

None the less, the shortcomings of the constitution were to show soon after the merger. As the Syrian leader, Faris el-Khuri, reportedly said, the UAR 'was done in a minute, in a foolish minute.'[4] The Ba'ath had hoped to imbue Nasser with their 'philosophy,' but instead Nasser tried to ignore them, though they were (and still are) powerful. To reassert themselves, the Ba'ath, through the Syrian army, decided after all that Syria was better off without Egypt.

The Syrian Secession

The Syrians suffered from many ills which swept the country: suppression of freedom, factionalism, detention, torture, mass arrests, abuse of individual powers, physical liquidation of opposition, outside clandestine activities and other evils. They expected Cairo to prescribe remedies for these ills. Instead of improving the situation, the union, by and large, made things worse for the Syrians. Thus, Syrian initial enthusiasm for union was soon to be replaced by disenchantment and discontent.

The desire for unity was stimulated by the popularity of Nasser among the Syrian masses. But Nasser alone was not enough to sustain that short-lived unity. The differences and the difficulties which existed inside the two countries were not the same nor was the external situation the same. For one thing Syria and Egypt were geographically far apart, separated by an enemy and the sea, which obstructed the consolidation of mass relationship, a fundamental aspect in any union. But there were other major factors which led to the failure of the UAR: the politics of the Ba'ath, the army, Nasser's strong man in Syria, Abdel-Hamid el-Sarra'j, and other powerful personalities in Syria; the apparent Egyptian sense of domination in the Syrian army and other key areas; Egyptian socialist programmes which were unfamiliar to many Syrians; and outside conspiracies originating from countries that opposed Nasser's policies. The final straw was when Nasser shocked the Syrians on 23 July 1961 by his socialist laws which nationalized all banks, insurance companies, industrial plants, and public utilities; feudal practices were officially liquidated; workers were to share profits with industries and to have their representatives on all management boards; acquisition by the government of a controlling interest in a long list of enterprises; and acquisition by the government of a 25 per cent interest in all importing agencies.[5] Through the socialist laws, Nasser wanted to eliminate all opposition to the union.[6] But the opposite of that happened: two months later the forces opposed to Nasser's laws seceded from the union. Moreover, Syrians resented Egyptian bureaucratization of Syria. The middle class suffered to some degree from Egyptian red tape and restrictions of economic and administrative reforms which were introduced by the Egyptians. In short the failure of the UAR came as a result of the need for 'a field for effective political participation and expression of opinion, so as to take the edge off the widespread sense of disillusion among soldiers, political notables, businessmen, and ordinary citizens that made the secession possible,'[7] a close observer wrote. Thus the stage was set to prove that Syria was 'a difficult country to govern', as Shukri al-Quwatli is said to have told Nasser.[8] At dawn on 18 September a group of Syrian officers took over the government in Syria, sent Marshal Amir back home, and proclaimed the separation of Syria from Egypt.

Nasser's Reaction to the Secession

The Syrian secession (*infisal*) dealt the most serious blow to Nasser's Arab unity campaign. It was a major reverse in his 'three circles' policy. The *infisal* made him furious. He criticized himself for trusting the Syrian politicians. Nasser's Arab policy turned from 'unity of rank' (*wihdat al-saff*) to the call for 'unity of purpose' (*wihdat al-hadaf*). He differentiated between 'Egypt as a state' and 'Egypt as a revolution'. As Nasser's spokesman explained:

As a state, Egypt deals with all Arab governments, whatever their forms or systems. It sits with them in the Arab League and at the United Nations, and concludes defence, trade, cultural, and other different agreements . . ..

As a revolution, *Egypt should deal only with the people.* And this does not imply intereference on our part in the affairs of others. Otherwise we contradict the fundamental premise of our struggle that the Arab people are a single nation. . . . Egypt as a revolution should never hesitate or halt at frontiers, but should carry her message across them . . . . *If the Arab League were to be used to paralyse our movement, we must be prepared to freeze the operations of that organization.*[9] (author's emphasis)

Nasser declared that he could no longer co-operate with Arab 'reactionaries' and therefore he could not accept their charges that he was wrecking Arab solidarity. 'I want Arab unity of purpose before I talk about Arab unity of rank,'[10] Nasser declared.

The implications of Nasser's and Heikal's declarations are clear. Internally, after the secession, Nasser launched radical social changes. Externally, Nasser broke off diplomatic relations with Jordan, accusing King Hussein of being involved in the secession; he terminated the loose confederation existing between the UAR and Yemen (see next chapter); he denounced King Saud, and he vowed not to recognize the new Syrian government. Nasser argued that for Arab unity to be achieved, Arab 'reactionaries' must go. This could be done through internal upheavals and agitations by the Arab masses, upon whom Nasser relied so much in achieving his Arab policy goals.

When the new leaders of Syria announced their separation of Syria from the UAR, the first thing Nasser did was to go to the radio station and tell his people that a 'handful of soldiers took over Damascus radio and surrounded the army headquarters.' He insisted that 'I could in no circumstances join the enemies of the Arab nation . . . and [I] declare the dissolution of the United Arab Republic,' and added, 'upon issuing orders, the First Army [the Syrian army] is now converging [on Damascus] from all sides in Syria to repress the mutiny.'[11] After his radio statement, Nasser hurried into the Egyptian army's headquarters in Cairo where he decided to send Egyptian troops to Syria to crush the 'rebels'. Some Egyptian paratroopers were in fact dropped in Latakia on 28 September. However, when it became clear that the new leaders in Syria were in control of the country, Nasser called off his military plan and ordered his paratroopers to surrender themselves to the Syrians, who later sent them back to their country.[12]

Meanwhile several Arab and non-Arab countries recognized the new regime in Damascus. Nasser, faced with the Syrian reality, spoke to his listeners on 5 October, telling them that although 'I am a champion of unity,' he felt 'at this moment that it is not imperative that Syria remains a part of the UAR, but it is imperative that Syria should remain as Syria.'[13] After defending the Egyptian role in Syria during the union, Nasser announced that the UAR would not stand against Syria's readmission to UN membership and that 'he would not hinder' the readmission of Syria to the League of Arab States, but he would 'not agree to recognize any government in Damascus except after a Syrian popular and free-will decision which chooses for itself its own road.'[14] Nasser also asked that the Arab League 'immediately' form a committee to investigate the questions of currency, detainees, and Egyptian troops and workers in Syria.[15] On October 29, 1961 Syria was re-admitted to the Arab League. The League's secretary-general initiated a series of meetings between Syrian and Egyptian representatives and an agreement was reached between the two countries on the outstanding questions between Cairo and Damascus. On 2 November Syria agreed to repatriate 870 Egyptian officers and other ranks, while Cairo reciprocated by allowing 960 Syrian officers to go back to their country.[16]

After his initial moderate opposition to the secession, Nasser and the Egyptian media machine stepped up their attacks and denounced the Syrian leaders as 'reactionaries', 'traitors', 'anti-Arab unity', 'oppressors', and so forth. In the 13 October cabinet meeting, Nasser told his aides and ministers that 'the coming struggle will be with the reactionary forces in the region — Saud, Hussein, and Damascus; it will be an ideological struggle,' and he called on his Cabinet to be ready for that by strengthening the Egyptian internal front.[17] Despite some of his close associates' reservations about Nasser's continuous attacks on the Syrians in the hope of arousing the masses against their regime,[18] Nasser insisted on opposing the Syrian 'reactionary' leaders. 'It does not mean that if the reactionaries, colonialists, and their agents succeeded in separating Syria from Egypt the call for pan-Arabism and Arab unity is finished,' Nasser declared. He insisted that the struggle for Arab unity would continue no matter how great the challenge was.[19] He accused the Syrian leaders, such as Ma'mun al-Kuzbari and Sabri al-Assali, of being American agents in the Middle East, and of receiving American bribes, before the union occurred, in order to serve US interests in Syria.[20] To win the sympathy of the army, he accused Akram Hurani and other Syrian leaders of arresting 92 pro-UAR officers and he charged that more officers were being arrested, one after the other.[21] Nasser's attacks against the Syrians climaxed in July 1962, during the 10th anniversary celebrations of the Egyptian revolution.

> The Syrian people struggle for nationalism, unity, Arabism, socialism and for social justice . . .. The disarmed Syrian people are standing up, challenging the financially strong reactionaries, imperialism, and their agents . . .. In no circumstances will the Syrian people be frightened . . . I am full of confidence that the heroic Syrian people can defeat the reactionaries, opportunism, and their agents.

Nasser declared that Egypt was wholeheartedly at the side of the '*Syrian Arab people in the northern region of the United Arab Republic*' (author's emphasis) in its struggle against 'reactionism, opportunism, and imperialism,'[22] referring to the Syrian regime. Nasser alleged that wholesale arrests were occurring in Syria, including the imprisonment of lawyers and intellectuals. He declared: 'I announced in the past that we had decided to disregard events in Syria, but now we cannot in any circumstances overlook what is happening there.' He added: 'With all our strength and possession, we are on the side of the struggling Syrian people. . . . We will ally ourselves with the Syrian people to eliminate the reactionaries, imperialism, opportunists, and the agents of imperialism.'[23] Alleging that dozens of Syrians were killed by Syrian 'reactionary dictators' during their fight against 'social and economic oppression' and for 'political and social liberty', Nasser declared that he hoped that by next year the Syrian people would topple their government.[24]

As a result of Nasser's speeches, agitations, and his media machine attacks, the Syrian government counterattacked and accused the Egyptian leader of sabotage and subversion by Egyptian agents infiltrating Syria through Lebanon. On 28 July one of the Syrian leaders, al-'Azma accused Nasser of 'instigating disorder and openly supporting subversion' against the Syrian government, 'thus uncovering his hostile intentions and his lust for domination of the entire Arab people.'[25] On 29 July the Syrian minister of the interior announced that the Damascus authorities had foiled a pro-Cairo plot to overthrow the Syrian regime, had destroyed 'sabotage rings' in Damascus, Homs, and Aleppo, and arrested 150 persons. The minister alleged that the Egyptian embassy in Beirut had been supplying weapons and ammunition for subversive activities in Syria. Based on the Syrian claims, Damascus on 29 July requested an urgent meeting of the Arab League council to study and act on its complaint about Egypt's 'flagrant interference' in Syrian internal affairs.[26]

The Arab League Council Meeting: Shtoura

The Syrian foreign minister in his complaint to the secretary-general of the Arab League requested an immediate meeting of the League's council to look into the situation created by 'President Gamal Abdel-Nasser's statements and actions toward Syria which amount to a frank attack on the sovereignty and dignity of the people of the Arab Republic of Syria'. Moreover, the Syrian foreign minister asked that the League meeting be held 'in any Arab state but Egypt'.[27]

At first Secretary-General Hassouna, perhaps on the initiative of Cairo, attempted to settle the dispute between the two countries without having the League council meet. Thus Hassouna went to Damascus and discussed their complaint with the Syrian leaders. The Syrians demanded an end to the Egyptian campaign. After ending his talks in Damascus, Hassouna returned to Cairo and conferred with Egyptian officials, hoping for an agreement between the two countries.[28] But apparently Syria did not trust the secretary-general's motives and Egypt refused to admit it was interfering in Syrian affairs. Therefore, his efforts led nowhere. The Syrians insisted that the League council meeting be held outside Egypt. Prior to the council's meeting, Saudi Arabia, Iraq (which boycotted the council meeting), and Jordan supported the Syrian complaint against Cairo. However, the council was not convened until 22 August, when it met at the Lebanese town of Shtoura. The extraordinary session at Shtoura was characterized by a violent confrontation between the Syrian and Egyptian delegations which brought the League near the point of collapse. Indeed this session was considered as 'the bitterest and most acrimonious meeting in the League's history'.[29]

The Syrian delegation, according to some sources, was composed of 300 members including 250 armed personnel.[30] To infuriate the Syrians, three of the Egyptian delegates, including its chief delegate, Akram Dayri, were pro-UAR Syrians. Lebanon, Jordan, Saudi Arabia, Algeria, Tunisia, Morocco, Yemen, Libya, Sudan, and Kuwait were also represented at the meeting. The Arab League delegation was led by Secretary-General Hassouna and his assistant Sayed Nofal.

At the beginning of the meeting, Syria submitted to the general secretariat of the League a statement, along with its formal complaint, asking the general secretariat to distribute its complaint to the member states. The complaint noted that, despite Syria's regaining its sovereignty and its international status, 'the rulers of Cairo continue to interfere in Syrian internal affairs and to launch a campaign of speeches against it, and to use the nationalized press and the instrument of radio and information to concentrate on propaganda warfare against the Syrian state and to its frank provocation for insurrection.'[31] The 'Cairo rulers' also were supporting 'elements' of 'destruction' to create 'unrest and instability' in Syria. The Syrian complaint went further and said that Egyptian intervention in Syria was climaxed by Nasser's speeches in July, 'which [were] considered a grave interference in the internal affairs of the state of Syria' and in which he attacked the Syrian system and vowed to support the opposition forces against the Syrian leaders and called Syria the 'northern region'.[32]

The Egyptian activities led to the worsening of inter-Arab relations, and thus, according to the Syrian complaint, Cairo's behaviour was considered a violation of article 2 of the League's pact which stated that the purpose of the League is 'the strengthening of the relations between the member states . . .,' and also a violation of article 8 of the pact which calls on each member state to 'respect the systems of government established in the other member states . . .' and 'to abstain from any action calculated to change established systems of government'. The Syrian government then called on the League council 'to take firm measures to prevent the rulers of Cairo from intervening in Syrian internal affairs'.[33]

The Syrian delegation at the outset of the session took strong exception to the fact that the leader and deputy leader of the Egyptian delegation were both pro-Nasser Syrians who held ministerial posts during the union and who had gone to Cairo after the UAR dissolution. 'The way Nasser has formed his delegation to the League of Arab States in itself shows all the appearance of challenge and aggression . . . 'the Syrian delegate protested. Warrants for the arrest of the Syrians in the Egyptian delegation were issued by the Damascus government during the Shtoura meeting.[34] Furthermore, to substantiate their claims, the Syrian delegation distributed documents exposing Egyptian 'crimes' during and after the union.[35] Khalil Kallas, the Syrian deputy chief delegate to the Shtoura meeting, spoke at the first session and strongly criticized Nasser and his former rule of

Syria; he asked the council 'to decide which [of Nasser's] actions constituted interference, and whether interference is permitted or not. At least once in the history of the Arab League we want this principle to be decided,'[36] a reference to the continuous Egyptian domination of that regional machinery. He was followed by another member of the Syrian delegation, As'ad Mahassin, who denounced Nasser's speeches and said that Nasser's interference in Syria as 'the northern region' constituted an attack on the sovereignty and independence of Syria.[37] Furthermore, the Syrian delegation charged *inter alia* that Nasser was plotting to topple the government in Damascus and aiming to 'annex' Syria; that the Egyptian embassy in Lebanon was fomenting subversive activities to this end; that the Egyptian ambassador in Lebanon and Akram Dayri and his deputy were personally involved in that plot; that Nasser was pursuing a 'soft' policy toward Israel ('the imperialist agent and the reactionary is he who lets Israel have a free passage in the Gulf of Aqaba'); that Nasser instructed his diplomats abroad to pursue a policy of noncommittal on the question of the Palestinian refugees in order to obtain American aid; and that substantial quantities of Syrian weapons had been removed to Egypt upon the dissolution of the UAR. The Syrian delegation presented documents to the League council to prove the truth of their charges against Egypt, including copies of Egyptian telegrams allegedly sent to pro-UAR agents in Syria.[38] Furthermore, to expose Nasser's interference in Syria, and while the League council meeting was in progress at Shtoura, Syria announced on 27 August that it had given political asylum to the Egyptian military attaché in Lebanon, Lieutenant-Colonel Zaghlul Abdel Rahman. He supplied the Syrians with a list of Egyptian agents in Syria. In a statement made in Damascus the same day, Rahman accused Nasser of personally directing a pro-Cairo terrorist and sabotage network which was operating in Syria.[39] Based on these allegations, the Syrian delegation to Shtoura demanded 'firm measures' by the League council to end the Egyptian 'interference' in the domestic affairs of the country. Using harsh words, the Syrian delegate explained that 'we are complaining to your respected council about this intruder [Nasser] on our principles, ethics, and tradition; we are complaining about this enemy of our nationalism, Arabism, and unity.'[40]

The Egyptian delegation in turn spoke with equally strong counter-allegations. It denied the Syrian charges *in toto*, and also denied the authenticity of the documents presented by Syria to the council. It discussed the gains of the union era and then turned to the internal situation in Syria; the very discussion of this matter was taken by Syria as justification for its complaint against Cairo. The Egyptian delegation said that the Syrian complaint was an attempt to distract attention from the Syrian internal strife, and that the purpose of the Syrian complaint was very similar to the Lebanese complaint of 1958: to hide what was underneath it.[41] The Egyptian representative described the Syrian leaders as 'a gang of reactionaries who are grinding down the people and suppressing freedoms in Syria'. Furthermore, the Egyptians alleged that As'ad Mahassin had embezzled UAR embassy funds while he was its ambassador in Rabat during the union.[42]

The Syrian-Egyptian allegations and counter-allegations were described as 'bad blood between the two countries [which] has shown itself in innumerable ways, and but for the vigilance of the Lebanese police would have led to fisticuffs, or more.' The Cairo and Damascus representatives 'almost came to blows' and were urged by the council to 'maintain a minimum of decorum in addressing each other.'[43] Each side was trying to win the support of the League's council.

The debate was so violent that Egypt asked the council to discuss the manner in which the discussion was proceeding. The council acted promptly and adopted a resolution whereby it decided 'to omit from the minutes of the meeting all offensive remarks about: 1) any Head of State; 2) any Head of Government; 3) the persons present at the session, whether within the council or outside it.'[44] This was clearly to erase any derogatory remarks about Nasser.

On 27 August the Syrian and Egyptian delegations exchanged similar allegations in the sixth and seventh meetings of the session. The Sudanese representative, as in the case of Lebanon, intervened and suggested the end of allegations and counter-allegations and the close of the discusssions, which the Egyptians favoured. The council, in line with Egyptian tactics, agreed on a broad draft resolution which called for strengthening Arab solidarity and support of the Arab League. Further enraging the Syrians, the draft resolution called for no more discussion of the Syrian complaint.[45]

On 28 August the council held its eighth meeting at which the Egyptian chief delegate, Akram Dayri, using a familiar Egyptian tactic, said that it was no longer possible for Egypt to tolerate Damascus' campaign of 'lies and insults' against his government: 'Unless the Council of the Arab League at the present session, pronounces expressly and plainly upon the whole subject of the lies and insults heard from its rostrum, the United Arab Republic will decide to withdraw from the League of Arab States.'[46] The Egyptian representative protested that the League 'has become a humiliation to its member states. It can do nothing for the aspirations of the Arab Struggle.' Thereafter, to make it appear that he was serious in his threats, Dayri and his delegation walked out from the Shtoura meeting. Listening to these arguments, Secretary-General Hassouna 'broke down in tears,'[47] to make the Egyptian action look genuine, thereby hoping for Arab support of Egypt's position.

The Egyptian walkout at the Shtoura meeting and its threat to withdraw from the Arab League seemed to deal a serious blow to that organization. Indeed, as Heikal wrote earlier, Nasser could 'freeze' the Arab League. Egypt was not only the largest financial contributor to the League, but also about 75 per cent of its staff and employees were Egyptians, and its headquarters were in Cairo. In effect Nasser would cripple the organization if it could no longer be used to serve his aims. The secretary-general and other League members were determined to avoid such a thing happening, the secretary-general because of his and Egypt's interests, and the other Arabs because at least of their emotional attachment to the League. They wanted to preserve it and this could be done now only if they could be on good terms with Nasser.

On 30 August the League council held the ninth and last meeting of its extraordinary session. Egypt did not participate. The Syrian delegation submitted in this meeting a memorandum at which the Syrian delegation attempted to win the sympathy of the Arab League explaining that Syria resorted to the League because Syria considered this organization the natural Arab institution to which the member states should resort in quest of solutions to their disputes within the framework of the pact of the Arab League. Upon exposing Nasser, the Syrian delegate argued,

> The ruling oppressor [Nasser] surprised the League by the comedy of withdrawal and by threatening to destroy the League if it did not respond to his desires and submit to his adventures as if the League is one of his government departments or one of his instruments of domination. He also wants it to be one of his propaganda systems . . . to placate his power madness which is turning his head.[48]

Furthermore, realizing the impact of Egypt's withdrawal from the League on its chances for survival, the Syrian delegation, in a statement on behalf of its government, announced that it

rejects strongly all the attempts to impose individual or state
domination on the League. . . . if the Arab League were to
serve the common Arab objectives, then its members must
[enjoy] the prevalence of understanding based on their
equality . . . no difference between its big or small
[members]. If sacrifices occur they should not be to please
the adventurism of oppressive rulers or because an Arab
country's population is larger than another.[49]

The Syrians, fearing that Egypt's withdrawal could influence other
delegation positions in the council to adopt at least a neutral stand,
announced that

the withdrawal of any country of the member states, or
threats to do so, cannot in any circumstances effect its [the
League's] being or expose it to collapse. But what in fact
exposes it to danger is that the Arab League becomes an
instrument in the hands of one of the individuals, or a means
to strengthen his authority or of the systems of his rule.
Anyone who tries to threaten the League by withdrawal and
to pressure its members will be alone responsible, for what
he has done before God, history, and the Arab people.[50]

The Syrian statement concluded by asking the council to 'condemn
the interference' of Nasser and his activities, reminding the council
that the 'hesitation' of the League's council in taking firm measures
would be 'considered encouragement to Mr Abdel-Nasser to continue
his violation of the pact of the Arab League and his challenge to its
dignity and the dignity of its members'.[51]

The Syrian fears of the League council's submission to Nasser's
threat were justified. The 'firm measures' suggested by Syria were
never taken and the Syrian pleas that the council should not bow to
Nasser's pressure were all in vain. The council, submitting to Egypt's
threats, in its last meeting on 30 August adopted a resolution, to
Syria's outrage, whereby it decided that:

The council of the Arab League in its meeting which was
held on the evening of 30 August 1962 to look into the
complaint of the Arab Republic of Syria against the United
Arab Republic, the text of which was submitted to the

member states, decides the following:

1 According to the provision of the League's pact it should not proceed with the mentioned complaint, owing to the withdrawal of the United Arab Republic from the council meeting.

2 The extraordinary session should remain open, pending another meeting to be held as soon as possible.

3 The member states should use their offices to consolidate the League through the respect for its pact, and the unification of its members, which in turn would enable the League to proceed with its mission.[52]

The secretary-general and the council viewed the Egyptian threat as serious and considered that the Arab League would have no value without Cairo's participation. Moreover, various Arab states were not in favour of 'freezing' that organization. To the satisfaction of Cairo, several Arab leaders such as Ahmad Ben Bella of Algeria and Fu'ad Shihab of Lebanon attempted 'mediation' to induce Egypt to resume participation in Arab League activities.

Shihab appealed to Nasser not to withdraw because the Arab League 'will have no value if the UAR withdraws from it as the UAR is its biggest and strongest member state.'[53] But Nasser insisted that the League council must first comment 'in frankness' on the manner in which the discussion proceeded at the Shtoura meeting.[54] In other words, despite its disregard of the Syrian complaint, the council should also condemn Syria. Abdel-Khaliq Hassouna held several meetings with Nasser to convince him of the harm his move might bring to the League if the Egyptian president carried out his threat. Following Hassouna's 'intensive efforts', Nasser agreed not to withdraw from the Arab League so long as the Shtoura meeting remained open.[55] In short, Nasser's tactics paid off and the League's Council was forcibly constrained from any action that might be considered not in Nasser's interest.

Nasser's Success: An Evaluation

Following the Syrian secession from the union, Nasser, as we have noted earlier, adopted a new 'revolutionary' slogan — 'unity of purpose' — and disregarded the old one, 'unity of rank'. Prior to the Shtoura meeting, and in light of his new slogan, Nasser was asked if he still believed that the continuing existence of the Arab League was acceptable to him. He replied:

> My view of the League of Arab States is that it is a picture which incarnates the realities of the Arab states. It is not Hassouna's league as some say, Hassouna is no more than an administrative official there. . . . In general all the differences in the Arab world are reflected in the Arab League. . . . It reflects the contradictions between socialism and reactionism . . . between exploitation and social justice, and between the goals of the people and the goals of imperialism. . . . Until the goals become united, the Arab League will only play its traditional role in the fields of economics and culture and in the co-ordination of the Arab efforts at the United Nations.[56]

Nasser's statement on the Arab League and his preceding formulation of his new slogan were no coincidence. Earlier we noticed that Egypt emphasized the nobleness of the League as a 'holy organization' to solve Arab disputes (see chapter 4). However, at that time Nasser was on the offensive and Iraq was on the defensive. At the Shtoura meeting the Syrians were on the offensive and Egypt was on the defensive. Moreover, the League secretary-general and his assistant could do no more than try to conciliate. Nasser, in an unprecedented manner, was subject to violent and bitter attacks on his activities and 'dreams to annex Syria'. He was unable to silence the Syrians who were supported, at least implicitly, by Iraq, Jordan, Saudi Arabia, Yemen, and Lebanon. Indeed, Egypt was cornered at the Shtoura meeting. The Egyptian delegation counterattacked with allegations that Syria's problems were internal. But where the Syrians substantiated their allegations with documents, Egypt could not. Egypt hoped, as in previous cases, that the council would adopt views similar to those of Cairo. But the council seemed to be attentive to Damascus. Thus Egypt had to act. Cairo made it clear that any resolution against Egypt would lead to serious consequences, including bringing into question the very existence of the Arab League. From the Egyptian point of view, as Heikal wrote, 'If the Arab League were to be used to paralyse our movement, we must be prepared to freeze the operations of that organization.'[57] At the Shtoura meeting it became clear that Egypt's capitalizing on its championship of Arab unity was not having the effect for which

Nasser hoped. As Arab nationalists admitted that there could be no Arab unity without Egypt, because it 'could and would successfully oppose any movement towards Arab unity which excluded her,'[58] so too Nasser knew that the Arab states realized that there could be no Arab League without Egypt and he knew that the Arabs were greatly attached to this body. Nasser felt that since Egypt paid more than any other member to the League's budget and that because the League was located in Cairo where the majority of its employees were Egyptians, Egypt should enjoy a distinguished role in the League and not be criticised by any other member state. In addition, Nasser's popularity among the Arab masses and his image as a leading Third World leader ought, he thought, to give him more weight in the League than the other Arab states.[59] Thus it should be no surprise when his delegation told the council at the Shtoura meeting on 28 August that Egypt concluded that the Arab League could no longer serve 'the true Arab action for the sake of the Arab future',[60] (meaning Nasser's foreign policy objectives). The Egyptian delegation explained that Cairo,

> emphasizes here before all the people of the Arab nation that this decision [withdrawal] in no circumstance means that the UAR would disregard its responsibility toward the comprehensive Arab struggle in all its arenas and forms. The matter is that the UAR, because of a feeling of trust, cannot consider saying before all the Arab people that the Arab League, in its present situation, is in shape as a good instrument to have the Arab struggle reach its goals, because of the reactionaries which are co-operating with imperialism.[61]

In effect Egypt was saying to the League council members that either Cairo was to have its own way in the League or it would destroy that organization. The council, realizing this fact, desired to avoid confrontation. Several Arab delegations preferred to deal with 'Egypt as a state' rather than with 'Egypt as a revolution'.

At first the League was regarded by both Egypt and Syria as the right forum to which to resort for the settlement of their dispute. Egypt believed, as on previous occasions, that it would have its way in the League, and Syria, by having the meeting outside Egypt, that it would enjoy the support of the other League members. But, at least in part, because of the council's lack of sympathy for Cairo's position, Egypt simply walked out of the Shtoura meeting and accused the League of not being able to stop the violent Syrian attacks on Nasser. Unlike Iraq's withdrawal from the League in 1961 and Tunisia's in 1958 and 1965, Cairo's withdrawal from the League would have constituted a major threat to the existence of that organization. At that time Egypt was the major member, with a distinguished position within the League. The loss of the largest financial contribution alone would seriously have undermined the functions and activities of the League. Realizing Egypt's position, as in the League's efforts, through its secretary-general, immediately following the session, and against the wishes of Syria, the League opted to attempt conciliation between the two countries rather than to oppose Egypt. The League could afford no adjudication in this case precisely because Egypt was the defendant.

Syria requested that the League council take 'firm measures' to stop Egyptian 'interference' in the internal affairs of Syria. It based its argument on article 6 of the Arab League pact dealing with the case of aggression or threat of aggression by a member state against another state. This article states, in part, that 'The Council shall by unanimous decision determine the measures necessary to repulse the aggression.' Furthermore, this article notes that 'If the aggressor is a member state, his vote shall not be counted in determining unanimity.' The council, against the Syrian warning, submitted to Nasser's threats and, therefore, did not adopt any resolution which could be interpreted as against Egypt's interests. It was the view of the council taken at the last meeting of its extraordinary session that it could not proceed with the examination of the Syrian complaint since the defendant party was absent. The council viewed Cairo's participation in the discussion as necessary first to give Cairo the chance to defend itself and second to determine whether or not aggression took place.[62] Such an argument is worth considering.

But the truth was that, due to the factors mentioned earlier, the council could not possibly point a finger at Egypt under Nasser as the 'aggressor'. Egypt threatened yet did not totally withdraw from membership. It may be argued that the intensive efforts of the secretary-general and the attempts of mediation by several Arab leaders to persuade Nasser not to withdraw helped to prevent total withdrawal. But it is equally true, it may be argued, that Nasser was not necessarily interested in total withdrawal, but rather he was manœuvring in inter-Arab politics to strengthen his position. This was done by not participating in the activities of the League for a year and by keeping alive the threat to withdraw totally. But to argue that the council could not reach a decision, as Syria demanded, because Egypt was absent is not convincing. The council, whether because of Nasser's domination or because it was concerned about the damage that Egypt could do to the League, opted for conciliation with Cairo and, in a sense, rejected Syria's allegation on the basis that the council could no longer examine its case since Egypt was absent. In other words, the council could not act or adopt a resolution which was unacceptable to Cairo. Otherwise, how can we explain the council's resolutions on several occasions when member states were absent, one example being the 1978 resolution on South Yemen?

In June 1978 the North Yemen president, Ahmad al-Ghashmi, was killed by a bomb which exploded in his office while he was meeting with a representative from the government of South Yemen (Aden). North Yemen accused Aden of being behind the murder and promptly called for an urgent meeting of the Arab League council to discuss this situation, in accordance with article 6. The council held its extraordinary session in Cairo and the North Yemeni foreign minister, Abdallah al-Assnaj, demanded 'severe punishments' for Aden,[63] in accordance with article 18 which in part states that 'The Council of the League may consider any state which fails to fulfill its obligation under this Pact as having become separated from the League' upon a unanimous decision of the member states, excluding the state concerned. In this case, the Egyptian foreign minister, Muhamad Ibrahim Kamil, called on the council to take strong measures against South Yemen.[64] At this extraordinary session, however, Aden and several other members (Algeria, Syria, Libya, Iraq, and the PLO) did not participate. Yet the council saw it appropriate to adopt a resolution calling for firm measures against South Yemen.[65] The council noted that Aden's actions fell under the provisions of article 6 of the pact and thus South Yemen's action was in violation of the provision of Article 8 (see Appendix A). Thereupon, the adopted resolution 'condemned' South Yemen and the council requested that 'diplomatic and political relations between the member states and the People's Democratic Republic of Yemen [Aden] be frozen,' and called for 'an end of cultural economical and technical aid which the Arab states extend to the People's Democratic Republic of Yemen'.[66]

The South Yemen resolution contradicted the view taken by the council during the extraordinary session at Shtoura. Explanation of this contradiction is difficult, yet one can safely conclude that the value of South Yemen's membership to the Arab League by no means approximated that of Egypt's.

For Nasser to protect his interest, from the Egyptian point of view, after Cairo's failure at Shtoura, Nasser adopted the 'revolutionary' method to isolate Syria and to assert Egypt's domination in and outside the Arab League. But the member states had other interests. Several League members, for example, preferred Arab solidarity over Egyptian revolutionary ideology which threatened Arab leaders' positions. On 13 September 1962 the League council held its first meeting after Shtoura, at which the secretary-general, in an opening statement, said that, 'Our meeting today, at the League's headquarters in Cairo, the capital of the UAR, and the centre of eternal Arabism is a sign of optimism.' It was a reference to the absence of Egypt in the council meeting and contained the hope that it would return to the League.[67]

To appease Nasser, the Arab League council, at a meeting on 15 September 1962, presided over by the Algerian delegate, Ahmad Tawfiq al-Madani, from which Egypt was absent, reappointed Abdel-Khaliq Hassouna for another five-year term as secretary-general. The Moroccan delegate, Abdel-Khaliq el-Trais, observed that the reappointment of Hassouna was

> a definite proof of our great eagerness to see the UAR amongst us. Our election of the secretary-general — who by citizenship belongs to the big sister — is great evidence that we cannot, for long, accept this situation of the absence of the UAR, which is the biggest member numerically and in terms of capabilities, from our meeting.
>
> Thus our election of the secretary-general today should be understood by the dear sister and its officials, particularly his excellency the beloved president, as our giving the UAR something by way of a compensation.[68]

Libya also noted that Hassouna'e election was an indication of the Arabs' faith in Nasser's leadership and that 'we strongly desire and are eager to see the big sister reoccupy its position of leadership in the League.'[69] Sudan too observed that 'our mere meeting in Cairo and our election of the secretary-general — a citizen of the UAR — is an indication of our insistence that the UAR return to the League.'[70] Other council members also spoke in favour of the return of Cairo to the League's meetings.

However, Nasser was not satisfied by what members of the League had offered him in return for the resumption of Egypt's activities in the

League. The re-election of Hassouna helped to calm down the situation resulting from the political crisis of Shtoura, but, as *al-Ahram* noted, the League now faced 'a sharp financial crisis' if Cairo did not pay its share.[71] Nasser was determined to work for the overthrow of the regime that had brought the complaint against him and to remind other League members that Egypt was more than just simply another member, and that he could act as he pleased. One of the methods that Nasser used to this end was an appeal to the Arab masses, since he remained champion of pan-Arabism. His revolutionary ideology was also to stimulate internal pressure on his adversaries and rivals. To prove that he meant business he soon dispatched thousands of Egyptian soldiers to Yemen to defend the new revolution which took place there in September 1962. Furthermore, as an indication that Egypt still could get its way in the League even if it was not active, was the dismissal in January 1963 of the commissioner of the Arab League office for the boycott of Israel. The commissioner, 'Abd al-Karim al-'Aidi, and the permanent headquarters of the boycott office were located in Damascus. Since 1950 the commissioner had been the highest Syrian official on the League staff. Egypt was angered in September 1962 when the commissioner met the Egyptian military attaché in Lebanon who had taken asylum in Syria. The latter presented al-'Aidi with certain documents presumably pertaining to Egyptian activities against Syria. It is believed that it was on the instructions of Nasser that Hassouna relieved the commissioner of his post and replaced him with an Egyptian, Muhamad Mahjoub.[72] The Syrian authorities, with Saudi, Jordanian, and Iraqi support, refused to recognize the legality of Hassouna's action. Syria maintained that the commissioner had been appointed by the League council and could only be replaced by a vote of the League council.[73] Egypt, however, prevailed, and Mahjoub did replace the Syrian commissioner.

Nasser's persistent pressures paid off. On 8 March 1963 Nasser was delighted to hear of a new Syrian coup that overthrew his adversaries in Damascus. He immediately sent his congratulations and extended diplomatic relations to the new leaders who expressed their commitment to Arab unity and denounced the secessionists.

The new Syrian prime minister, Salah al-Din al-Bitar, cabled the Arab League withdrawing its complaint against Egypt and requesting its removal from the agenda of the League's extraordinary session. Bitar added that 'the revolution of the Arab people in Syria came about as a revenge for the Shtoura quarrel and for the tragic secession.'[74]

The Egyptian foreign ministry, in a memorandum to the Arab League general secretariat, said that it considered 'the historic events in Damascus' of 8 March as a complete and decisive response to the whole 'poison campaign' launched by the former Syrian government against Egypt. 'Therefore, the UAR decided to resume fully its activities in the Arab League at this historic period.'[75]

At its 23 March meeting the League council agreed to a Syrian suggestion which stated that

> the League council expresses the happiness of all [?] its members at the return of the big sister UAR to its full activities in the League . . . hoping this move will be a beginning of a new era to support and strengthen the League . . . and decides to expunge from its records, documents, and minutes all mention of the Syrian complaint . . . as if it had not taken place and to close the [Shtoura] extraordinary session.[76]

The new Egyptian representative at the Arab League, Sayed Abdel-Hamid, spoke positively of the new rulers in Syria and emphasized that 'every victory for the advancement of the Arab nation and for the liberation of its territory from imperialism and its collaborators and from the reactionaries and opportunists is a strength to our Arab League which draws upon its power and effectiveness from the currents of Arab Liberation.'[77]

Thus Nasser succeeded in preventing the League from taking any measure against his interests. After several months of intensive efforts to oust the Syrian regime, Nasser was able to reassert his 'distinguished' position in the League and to claim, rightly or wrongly, that he had brought down those 'handful' of secessionists, who, in his view, were 'anti-Arab unity'.

Notes to chapter six

1   For a comprehensive study of the Syrian situation between 1945 and 1958 see Patrick Seale, *The Struggle for Syria: A Study of Post-War Arab Politics, 1945–1958*, London, New York, Toronto, Oxford University Press, 1965; for those who read Arabic see Salah Nasr, *Abdel-Nasser and the Unity Experience*, Cairo, al-Watan al-Arabi, 1976.

2   Mohamed Hassanein Heikal *Matha Jara fi Soria*, (What Happened in Syria), Cairo, al-Dar al-Qawmiyyah lil-Tiba'ah wal-Nashr, 1962, p. 40.

3   *Report of the Secretary-General to the League Council*, 29th ordinary session, March 1958, p. 7.

4   Seale, p. 324.

5   George Lenczowski, *The Middle East in World Affairs*, Ithaca, Cornell University Press, 3rd edn, 1962, pp. 537–38.

6   Anwar el-Sadat, *October* (Cairo), 24 July 1977, p. 17.

7   Malcolm H. Kerr, *The Arab Cold War: Gamal 'Abd Al-Nasir and his Rivals, 1958–1970*, London, Oxford University Press, 3rd end, 1971, p. 25.

8   Ibid., p. 21.

9   Heikal, pp. 191–92.

10 Speech of 22 February 1962, *President Gamal Abdel-Nasser Speeches and Press Interviews*, part IV, February 1962–June 1964, p. 20.

11 Nasser's statement on 28 September 1961, *Khutab wa-Tasrihat al-Rais Gamal Abdel-Nasser, President Gamal Abdel-Nasser Speeches and Press Interviews*, part III, February 1960–January 1962, pp. 522–25.

12 Nasr, pp. 269–70.

13 Royal Institute of International Affairs, *Documents on International Affairs, 1962*, London, Oxford University Press, 1971, p. 846.

14 Ibid., pp. 846–47.

15 Ibid., p. 847.

16 *Keesing*, 1962, p. 18440.

17 Abdel-Latif al-Baghdadi, *Memoires of Abdel-Latif al-Baghdadi* (in Arabic), part II, Cairo, Alexandria, al-Maktab al-Misri al-Hadith, 1977, p. 156.

18 See ibid., p. 129.

19 Speech of 23 December 1961, *President Gamal Abdel-Nasser Speeches and Press Interviews*, part III, February 1960–January 1962, pp. 654–55.

20 Speech of 22 February, 1962, ibid., part IV, February 1962–June 1964, pp. 14–19.

21 Speech of 27 May 1962, ibid., pp. 76, 100.

22 Speech of 2 July 1962, ibid., pp. 188–89.
23 Speech of 24 July 1962, ibid., p. 214.
24 Speech of 27 July 1962, ibid., p. 222.
25 *Keesing*, 1962, p. 18913.
26 Ibid.
27 Documents of the Syrian Complaint (in Arabic). *Texts and Documents of the Syrian Complaint Before the Arab League against the Nasserite Intervention in Syrian Affairs*, Shtoura, 22–30 August 1962 (Syrian Government, n.d.), pp. 24–25.
28 Hussein Hassouna, *The League of Arab States*, Dobbs Ferry, N.Y., Oceana, 1975, p. 169.
29 *Keesing*, 1962, p. 18957.
30 Zakaria Neil to the author, Cairo, 10 July 1978.
31 *Documents of the Syrian Complaint*, pp. 15–16.
32 Ibid., pp. 17–19.
33 Ibid., p. 20.
34 *Keesing*, 1962, p. 18957.
35 Kerr, p. 38; Hassouna, pp. 169–70.
36 *Documents of the Syrian Complaint*, p. 24.
37 Ibid., p. 25.
38 *Keesing*, 1962, p. 18957; *Documents of the Syrian Complaint*, pp. 28–53, 155–245.
39 A. I. Dawisha, *Egypt in the Arab World*, London, Macmillan, 1976, p. 37; *Keesing*, 1962, p. 18957.
40 *Documents of the Syrian Complaint*, p. 141.
41 Boutros Boutros-Ghali, *Jamiá t al-Dowal al-Arabiyyeh wa-Hal al-Munazáat al-Iglimiyyeh*, (The League of Arab States and the Settlement of Regional Disputes), Cairo, Dar al-Tiba'ah al-Hadithah, 1977, p. 98.
42 *Keesing*, 1962, p. 18957.
43 Ibid.
44 *Report of the Secretary-General to the Arab League Council*, 39th ordinary session, 30 March 1963, p. 58.
45 Ibid.
46 *Minutes of League Council*, 37th session, 8th meeting, 28 August 1962, p. 9; quoted in Hassouna, p. 170.
47 Kerr, p. 39.
48 *Documents of the Syrian Complaint*, p. 150.
49 Ibid.
50 Ibid., p. 151.
51 Ibid.
52 *Report of Secretary-General to the League Council*, 39th ordinary session, 30 March 1963, p. 59.
53 *al-Ahram*, 9 September 1962.
54 Ibid.
55 *Keesing*, 1962, p. 18957: Hassouna, p. 171; Boutros-Ghali, *op. cit.*, p. 101.

56 Interview of President Gamal Abdel-Nasser on 13 May 1962 with the Lebanese *Kul Sha'i* magazine. *President Gamal Abdel-Nasser Speeches and Press Interviews*, part IV, February 1962–June 1964, p. 30.

57 Heikal, p. 192.

58 Seale, pp. 310–311.

59 Abdel-Mun'im el-Rifa'i to the author, Amman, 12 August 1978.

60 Abdel-Fatah Mustafa al-Saifi, *al-Mujtama'al-Watani al-Arabi: Imkaniyatuh wa-Qudratuh wa-Mashakiluh*, (The Arab National Society: Its Potential, Capabilities, and Problems), Alexandria, al-Maktab al-Misri al-Hadith lil-Tiba'ah wal-Nashr, 1969, p. 101.

61 Ibid., p. 102.

62 For discussion of this view see Hassouna, pp. 173–174; Boutros-Ghali, *op. cit.* pp. 104–05.

63 *al-Ahram*, 2 July 1978, p. 1.

64 Ibid.

65 Ibid., 3 July 1978, p. 1.

66 Ibid.

67 *Minutes of the League Council*, 38th ordinary session, 1st meeting, 13 September 1962, p. 8.

68 *Minutes of the League Council*, 38th ordinary session, 2nd meeting, 15 September 1962, p. 14.

69 Ibid., p. 15.

70 Ibid., p. 17.

71 *al-Ahram*, 18 September 1962.

72 Kerr, p. 40.

73 Ibid.

74 *Minutes of the League Council*, 38th ordinary session, 3rd meeting, 23 March 1963, p. 32.

75 Ibid., pp. 32–33.

76 Ibid., p. 34.

77 Ibid., p. 38.

Chapter Seven

Yemen: 1962–67

Until the 1962 revolution, Yemen was the most isolated country in the Arab world. It is a mountainous country which was ruled for centuries by imams. There have been several attempts to change forcibly the system in San'a. The most successful one was the coup d'état of 1962 led by Colonel Abdallah al-Sallal. However, his coup was not totally successful as the tribal royalists launched a civil war to regain their authority in San'a. To sustain his shaky coup, al-Sallal called on his hero, President Nasser, to send aid before the new republican regime collapsed. For Nasser, this was a good opportunity to teach King Saud and the 'reactionaries' a lesson for their role in the Syrian secession and to reassert Nasser's support of Egypt's claim to pan-Arabism's leadership. Egypt responded positively and thousands of fully equipped Egyptian soldiers were rushed to Yemen, without any idea as to how long this Egyptian operation would last. Little did Nasser realize that it would bog down his troops for five years and that it would create an international and inter-Arab crisis that was to involve both the UN and the Arab League.

The Internal Crisis

Until 1918 Yemen was under the rule of the Ottomans, who had occupied it since the latter part of the nineteenth century. Imam Yahya Hamid al-Din, of the dominant Zaidi sect of the Shi'a branch of Islam, emerged as the effective ruler of that country. Yahya's rule

136

was marked by isolation, oppression, and by little, if any, progress and modernization.[1] He was assassinated in 1948 and was succeeded by his son Ahmad. Like his father Imam Ahmad relied on tyrannical rule and purges to ensure the security of his position. Despite his xenophobic suspicion of foreigners, Imam Ahmad relaxed his restrictions on foreign deals and permitted a small degree of modernization, for example, wider use of electricity, greater use of motor vehicles, and a new radio station.[2]

But discontent and revolt were the main results of the imam's policies. The uprising by the powerful Hashid and Bakil tribes made it necessary for the army to put them down at the same time as the tribes in the Khawlan region also revolted. In addition, subversive pamphlets relating to the 'Yemeni Officers' Movement' were discovered in the city of Ta'iz, where several bombs exploded. The 'Voice of the Arabs', after the Syrian secession, added to the already difficult situation by attacking the imamate. The unrest became more widespread, and in May 1962 Imam Ahmad ordered two villages to be razed for harbouring anti-imamate nationalists. In August, in something unheard of in Yemen, Yemenis marched in San'a against the imam's alleged approval of the American bases in Saudi Arabia. Several demonstrators were killed by soldiers, several were executed, many were detained, and the secular schools, where Egyptian influence was considerable, were closed. In early September there were more demonstrations in San'a and Ta'iz at which pictures of Nasser were displayed.[3]

On 18 September 1962 Imam Ahmad, a most hated and feared ruler who had survived many assassination attempts, died in his bed. Noting the minimal changes in Yemen, the London *Times* wrote: 'Imam Ahmad will be remembered for his success in preserving his kingdom virtually intact against all the political and social ideas of the twentieth century.'[4] Crown Prince Muhamad al-Badr succeeded his father with the firm intention of modernizing the still medieval kingdom. But it was impossible for him to do that in one week, for his imamate in San'a came to an end on 26 September through a military coup d'état, by which Yemen became a republic.

Egyptian Military Intervention in Yemen

On 26 September units of the Yemeni army shelled the imam's palace all night and the Yemeni Arab Republic was proclaimed. Al-Badr, however, managed to escape to the northern region where loyal Zaidi tribesmen vowed to regain San'a for him and to punish the rebels. Abdallah al-Sallal, the new chief-of-staff of al-Badr's army, joined the revolutionaries when the shooting had already begun, and was named the first president of the new republic. But the new leaders were not in full control of the country and knew that previous coup attempts had been crushed by surviving members of the imamate with the help of loyal Zaidis. To ensure their success the revolutionaries executed many supporters of the imam,[5] but, by and large, the inhabitants of San'a, Ta'iz, and Hodeida were joyful at the proclamation of the new republic. Al-Sallal announced that his aim was to build a socialist country on the Egyptian model. In the northern region the imam had many followers. Immediately after the revolution Prince Hassan, the imam's uncle, flew from New York, where he was Yemen's representative at the UN, to Saudi Arabia, where he was joined by other members of the imam's family, to set up a government in exile. Moreover, clashes between the imam's supporters and al-Sallal's troops broke out, especially on the borders with Saudi Arabia, where Saudi troops were reported on 1 October to be concentrated.[6] Aware of the grave situation within and without, al-Sallal turned to Nasser for support against possible 'foreign' intervention.

Nasser was presented with a golden opportunity to break out of his isolation, 'to teach King Saud a lesson' for his role in the Syrian secession, to confront the 'imperialist' British in Aden, to be close to the oil resources on the peninsula, and to make credible his new revolutionary ideology. Accordingly, Nasser (supported by other Egyptian leaders) responded to al-Sallal's urgent appeal by swiftly dispatching Egyptian troops to San'a. Nasser said that, one day after the Yemeni revolution occurred, he decided that he would not let 'reactionism defeat the revolution in Yemen [since if that should occur, it] would turn toward us and transfer the struggle to one against socialism, progress, and the people of Egypt in Cairo. . . . We must defend our principles in the heart of the Arabian Pensinsula against the reactionaries, imperialism, and Zionism.'[7] To Nasser, then, Yemen was more than an internal quarrel.

But Egyptian involvement in Yemen was to lead to a protracted war. Nasser's successor noted that 'the one Egyptian brigade initially sent to the Yemen multiplied until one day the Egyptian force in the Yemen numbered 70,000,' and added that his country's military intervention in Yemen 'was a military failure for Egypt.'[8] Indeed, Yemen was to become a morass for Egyptian operations there due to Nasser's 'miscalculations', especially with regard to Saudi intentions.

King Saud, sensing a threat to his kingdom from revolutionary Nasserist Yemeni leaders, did not hesitate to denounce them, and from the early days of the Yemeni revolution, he proclaimed his recognition of the imamate as the legitimate authority in Yemen. Saud's material and moral support for the surviving royal Yemenis was forthcoming too. The armies raised by al-Badr and supported by the Saudis (and to some extent by Jordan, Iran, and Pakistan), inflicted heavy losses upon the Egyptians and the Yemeni republicans throughout 1962, 1963, and the first part of 1964. Although the imamate forces suffered a setback in the second half of 1964, from early 1965 on the Egyptian forces experienced a series of disasters.[9]

The United Nations Initiative

Arab and non-Arab countries attempted to mediate in the Yemeni conflict. On 6 November 1962, President Nazim al-Qudsi of Syria proposed to Iraq that consultations over mediation of the Yemen conflict be held by the Arab League council, while Tunisia and Lebanon agreed to make a joint effort as well to end the crisis. Iraq responded to the Syrian appeal favourably. But the secretary-general of the League sent a memorandum to League members suggesting that meeting on Yemen would not be useful at present (see next section). The USA too offered its good offices to solve the Yemeni conflict; it hoped to bring the UN in to try to mediate between the quarrelling parties. President John F. Kennedy wrote to the leaders of the parties concerned, offering his services to bring about a peaceful settlement to the war in Yemen. President Kennedy suggested a formula in which he proposed the withdrawal of Egyptian troops and the severance of Saudi support to the Yemeni royalists. Abdallah al-Sallal and Egypt welcomed Kennedy's offer. The Egyptian acceptance of the US offer led to Washington's recognition of the republicans on 19 December 1962. The following day 50 states followed the American lead, and the republicans, rather than the royalists, were admitted, by a majority vote, into the UN.[10] This was a major victory for Egypt and the Yemeni republicans and a severe blow to the Saudis and the Yemeni royalists.

Contrary to Washington's hopes, however, the al-Sallal regime was too insecure to be left on its own, and the American recognition was not followed by gradual evacuation of Egyptian troops; Egypt actually increased its military build-up in Yemen, and its aircraft bombed Saudi towns. The Saudis too continued their military support for the imamate forces.[11] However, in early March 1963 President Kennedy dispatched former Ambassador Ellsworth Bunker to mediate between the conflicting parties. Bunker visited Egypt and Saudi Arabia. A few days earler, Dr Ralph Bunche visited Yemen and Saudi Arabia on a fact-finding mission on behalf of UN Secretary-General U Thant. Bunker and Bunche met with the leaders in these countries and their independent missions resulted in 'a disengagement agreement' between Cairo and Riyadh to end the war in Yemen. The terms of the agreement were announced by U Thant, in a report to the Security Council on 29 April as follows:

1   Saudi Arabia would terminate all aid to the royalists and would prohibit the use of its territory by royalist leaders to carry on the struggle.
2   The U.A.R. [Egypt], simultaneously with the suspension of Saudi support for the royalists, would begin a phased withdrawal of its troops from Yemen as soon as possible.
3   The U.A.R. would not take any punitive action against royalists, and would abstain from any action against Saudi territory.
4   A demilitarized zone would be established , extending 20 kilometers on each side of the demarcated border of Yemen-Saudi Arabia.
5   UN observers would be stationed in the demilitarized zone to check on the observance of the agreement. They would ensure that neither side tried to introduce troops or arms into this zone, verify the repatriation of the Egyptian forces and the cessation of royalist activities on Saudi territory, and go inside the zone to check on the military disengagement if it became necessary.[12]

In pursuance of the 'disengagement agreement', U Thant ordered Major-General Carl von Horn, chief-of-staff of the UN truce supervision organization in Palestine, to visit Egypt, Saudi Arabia, and Yemen with the task of setting up a UN observation mission in Yemen. This agreement failed to end the Yemeni war. Mutual distrust between Cairo and Riyadh made each suspect that the other party was not carrying out its side of the agreement. Furthermore, the royalist leaders refused to accept it. On 4 May the Saudis charged Egypt with replacing the troops withdrawn by reinforcements, and the Egyptians countercharged that Riyadh was continuing to aid the imamate forces. Later the UN mission confirmed both allegations[13] as the secretary-general continued his efforts to bring about an implementation of the agreement.

On 27 May 1963 U Thant, after receiving General von Horn's report on his findings, stressed his 'concern that the United Nations observation assistance called for under the terms of disengagement in Yemen, as agreed upon by the parties, should be provided with the least possible delay.'[14] The secretary-general noted that the observation mission was to consist of no more than 200 people. Egypt and Saudi Arabia agreed to pay the cost of this mission, originally to last four months.

Unsatisfied with these developments, the Soviet Union requested that the Security Council meet, which it did on 10–11 June 1963, to consider U Thant's reports on Yemen. The Soviet representative, while not opposing sending an observation mission to Yemen, none the less argued that UN observation missions and peacekeeping undertaken by the UN should be authorized and financed by the Security Council.[15] U Thant, on the other hand, stressed 'the growing urgency of the need for the United Nations observation operation', and argued that on his own responsibility he was empowered to undertake such operations.[16]

A compromised resolution was submitted to the Security Council by Ghana and Morocco. The resolution noted with satisfaction the initiative by U Thant and the agreement of Cairo and Riyadh to finance the observation mission over a period of two months. The resolution also:

1 *Requests* the Secretary-General to establish the observation operation as defined by him;
2 *Urges* the parties concerned to observe fully the terms of disengagement [mentioned earlier] and to refrain from any action which would increase tension in the area.
3 *Requests* the Secretary-General to report to the Security Council on the implementation of this decision.[17]

After debate the resolution was approved by ten votes to none, with one abstention, the Soviet Union.[18]

The advance party of the UN Yemen Observation Mission (UNYOM) reached San'a, where it established its headquarters, on 13 June 1963, and the formation of the main body of UNYOM was completed on 20 July and deployed in San'a, Hodeida, Sada, Najran, and Jizan. From the beginning of its operations, UNYOM met with a lack of co-operation and hostility in Yemen. The April 'Disengagement Agreement' had failed to end the fighting there, and indeed, the war seemed to be escalating. The Saudis alleged that Egyptian aircraft were dropping poison-gas bombs in northern Yemen, and the secretary-general instructed General von Horn, the commander of UNYOM, to investigate the Saudi charges, but he was unable to confirm them.[19] Von Horn resigned his post on 20 August 1963 because he believed that U Thant had refused to send him enough aircraft and funds without which, he felt, UNYOM was unable to do its job satisfactorily. He was replaced by General P.S. Gyani of India, but the observation mission achieved nothing in its first four months of operations in Yemen. U Thant admitted, in his 4 September report to the Security Council, that no significant progress had been made in the UNYOM efforts to implement the 'Disengagement Agreement', and that in some respects neither Cairo nor Riyadh had fulfilled their obligations in the agreement.[20]

The secretary-general's second report on the mission to the Security Council, on 30 October, was no different from the first one. He announced that UNYOM would be withdrawn by 4 November, as Riyadh would not pay any more of the mission's cost in Yemen, but it was later announced that Egypt and Saudi Arabia would continue to defray the mission's cost. In an effort to mediate the fighting, U Thant announced on 4 November that he had appointed the director of the UN European office at Geneva, Signor Pier Spinelli, to head the UN mission as his special representative in San'a, where he arrived on 8 November. In pursuance of his task, Spinelli visited Egypt and Saudi Arabia for talks with their respective leaders.[21] Throughout 1963 and into 1964 UNYOM was, with some difficulties, extended every two months but with no success in inducing the parties to stop the war. On 2 September 1964 U Thant announced that UNYOM would terminate its activities (restricted to observation and reporting only) on 4 September. Thus the observation mission in Yemen was ended with very limited, if any, progress.

The Arab League Efforts

From the beginning of the Yemeni conflict, the Arab League was unable to play any constructive role to settle the war peacefully. Egypt, after what happened to it at Shtoura, could not effectively utilize the League to serve its interests in the Yemeni case. Contrary to what happened in the Iraqi case, for example, Egypt's major opponent in this conflict was Saudi Arabia, which had its own supporters in the League. Thus Egypt was determined, at first, to achieve its objective in Yemen, namely to secure a pro-Cairo republican regime in San'a, without having to go to the League if possible. Nevertheless, when the republicans asked for recognition by the League, the latter had to be involved in the presentation.

The Yemeni representation to the League was controversial. A few days after al-Sallal's coup, the republicans and the imamate requested a meeting of the League council to consider the situation in Yemen. The legation of Yemen in Amman, which was loyal to the royalists, requested in the name of the imam an urgent meeting of the League council. A similar request by the Yemeni republican regime followed. The Saudis and their supporters strongly opposed the republican request. Similarly, Egypt and its supporters, which were few at the time, viewed the republicans as the legitimate authority in Yemen and, therefore, felt that the League should ignore the royalists and respond only to the republicans. Because of this split in the League over the recognition of the legitimate government of Yemen, and because of the uncertainty of the Yemeni internal situation, the majority of the member states saw that a League council meeting would be inappropriate at that time.[22] But when the League council met in its 38th ordinary session, the situation in the Arab world had changed in favour of Egypt: two pro-Nasser regimes had taken over, in Damascus and Baghdad, and Nasser once again was riding high. In March 1963 the majority of the League member states now recognized the republicans in San'a. Thus with the new strongly pro-Nasser alliance in the League, the League council, despite strong Saudi and Jordanian opposition, decided to recognize the republican regime in San'a as the legitimate government of Yemen and thus admit it as the representative of Yemen in the Arab League.[23] This move by the League did not ameliorate the situation in Yemen. In fact it was deteriorating. Undoubtedly, with the encouragment of Cairo, al-Sallal's government, after the failure of UNYOM, appealed to the League to attempt to put an end to the dispute between Yemen and its adversaries, namely Saudi Arabia and Jordan. On 16 September 1963, the political committee responded to the Republic of Yemen's appeal by sending a recommendation to the council which was adopted as a resolution during the council's 40th ordinary session on 19 September. Shaped by Egypt, the resolution was biased in favour of the Yemeni republic; it called on all member states to support the Yemeni request for the restoration of normal relations between the Arab states and for promotion of peace and stability in Yemen. The council also called on Abdel-Khaliq Hassouna, the League's secretary-general and the chairman of the council, to initiate contacts with the parties concerned in order to achieve these objectives.[24] Again Saudi Arabia abstained from voting, and Jordan expressed reservations on the status of Yemen as a republic since Amman still recognized the imamate rather than the republicans in Yemen. In effect, the two countries disagreed with the council's initiative, but the resolution of the council was adopted anyway. Soon afterwards Hassouna and other League officials held a series of consultations in Cairo at which a 'peace mission' was formed to visit the parties concerned in order to attempt to end the Yemeni conflict, which UNYOM had failed to achieve.

On 24 September the Arab League mission, headed by Hassouna, visited Beirut where it discussed the Yemeni question with Lebanese leaders. On the following day the mission arrived in Taif where it held meetings with Prince Faisal (*de facto* ruler of Saudi Arabia) and with other Saudi officials. The secretary-general and other members of the mission detailed to Faisal the events of the council meeting of 19 September in which the Yemeni Republic's delegate called for peace and aid for his country and expressed his hope that normal relations would be established between the Republic of Yemen and its neighbours. The Mission expressed the League's hope that the Saudi government would recognize the importance of the restoration of peace and stability in Yemen. The secretary-general reported that 'we [the League mission] expressed our hope that the Kingdom of Saudi Arabia would do its utmost to eliminate the tension along the borders . . . .'[25] In other words, the League wanted the Saudis to change their view of the San'a regime and recognize the republican system there.

Prince Faisal explained that his government carefully avoided having any Saudi soldiers cross the border into Yemen. Faisal also welcomed efforts to 'clear the Arab atmosphere' which first 'requires the end of the broadcasting and press campaign between the sister Arab states', a pointed reference to the hysterical Egyptian media attacks on his country. At the end of the League mission's visit, the Saudi government issued an official communiqué in which it 'welcomed all attempts undertaken to promote [Arab] solidarity and resume normal relations between the sister Arab states.' The Saudi communiqué emphasized the Saudi government's eagerness to co-operate towards the realization of that end and its hope that the League mission would find in the responses of the other parties concerned that which would facilitate the realization of the interests of the Yemeni people.[26] Riyadh, however, did not end its support for the royalists nor did it agree to recognize the republicans in Yemen.

The League mission then went to Jordan on 1 October. In Amman the mission met with King Hussein and Jordanian officials. According to Hassouna, the meeting with Jordanian officials made it clear to them that the government there did not consider itself as a party to the Yemeni conflict. The League mission was informed that Amman had ended its co-operation and aid for the Yemeni royalists and that establishment of normal relations with the Republic of Yemen was attendant only on its recognition of the government of San'a. Like the Saudis, the Jordanians expressed their hope for restoration of Arab solidarity 'particularly with the United Arab Republic'. They too emphasized the need for ending the propaganda campaign, particularly violent Egyptian attacks against the 'reactionaries'.[27]

A few days later the League mission arrived in Yemen, where Hassouna and his companions met Field Marshal al-Sallal, president of the Republic of Yemen, but did not meet any royalists. The mission told al-Sallal of the good news it brought from Amman and Taif. The Yemeni republicans expressed their gratitude and satisfaction over the League Council efforts. The secretary-general observed, while in Yemen, the urgent need for the Arab states to send all kinds of aid to the Yemeni people. At the end of the mission's visit, al-Sallal's government issued an official communiqué that expressed its thanks for the League's efforts and reaffirmed 'its readiness to continue its effective positive policy . . . to consolidate Arab solidarity and resume normal relations between the sister Arab States.'[28]

After visiting Saudi Arabia, Jordan, and republican Yemen, the League mission returned to Cairo where it reported its findings to Egyptian officials, including the foreign minister. The latter informed Hassouna and other members of the League mission that his government had in fact gradually withdrawn some of its forces from Yemen as the 'Disengagement Agreement' required. The Egyptian foreign minister expressed Cairo's hope that the other parties involved in the Yemeni conflict would also carry out their obligations under that agreement.[29]

By and large, however, the League mission proved to be impotent, since it did not put an end to the conflict and the Yemeni war continued on a larger scale than when it began. Egypt now, despite substantial Soviet contributions to its Yemeni war efforts, began to realize that it could not continue for long to bear the human and material cost, especially in light of the fact that it was one of the poor Arab countries.

Nasser's Call on the Arab League to Arrange an Arab Summit Meeting: Arab Summits and the Yemeni Conflict

Against the background of increasing Egyptian losses, Nasser called for an Arab summit meeting to discuss Arab affairs. The pretext for this meeting was Israel's diversion of the river Jordan, but the Yemeni conflict was undoubtedly the main question on Nasser's mind. Indeed, perhaps the river Jordan matter was a cover-up for his real intentions: to get the Arab leaders together to work out an acceptable solution to the war in Yemen on the excuse that Egyptian forces were needed in the Sinai to face the Israeli war machine.

On 23 December 1963 Nasser spoke in Port Sa'id and said:

> In order to confront Israel, a summit meeting of the Arab
> kings and heads of state must take place as soon as possible,
> regardless of the strife and conflicts between them. We are
> willing to sit with our adversaries. . . . For the sake of
> Palestine we are ready to sit with them. . . . Egypt is
> prepared to shoulder its responsibility completely . . . We
> [would] *bring back our brothers from Yemen* [author's
> emphasis] We want to talk about the diversion of the river
> Jordan . . . I propose a meeting between the kings and heads
> of state and I will send to the Arab League this proposal to
> hold this meeting as soon as possible.[30]

Egypt's return to the Arab League as an appropriate forum to settle Arab disputes was greatly welcomed by Arab and League officials. As a high Arab League official put it: 'Nasser's call for a summit meeting restored a golden era to the League.'[31]

On 24 December the general secretariat of the Arab League received a note from the Egyptian foreign ministry embodying Nasser's request for convening an Arab summit meeting of the Arab League to deal with the problem of the diversion of the Jordan waters.

Part of the Egyptian note read:

> the Ministry of Foreign Affairs, in accordance with instructions from the Presidency of the Republic has the honour to request the Arab League General Secretariat to address invitations to the other Arab States for this proposed meeting, to be held at the Arab League Secretariat in Cairo, as the place in which the Arab governments can meet, irrespective of any difference between them.[32]

On the same day the League secretariat invited member states to a summit meeting in Cairo the date of which was set for 12 January 1964. Hassouna was so instrumental in gathering all the Arab leaders together that one observer wrote that he 'reestablished the prestige of the organization.'[33] But the secretary-general's efforts were really to serve Egyptian foreign policy since Nasser requested the meeting.

At the outset of the summit the Egyptian president struck a conciliatory note toward 'reactionary' Arabs. The main result of the summit was the change of Nasser's attitude that led to the resumption of diplomatic relations between Cairo on the one hand and Riyadh and Amman on the other.

The second Arab summit meeting[34] was held within the framework of the Arab League and in private, primarily to discuss the river Jordan problem. The Yemeni case, however, was a prominent topic in the Arab leaders' discussions. The summit meeting was rather conciliatory in its approach. During the conference the Iraqi and Algerian leaders, who were pro-Nasser, tried to mediate between Riyadh and Cairo in an attempt to settle the Yemeni war. They also tried to induce Saudi Arabia to recognize the Republic of Yemen.[35] At the end of the summit meeting a communiqué was issued which charged the Israelis with aggression against the Arab states by diverting the river Jordan waters. To unify their ranks against Israel, the Arab leaders 'unanimously agree[d] to settle all differences, to clear the Arab atmosphere of all blemishes, to suspend all campaigns by information media, to consolidate relations between the Arab sister states, to ensure collective co-operative reconstruction, and to ward off the aggressive expansionist designs menacing all Arabs alike.'[36] No explicit reference to Yemen was mentioned in the communiqué, but Nasser must have hoped that 'the consolidation of relations between the Arab sister states' would lead to a rapprochement with Riyadh over the Yemeni crisis. On 3 March 1964

Secretary-General U Thant reported to the Security Council on the impact of the Arab summit meeting on the crisis in Yemen. He noted:

> the increasing unity of feeling and purpose within the Arab World arising from the Conference of Arab Heads of State held in Cairo in mid-January and the improvement in relations between Saudi Arabia and the United Arab Republic which resulted therefrom. Both before and after the Conference, I and my special representative on my behalf, had been urging the two governments concerned to hold direct conversations on the Yemen question. After the Cairo Conference this task was also undertaken by a mission composed of representatives of the presidents of Algeria and Iraq. I was please to learn from a communiqué issued by the Saudi Arabian Government, after discussions with the Arab Mission, that it welcomed the resumption of political relations with the United Arab Republic provided a meeting would be held between the two parties in Saudi Arabia which would be attended also by the mediating delegates . . .[37]

On 1 March 1964 an Egyptian delegation led by Field Marshal Abdel-Hakim Amir, the Egyptian vice-president, visited Saudi Arabia and held talks with Prince Faisal and other Saudi officials on the Egyptian withdrawal from Yemen and the ending of Saudi aid to the royalists. At the end of the Egyptian delegation's visit, the two governments announced their intentions of resuming diplomatic relations, and that 'the U.A.R. and Saudi Arabia, having no aims in the Yemen, declare themselves in favour of the absolute independence of that country and are ready to oppose any imperialist attempt against the freedom of the Yemeni people.' Furthermore, Prince Faisal agreed to visit Egypt in the near future for talks with President Nasser aimed at achieving 'a definite solution of the Yemeni problem'.[38] Owing to Nasser's change of slogan from 'unity of purpose' to once again 'unity of rank', King Hussein made four visits to Cairo in 1964. Nasser even persuaded the king in July to recognize the republican government in San'a.[39] This was a diplomatic coup for Cairo and a serious setback to the Saudis and the royalist Yemenis.

The third Arab summit meeting was held in September 1964 in Alexandria, Egypt. Most of the talks in this conference were focused on the Israeli plan to divert Jordan's water. But when the conference was over, Faisal of Saudi Arabia remained in Egypt for several days in order to discuss the war in Yemen with Nasser. At the end of their discussions the two leaders announced that they agreed to co-operate in mediation with the concerned parties (royalist and republican Yemenis) in order to reach a final peaceful solution to the continuing crisis.[40] Faisal's talks with Nasser led to a meeting between the representatives of the Yemeni republicans and royalists in Sudan on 30 October.

Arab Attempts to End the Strife in Yemen

We have noted that the Arab League arrangements for the summit conferences led to rapprochement between Saudi Arabia and Egypt. As a result of this rapprochement, the two countries resumed their diplomatic relations and held a series of intensive talks on the question of the war in Yemen. They vowed to strive for a 'definite' peaceful solution to the continuing Yemeni war, especially after the costly failure of Egypt's offensive in the summer of 1964 to achieve ultimate victory; Nasser began to refer to his involvement in Yemen as 'my Vietnam'.[41]

As a result of the September meeting between Faisal and Nasser, peace talks between republican and royalist delegations were held at Erkwit, Sudan, on 1–3 November 1964. The two delegations agreed on a ceasefire which would have come into force on 8 November, and a national congress attended by representatives of the two factions would meet in a Yemeni town on 23 November. While the ceasefire came into effect on 8 November as arranged, the national congress never met because of disagreement over where the congress should take place and over the choice of representatives. Furthermore, on 14 November Imam al-Badr declared that the withdrawal of Egyptian forces must be guaranteed before there could be an armistice.[42]

In early December intensive fighting broke out with the royalists taking the offensive and capturing several key areas in northwestern Yemen and in the southeastern area. The royalist success was reportedly due to generous Saudi aid. King Faisal (he succeeded his brother as king in November 1964) confirmed that he was actively supporting the royalists because Egypt had not observed the September agreement.[43] The confusion in Yemen was further intensified when several republican leaders resigned from al-Sallal's cabinet and accused his regime of corruption and incompetence. Even among the republicans, resentments arose against Egyptian domination in Yemen; some republican leaders tried to negotiate separately with Riyadh and with Yemeni royalists.[44]

The deterioration of the situation in Yemen led to renewed attempts to mediate the crisis which were undertaken by various Arab leaders. On 6 June 1965, the Jordanian prime minister said that King Hussein was working to achieve a peaceful settlement of the war in Yemen, and that his initiative had led to agreement in principle between Cairo and Riyadh. The king sent a letter to Nasser and Faisal on 14 June, in which he proposed the creation of a joint republican and royalist administration under a neutral leader to rule Yemen until the people expressed their wishes through a national referendum, until the withdrawal of all foreign forces, which were to be replaced by an inter-Arab peace force, and until the Arab fund to finance the reconstruction of the country's war-torn economy was established.[45]

Kuwait, too, attempted to act as peacemaker. The crown prince and prime minister of Kuwait visited Saudi Arabia on 12 June and held talks with King Faisal at the Yemeni republicans' request. At the end of the talks a joint communiqué was issued which declared that the two countries had agreed to persevere to find means that would pave the way to a solution to the problem of Yemen. President Ahmad Ben Bella of Algeria dispatched a special envoy to Egypt, Yemen, and Iraq. After talks with the leaders in these countries, the Algerian envoy said in Baghdad on 12 June that a peace formula had 'crystallized'.[46] These initiatives led to more talks between Saudi and Egyptian officials that resulted in the Jiddah agreement. On 20 July, at Nasser's request, the Saudi under-secretary for foreign affairs held talks with the Egyptian president. Two days later Nasser spoke of a plan which, with King Faisal's co-operation, would enable Nasser to withdraw his forces from Yemen in less than six months. But Nasser emphasized that he would not tolerate attacks by British and Saudi 'mercenaries' and that, if the negotiations failed, Egypt would have to 'liquidate the points of agression' (meaning Saudi Arabia). A few days later, Nasser sent a personal envoy to Riyadh and held talks with Faisal who warned Egypt that he was not prepared to talk under Cairo's threats. In the first half of August the Saudi ambassador in Egypt shuttled between Cairo and Riyadh, which led to an invitation to Nasser to meet with Faisal in Jiddah.[47]

The Nasser-Faisal meeting at Jiddah resulted in the signing of an agreement on 24 August which temporarily put an end to the fighting in Yemen. Nasser (as on several previous occasions) agreed to withdraw Egyptian forces from Yemen. At Jiddah it was reported that Nasser said to Faisal: 'I beg you to save the prestige of the Egyptian Army.'[48] The agreement also called for the ending of Saudi military aid to the royalists and for holding a plebiscite no later than 23 November 1966, through which the Yemeni people could decide for themselves the kind of regime they wanted. The two leaders agreed to 'co-operate in forming a "Transitory Conference" composed of 50 members representing all popular forces and "those who loose and bind" (i.e., the religious leaders) in the Yemen' to be held in Haradth, Yemen, on 23 November 1965, in order to determine the system of government during the transitional period up to the time of the plebiscite, to form a provisional government, and to determine the form and ways of carrying out the plebiscite.[49]

With the exception of Syria (the Ba'athists at this stage were engaged in bitter attacks on Nasser), the Arab countries welcomed the Jiddah agreement. Between 13 and 17 September 1965 the fourth Arab summit meeting was held at Casablanca. At the end of the meeting an official communiqué declared, among other things, that the Arab heads of state reiterated their belief in Arab solidarity and called on the Arab League member states to respect the sovereignty, independence, and the systems of government established in the other member states. The summit also called on the Arab media to serve the Arab cause rather than attack Arab heads of state.[50] Through this communiqué, Egypt hoped that Saudi Arabia would respect the republican system in Yemen, thereby ending its support for the royalist forces.

In accordance with the Jiddah agreement, the Haradth conference of royalists and republicans convened on 23 November 1965. However, the two groups proved to be adamant and stubborn in their positions on some basic provisions of the Jiddah agreement. The royalists and republicans failed to reach consensus on the three principles, mainly because of republican insistence upon the use of the word 'republic' to describe the transitional government provided for the Jiddah agreement. The Haradth talks broke down on 24 December 1965 and they were never resumed.[51] It is worth noting, however, that while the Haradth conference was still in session. Nasser sent more troops to Yemen, and the Soviet Union and China shipped more arms to the republicans in San'a.[52] It is conceivable that to counter the increased Soviet arms supplies to Egypt and Yemen, the USA, Britain, and Saudi Arabia concluded an arms agreement. This deal amounted to

$350 million and was announced in December 1965.

In the same month Faisal visited Iran, and in an unmistakable reference to Nasser's socialism, Faisal and the Shah of Iran proposed that the two countries unite in fighting elements alien to Islam.[53] Faisal visited Jordan in January 1966, and later went to Turkey, Sudan, Pakistan, Morocco, Tunisia, Guinea, and Mali, during which tour he launched his idea for the holding of an Islamic summit in Mecca. To disguise his dislike of Nasser's socialism, Faisal, when asked if Nasser would be invited to his proposed Islamic meeting, said that it was natural since Nasser was a Muslim and a brother Arab.[54] King Faisal's activities, none the less, were suspected by Nasser, and the Egyptian media unsurprisingly renewed its criticism of the Saudi tactics. Nasser suspected in particular Iran's role in Faisal's proposed Islamic alliance, since the Shah was supplying Israel with oil and because of his military aid to the royalist Yemenis, his close alliance with the West, and his country's membership in the Central Treaty Organization. Consequently, Nasser perceived the proposed Islamic summit meeting as a renewed drive to contain him and his revolutionary ideology.[55] In Nasser's mind the success of Faisal's plans for an Islamic conference would be to his advantage and thus he was definitely opposed to it.

In February 1966 Britain issued a White Paper on Defence which said that British troops would withdraw from the Aden protectorate by 1968. The British announcement caused Nasser to re-evaluate his strategy in Yemen, especially in light of Faisal's Islamic moves. The departure of the British would leave a vacuum that Nasser could not resist filling. Nasser boasted that the Egyptian presence in Yemen had forced Britain to evacuate Aden.[56] The new British policy, along with Faisal's activities and the resumption of hostilities between the royalists and republicans, may have been factors behind the change of Nasser's earlier desire to withdraw from Yemen. On 22 February 1966 Nasser, speaking on the anniversary of the union with Syria, said that unless a government was formed in San'a to hold the plebiscite and then settle the Yemeni problem, he would not withdraw his troops from Yemen. He stressed that, 'We [Egyptians] can stay in the Yemen one year, two, three, four, or five years. We can make sacrifices. We can stand it, for we believe in the Arab masses, the Arab revolution, and the unity of Arab struggle.' He added that 'Britain had decided to grant [Aden] independence in 1968. We will stay there till after 1968.'[57] Then Nasser, in a reference to Faisal's proposed Islamic summit meeting, went on to explain the Shah's involvement with the Western countries against the 'progressive Arabs'. 'We never refused Islamic co-operation, but such co-operation must be for the sake of God and Islam and not the outcome of American and British policy.' Nasser added that 'the presence of Tehran emphasizes that the pact is against the Arabs and the Muslims and for the protection of reaction. . . . What does the Shah know about Islam?'[58]

Nasser's speech spoiled the friendly atmosphere that prevailed in inter-Arab relations during 1964 and 1965, and by early 1966 the old adversaries were back at each other's throats. Nasser repeated his charges in a speech he gave on 22 March in which he said:

> Reaction in the Arab World had exploited the good faith of the revolutionary powers and allied itself to imperialism to destroy the progressive powers in the Arab world. Therefore, if this is allowed to go on, the ultimate result will be a return to the state we were in before the policy of unified Arab action and of summit conferences. . . . We are today revising our plans so that we may stay in the Yemen five years or longer if necessary. . . . I am saying that we shall stay 20 years and anyone who interferes in the Yemen shall get a hiding from us.

The last remark was an obvious reference to Saudi support of the royalists.[59]

The Arab League's fifth summit meeting was to be held in Algiers in September 1966. But on 22 July 1966 Nasser spoke of Arab 'reactionaries' collaboration with British and American 'imperialism' against the Arab progressive forces, in particular against Egypt. 'We, the liberated forces, cannot sit with these reactionary forces in forthcoming summit conferences. . . . We will ask the Arab League to postpone the [September] summit conference indefinitely.'[60] On 25 July the Egyptian foreign ministry informed the Arab League secretary-general of Nasser's request for the postponement of the coming Arab summit meeting, because, in Egypt's view, the conference under present circumstances 'will not achieve the objectives for which Egypt suggested the holding of these conferences.'[61] These objectives obviously included the securing of a republican system in Yemen which did not materialize by then. Several Arab countries rejected Nasser's request to postpone the summit meeting. Jordan wanted the meeting to be held as scheduled, and Saudi Arabia notified the League that the problem of Palestine made the holding of the summit imperative, regardless of inter-Arab differences.[62] Certainly the man who initiated this process was able to end it at will, and the Arab heads of state were to meet only after Egypt was defeated in the 1967 war.

Despite the serious deterioration in relations between Cairo and Riyadh, the ruler of Kuwait continued his mediation efforts, and peace talks between Saudi Arabia and Egypt were opened in Kuwait on 17 August 1966. At the conclusion of the talks on 19 August the negotiators reached an agreement on a peace plan based on the Kuwaiti formula. This formula envisaged the formation of an interim government drawn from all Yemeni factions, where the republicans would be the majority, but members of the imamate would be excluded to avoid the use of the term republic or imamate. For a transitional period of ten months the country would be known as 'the state of Yemen'. A joint Arab force would replace Egyptian forces and would supervise a plebiscite on the future form of regime. But the Kuwaiti agreement was never implemented, mainly because, once again, Egypt refused to withdraw its forces from Yemen.[63] Also the Saudi and Egyptian negotiators did not consult with the Yemeni factions. 'Royalists were as disgusted with Riyadh as were republicans with Cairo at being kept out of all knowledge of Kuwait's mediation effort,' reported the *Economist* of London.[64]

By early 1967 the situation was more complicated than before. On 24 January Jordan demanded the withdrawal of all non-Yemeni forces from Yemen territory as soon as possible and 'the direction of those forces against Israel'. Furthermore, Saudi Arabia alleged that Egypt was using poison gas against royalist and dissident republican areas. In February the governments of Tunisia and Jordan withdrew their recognition of al-Sallal's regime on the grounds that the republican government no longer had any stability and effective authority.[65] Fighting and Egyptian bombing continued throughout the first quarter of 1967.

The outbreak of the June war signalled unmitigated disaster for the overconfident Nasser. Yet the emotional spirit of Arab solidarity re-emerged in time of crisis, and the Arab heads of state met in Khartoum, Sudan, in August 1967 to see what they could do about Nasser's latest and most devastating troubles. There Nasser turned to Arab leaders, including the 'reactionaries' led by Faisal, 'who took the initiative and decided that Saudi Arabia would pay Egypt £50 million per annum.'[66] The Kuwaiti and Libyan leaders also agreed to support Egypt financially.

During the Khartoum conference, an agreement for a peaceful solution to the Yemeni war was reached between Nasser and Faisal on 31 August. The agreement provided that Egypt should withdraw all its forces from Yemen; that Riyadh should put an end to its aid to the royalists; and that a three-member committee, consisting of the foreign ministers of the Sudan, Iraq, and Morocco, should attempt to form a new government which would include representatives of all factions in Yemen. Complete Egyptian evacuation was set for December 1967.[67] Despite al-Sallal's opposition to the Khartoum agreement, Nasser meant what he said this time, and Egyptian troops completely evacuated Yemen in December. The tripartite committee visited Beirut and Riyadh (where it met with royalists in exile) and arrived in Yemen on 3 October to carry out its charge. But due to republican and royalist disagreement, the committee decided on 19 January 1968 to refer the problem back to Nasser and Faisal.

Meanwhile, while in Baghdad en route to Moscow, al-Sallal asked for and received political asylum after the Yemeni army toppled his regime on 5 November. A new presidential council was established on the same day. The new government said it did not reject the Khartoum agreement, but would oppose outside mediation (the tripartite committee). Furthermore, before the end of 1967, the British left Aden and a republic (South Yemen) was proclaimed. The new Aden government was in favour of a republic in Yemen and opposed the royalists who launched a major offensive to capture San'a, but failed. Ultimately the Saudis ceased their support of the royalists, many of whom defected to the republican side, to which Soviet armaments were now directly sent.[68] Moreover, in June and July 1969, Saudi officials made secret contacts with the republican government in San'a, and the facade of imamate unity was now rapidly falling apart.[69] In March 1970 an Islamic conference of foreign ministers was held in Jiddah, and a republican delegation from Yemen, led by Muhsin al-'Aini, prime minister and foreign minister, was invited to attend. At the end of the conference, with Saudi support, the remaining royalists and republicans reached a consensus to end the war, under which several royalist leaders were appointed in presidential, governmental, and legislative bodies. They also agreed that no member of the imamate would be allowed to return to Yemen, thereby fulfilling a long-held republican condition and thus clearing the way for national reconciliation. After eight years of strife, the Yemeni war came to an end.[70]

The Impotence of the Arab League in the Yemeni Crisis

Despite the fact that article 5 of the League's pact states, in part, that the League council 'shall mediate in all differences which threaten to lead to war between two member states . . . with a view to bringing about their reconciliation,' the Arab League could not do much about the fighting in Yemen, even if it wanted to. It was clear that a threat of war between Saudi Arabia and Egypt existed from September 1962 until May 1967 because of Yemen. However, the League, due to the machinations of the parties involved in the conflict, was left on the sideline.

After the Syrian secession, Nasser adopted his revolutionary tactic of supporting revolutionary forces, which attempted to overthrow 'reactionaries' in the Arab world. Nasser vowed that he would not be restricted by any body, including the Arab League, which he said he would 'freeze' if it stood in his way. This strategy was clear during the Shtoura meeting of August 1962 when Egypt simply walked out, threatening to break up the League. Shortly afterward, the fragile Yemeni coup against the imamate occurred. On the request of the leader of the coup, Nasser promptly dispatched Egyptian troops to Yemen to ensure that the new republican regime would be secured, in order that he might teach King Saud and the British 'imperialists' a lesson for their opposition to his pan-Arabism policy. However, Nasser 'miscalculated' the situation in Yemen and soon it became clear that in order to remain there he would have to sacrifice Egyptian soldiers and the near-bankrupt Egyptian treasury. Therefore, he seemed to have been convinced of the advantages of seeking a peaceful settlement that would ensure the survival of the Yemeni republic. President Kennedy and the UN secretary-general attempted to mediate, but, by and large, due to Saudi dissatisfaction and the strong royalist opposition, these efforts failed.

In early 1963 the Arab League Council, because of Egyptian influence and despite Saudi and Jordanian objections, recognized the republican regime as the legitimate authority in Yemen. This move, seen from Cairo, would lead to the eventual victory of the republicans (backed by Egyptian forces) over the royalists. But this conception failed and soon it became clear that Egypt was engaged in a costly and protracted war. However, Cairo showed signs of interest in a League attempt to bring about a solution to the Yemeni problem. Thereupon, Egypt encouraged a League mission, headed by the secretary-general, to visit the parties concerned, mainly Saudi Arabia and

Jordan; the mission also visited San'a in order to attempt to end Saudi and Jordanian aid to the royalists and to induce them to establish normal relations with the republican regime in San'a. Achieving such an objective would have been in the Egyptian interest. But the League mission failed to achieve this end.

Meanwhile the fighting was continuing, and increasing criticism was voiced inside and outside Egypt. Nasser, encouraged by Soviet aid in his Yemeni involvement, vowed not to withdraw from Yemen, despite his heavy losses, unless the republican government was secured. But by the end of 1963 the situation in Yemen became unbearable, and Nasser and other Egyptian leaders began to question their wisdom and to talk about their 'miscalculation' in Yemen. Before the end of December 1963 Nasser attempted a new method to utilize the Arab League to achieve his end. He called on the Arab League to arrange a summit meeting in Cairo. The reason given behind this move was Israel's diversion of the river Jordan. While the catalyst for this call could very well have been Israel's plans, undoubtedly the Yemeni war also figured prominently in Nasser's mind. As an Arab commentator said: 'The Egyptian government lost hope in its revolutionary policy of dealing with the people and ignoring the governments'. Egypt became 'exhausted' because of its differences with the Arab countries, particularly Saudi Arabia. Thus Nasser called for the second Arab summit meeting because 'Egypt wanted to end these disputes and put an end to the fighting in Yemen'.[71] That explains why Nasser during the summit spent more time talking to King Faisal rather than to the Syrian leader, Hafiz Amin, who was far more important as far as the diversion of the Jordan waters was concerned. But when the Yemeni conflict was not solved by the summit conferences, Nasser bitterly attacked Saudi Arabia and allied himself with Syria in an axis against Riyadh.

To illustrate the importance that Nasser attached to Yemen, even on 20 June 1967, after Egypt's defeat in the Arab-Israel war, Kamal al-Din Hussein, a close friend and aid to Nasser, tried to convince Nasser to forget his differences with Arab 'reactionaries' so that he could use them to serve Egyptian interests and to work toward an understanding with King Faisal to settle the Yemeni conflict. Nasser replied, 'And let al-Badr enter the Yemen?' Kamal said, 'Egypt is more important to us than Yemen.' Al-Baghdadi, another close associate of Nasser, observed that Nasser at this time 'was still thinking in Yemen on how not to allow al-Badr to enter it in spite of the fact that Egypt itself became occupied by Israel.'[72]

In short, after his military failure in Yemen, Nasser attempted to utilize the Arab League and, later, its summit conferences, to help in extricating himself from the war in Yemen. But this failed simply because of Saudi perseverence in and out of the Arab League in opposing Nasser's Yemeni objectives. The Saudis ultimately succeeded in resisting the League's efforts to settle the dispute. Indeed, the failure of the League signalled the beginning of the decline of Egyptian predominance in the League.

Notes to chapter seven

1 For discussion of Yemen during the imamate period see Edgar O'Ballance, *The War in the Yemen*, Hamden, Conn. Archon Books, 1971; Harold Ingrams, *The Yemen*, New York, Praeger, 1964; George Lenczowski, *The Middle East in World Affairs*, Ithaca and London, Cornell University Press, 1962, pp. 573–87; Eric Macro, *Yemen and the Western World since 1571*, New York, Praeger, 1968; Dana Adams Schmidt, *The Yemen: Unknown War*, New York, Holt, Rinehart and Winston, 1968.
2 O'Ballance, p. 49.
3 Ibid., pp. 63–64.
4 Stanko Guldescu, 'Yemen: The War and the Haradth Conference', *The Review of Politics*, vol. 28 no. 3, (July 1966), p. 320.
5 Robert Stephens, *Nasser: A Political Biography* (New York: Simon and Schuster, 1971), pp. 388–89.
6 *Keesing*, 16–23 March, 1963, p. 19298.
7 *Speech on 23 December 1962, President Gamal Abdel-Nasser Speeches and Press Interviews*, part IV, p. 261.
8 Anwar el-Sadat, *In Search of Identity* (New York: Harper and Row, 1978), p. 163.
9 Guldescu, p. 323.
10 A. I. Dawisha, 'Intervention in the Yemen', *The Middle East Journal*, vol. 29, no. 1 (winter, 1975), p. 51.
11 *Keesing*, 16–23 March 1963, p. 19302.
12 *Keesing*, 8–15 February 1964, p. 19891.

13 Ibid.

14 *Security Council Official Records (S.C.O.R.)*, 18th year, 1037th meeting, 10 June 1963, p. 1.

15 Ibid., 1038th meeting, 11 June 1963, p. 4.

16 *Keesing*, 8–15 February 1964, p. 19892.

17 *S.C.O.R.*, 18th year, 1038th meeting, 11 June 1963, p. 6.

18 Ibid., 1039th meeting, 11 June 1963, p. 2.

19 *Keesing*, 8–15 February 1964, p. 19892.

20 O'Ballance, p. 104.

21 Ibid., p. 105; *Keesing*, 8–15 February 1964, p. 19894.

22 Boutros Boutros-Ghali, *Jamia t al-Dowal al-Arabiyyeh wa-Hal al-Munaza'at al-Iqlimiyyeh*, (The League of Arab States and the Settlement of Regional Disputes), Cairo, Dar al-Tiba'ah al-Hadithah, 1977, p. 115.

23 *Minutes of League Council*, 38th ordinary session, 3rd meeting, 23 March 1963, p. 35.

24 Hussein A. Hassouna, *The League of Arab States and Regional Disputes*, Dobbs Ferry, N. Y., Oceana, 1975, pp. 184–85; Boutros-Ghali, *op. cit.* p. 116.

25 *Report of Secretary-General to the League Council*, 41st ordinary session, March 1964, p. 14.

26 Ibid.

27 Ibid.; Hassouna, p. 186.

28 Ibid., p. 16.

29 Boutros-Ghali, *op. cit.* p. 119.

30 Speech on December 23, 1963, *President Gamal Abdel-Nasser Speeches and Press Interviews*, part IV, February 1962–June 1964, pp. 492–93.

31 Sayed Nofal to the author, Cairo, 19 June 1978.

32 *Report of Secretary-General to the League Council*, 41st ordinary session, March 1964, p. 179.

33 Robert W. MacDonald, *The League of Arab States: A Study of the Dynamics of Regional Organizations*, Princeton, N. J., Princeton University Press, 1965, p. 159.

34 The first Arab summit meeting was held in Anshas (Cairo), on 26 May 1946, to discuss the Zionist threat in Palestine. Egypt, Saudi Arabia, Iraq, Yemen, Jordan, Lebanon, and Syria attended this conference.

35 *Keesing*, 4–11 April 1964, p. 19998.

36 *Statement by the Council of the Kings and Heads of State of the Arab League*, Cairo, 17 January 1964, pp. 6, 7.

37 U.N. Doc. S/5572, quoted in Hassouna, p. 187.

38 *Keesing*, 4–11 April 1964, p. 19998.

39 A.I. Dawisha, *Egypt in the Arab World*, London, Macmillan, 1976, p. 44.

40 Manfred Wenner, *Modern Yemen: 1918–1966*, Baltimore, Johns

Hopkins University Press, 1967, p. 214; Hassouna, p. 187; Boutros-Ghali, *op. cit.* p. 120.

41 Anthony Nutting, *Nasser*, London, Constable, 1972, p. 349.

42 *Keesing*, 16–23 January 1965, p. 20530.

43 Ibid., 9–16 October 1965, p. 21001.

44 Malcolm Kerr, *The Arab Cold War: 1958–1970*, London, Oxford University Press, 1970, p. 107. On 5 May 1965, a peace conference was held in Khamer, Yemen. Abdel-Rahman al-Iryani, member of the Yemeni presidential council chaired this conference. The royalists boycotted it. But the conference called, among other things, on Yemenis (including the royalists) to start solving their problems by peaceful means.

45 O'Ballance, p. 146; *Keesing*, 9–16 October 1965, p. 21002.

46 Ibid.

47 *Keesing*, p. 21003; Dawisha, *op. cit.*, p. 45.

48 Editor Hamed Mutawi' of the Saudi morning journal *al-Nadwa*, 26 March 1966; quoted in Guldescu, p. 323.

49 For the text of the Saudi-Egyptian agreement on Yemen (the Jiddah agreement) see *The Middle East Journal*, vol. 20, no. 1 (winter, 1966), pp. 93–94.

50 *Report of the Secretary-General to the League Council*, 48th ordinary session, September 1967, annex. no. 8, pp. 167–168.

51 For more details on the Haradth conference see Guldescu, pp. 323–31; see also O'Ballance, pp. 154–70, and Muhamad Tal'at al-Ghuneimi, *Jamiá t al-Dowal al-Arabiyyeh*, (League of Arab States), Alexandria, Minsha'at al-Ma'arif, 1974, p. 285.

52 Guldescu, p. 325.

53 Peter Mansfield, *Nasser's Egypt* Baltimore, Md., Penguin Books, 1969, p. 76.

54 Ibid.

55 A. I. Dawisha, 'Intervention in the Yemen', pp. 57–58.

56 Mansfield, p. 77.

57 *Address by President Gamal Abdel-Nasser at the Great Popular Rally Held by the Arab Socialist Union in Celebration of the Anniversary of Unity Day* (translated into English), Cairo, 22 February 1966, pp. 14–15.

58 Ibid., pp. 35–36.

59 *Address by President Gamal Abdel-Nasser at the Great Popular Rally Held in Suez on the Occasion of its National Day*, 22 March 1966 (translated into English), Cairo, Ministry of National Guidance, Information Department, pp. 44–46.

60 *Address by President Gamal Abdel-Nasser at the Great Popular Rally Held in Midan al-Gumhuriyyah on the Occasion of the 14th Anniversary of the Revolution*, 22 July 1966, Cairo, Ministry of National Guidance, Information Department, pp. 37–38.

61 *Report of the Secretary-General to the League Council*, September 1966, pp. 102–03.

62 Ibid., p. 107.

63 *Keesing*, 25 February–4 March 1967, p. 21891.

64 8 October 1966, p. 147.

65 *Keesing*, 25 February–4 March 1967, p. 21894.

66 el-Sadat, *In Search of Identity*, p. 188.

67 *Keesing*, 24 February–2 March 1968, p. 22547.

68 See ibid., pp. 22548–50.

69 O'Ballance, p. 201.

70 Hassouna, p. 193; *Keesing*, 1970, p. 24053; and in Arabic see Adel Rida, *Muhawalah li-Fahm al-Thawrah al-Yemeniyyeh*, (An Attempt to Understand the Yemeni Revolution), Cairo, Alexandria, al-Maktab al-Misri al-Hadith lil-Tiba'ah wal-Nashr, 1974, pp. 88–90.

71 *Muthakarat Massó ol Arabi Muttali*, (Memoire of an Informed Arab Official), (Anonymous), *al-Ahram* 4 May 1978, p. 5.

72 *Abdel-Latif al-Baghdadi Memoire*, part II, Cairo, Alexandria, al-Maktab al-Misri al-Hadith, 1977, pp. 310–11.

Chapter Eight

The Arab League Under Nasser: Conclusions

The world has seen many regional organizations. The purpose of establishing these organizations has been, more or less, to serve the interests of their members. Members' security has often been cited as the main goal of these organizations. But history and experience have shown that the major power in a given regional body is the main beneficiary. The major power becomes the predominant one where the other members often adopt its policy recommendations. This fact has been acknowledged by world leaders. As one writer aptly observed, 'regional organizations are often built around the local great power, taking on the character of a solar system, with subsidiary members revolving about the central sun.'[1] Winston Churchill, for example, emphasized the potential role of regional organizations as instruments for the leadership of the major powers. Franklin D. Roosevelt too held a similar view of regional councils.[2] Indeed, major powers in certain organizations behave in a hegemonic way.

The case of Egypt in the League of Arab States during the tenure of President Gamal Abdel-Nasser clearly shows the validity of those leaders' assertions. Although Nasser had multiple foreign policy goals, his primary objective was the preservation of Egypt's independence and the enhancement of Egypt's power and influence in the Arab world. During Nasser's reign the Arab League was predominantly Egyptian and was often used to help in accomplishing these goals. The four cases I have examined show how the League was used to accomplish Nasser's aims.

When in 1955 Iraq concluded the Baghdad Pact, Nasser saw this as a threat to his position in the Arab world. At first he tried, through personal emissaries to Baghdad, to convince the Iraqi leaders not to conclude the pact because, he argued, it would serve the interests of the West and not the Arab countries. But what in fact Nasser believed was that the pact might increase Iraq's power and influence, especially if other Arab states joined it. Nasser's initial attempts failed. He then resorted to his second tactic: an Arab League premiers' conference which was held in the Egyptian foreign ministry under his chairmanship. Aided by the League's secretary, Nasser persuaded the Arab leaders, on the surface at least, that the Baghdad Pact was contrary to the League's pact and the Arab collective security pact. Egypt effectively argued on the basis of article 10 of the security pact that 'the contracting states undertake to conclude no international agreements' contrary to the pact. Nasser succeeded, by having the Arab League adopt his policy, and through personal and diplomatic pressure, threats, public appeals, and other means, in isolating Iraq from the rest of the Arab world; this isolation contributed to the overthrow of the monarchy in 1958 and the collapse of the Baghdad Pact. The significance of the use of the Arab League was obvious: without having an Arab League conference and without arming his arguments by interpreting to his advantage the League's and the Arab collective security pacts, Nasser undoubtedly would not have succeeded in preventing other League members from joining the Baghdad Pact, and therefore isolating Iraq from the rest of the Arab world. His use of the Arab League in 1955 and the overthrow of the Iraqi monarchy enhanced both Nasser's dominance in the Arab League and the weakening of his traditional adversaries, the Hashemite kingdoms.

In the second case, Lebanon requested an urgent meeting of the Security Council to consider the Lebanese crisis which resulted, Beirut alleged, from Nasser's meddling in Lebanese internal affairs. But Egypt objected to Lebanon's resort to the Security Council and manœuvred to keep the Lebanese complaint confined to the Arab League, where it could quietly and effectively deal with Lebanon as it pleased. Egypt charged that Lebanon's efforts to bypass the regional organization were a violation of article 52 paragraph 2 of the UN charter. Inspired by strong Egyptian opposition to Lebanon's resort to the Security Council, the Arab League secretary-general succeeded in having the Security Council postpone its consideration of the case until the League had first dealt with it. After six sessions of the League council, Egypt pressed for, and the League council adopted, a very broad resolution which avoided the heart of the Lebanese complaint. Lebanon then took its case to the Security Council and later to the General Assembly where the secretary-general of the Arab League, after intensive efforts, promoted the League's schemes. In doing so, he was working in line with Egyptian foreign policy. He pressed for the Arab delegations' support of a League resolution which they unanimously approved. The Arab League then successfully urged the General Assembly to adopt the League's resolution which was broad and acceptable to Egypt. Lebanon too, frustrated by the secretary-general and by Egypt's manœuvres, accepted the League's resolution. Thus Egypt at first successfully prevented the League from addressing the heart of the Lebanese crisis at the Benghazi League council meeting and then effectively used the League's secretary-general who won the support of the General Assembly for an Arab League resolution which was consistent with Nasser's foreign policy.

A third episode in which Egypt's predominance in the Arab League paid off was in the Syrian case. Damascus, after submitting evidence in support of its claims against President Nasser, requested the League 'to take firm measures' against 'the rulers of Cairo'. Egypt countered no less aggressively and demanded — and the council adopted — a resolution that omitted from the minutes of the meeting all offensive remarks — clearly referring to Syrian remarks about Nasser. Moreover, under pressure from Egypt, the council, to the dismay of Syria, agreed on a draft resolution which, as in the Lebanese case, failed to address the substance of the Syrian grievances. Egypt wanted the council to go even further and condemn the 'rulers of Damascus' and threatened that unless the League did so Egypt would 'withdraw from the League of Arab States'. The League's secretary tried helplessly to moderate the Syrian position and he promoted Nasser's view that an Egyptian walkout from the League would mean at best the paralysing of the functions of the regional machinery. Cairo's threat included the withholding of the substantial Egyptian financial share of the League's budget. Egypt indeed could, at that time, 'freeze' the operations of the League, and this the members certainly wanted to avoid. To appease Nasser, the Shtoura council meeting rejected the Syrian requests. Not heeding the Syrian warning of Egyptian domination of the League, the council acquiesced in Nasser's views that the League would have no value without Egypt. Two weeks after the Shtoura episode, the League council reappointed Abdel-Khaliq Hassouna as secretary-general of the League as a gesture of 'appeasement' of Nasser. The Egyptian president did not return to 'active participation' in the League until a new pro-Cairo Syrian regime withdrew its complaint against Cairo. Thus Egypt not only used its predominance in the League to block any League Council resolution that Egypt regarded as contrary to its foreign policy goals, but it also threatened to 'freeze' the League, a threat that led to various Arab attempts, including those of the League's secretary-general, to secure Cairo's return to the League.

In the first case we have seen that Egypt successfully used the Arab League conference and the interpretations of the League's pact and the Arab collective security pact to its advantage to isolate Iraq and win Arab support for Egypt's stand in the Arab world. In the case of Lebanon, Egypt succeeded, through the League's council and secretary-general, in preventing Lebanon from winning Arab League or UN support for its claims against Egypt. In the case of Syria, Nasser shrewdly threatened to destroy the Arab League if the League addressed the heart of the Syrian complaint, and he eventually won his way in the League. In the final case, however, Nasser attempted to use the League to his advantage, but, largely due to Saudi perseverance, the League proved to be impotent in the Yemeni case. Although he scored a significant victory in early 1963 when the League, due to Egypt's pressure, recognized the republican regime as the legal representative of Yemen, Nasser was unable to score a swift victory in Yemen. His losses in men and money soon became unbearable. When non-Arab efforts (the USA and UN) proved unsuccessful in resolving the dispute, Nasser once again tried the Arab League. He supported, and perhaps, initiated the mission of the League led by the secretary-general which visited the concerned parties, principally Saudi Arabia. He knew that the mission would try to sell the Egyptian policy line: mainly to push for Saudi recognition of the republicans in Yemen. In effect that was what the mission did. But Saudi leaders, particularly Faisal, were not the same as they were in the 1950s when Saudi Arabia often supported Egyptian foreign policy goals (in part because of Saudi rivalry with the Hashemites). Faisal now believed Nasser's revolutionary ideas were getting closer to his own home, which he viewed as a threat to the ruling royal family. Thus the League's mission, to Nasser's displeasure, returned to Cairo empty-handed. Shortly afterwards, and at the height of the Yemeni conflict, Nasser, using Israel's plan to divert the waters of the river Jordan as a pretext to cover his real intentions, requested the

Arab League to arrange for an Arab summit meeting so that he could meet with the parties involved in Yemen. In a short time, the League's secretary and his assistant (another Egyptian citizen) succeeded in assembling the Arab leaders at the League's headquarters in Cairo. Not unexpectedly, Yemen was a major topic at this summit and at the following two conferences. But the Arab League summit strategy failed to accomplish what Nasser hoped: an end to the Yemeni conflict. Nasser, after three League conferences, abruptly called off future Arab League summit conferences. In fact by this time, Egyptian predominance in the League was beginning to erode, a process which accelerated after Egypt led the Arab confrontation states into defeat in June 1967.

Manipulating the League

How was Nasser able to use the League for so long? There are several important factors which helped Nasser in using that regional machinery. First, the personality and charisma of Nasser himself were critical factors in Egyptian hegemony in the Arab League. Unlike some parts of the world, the Middle East is an area where personality plays a distinct, if not exaggerated, political role. It is indisputable that Nasser's charisma held great appeal for the Arab masses. Nasser, whom a prominent Iraqi poet described as 'Adeem al-Majd wal-Akhda' (Great in glory and errors),[3] was blessed by both. Nasser used these characteristics for both psychological and political reasons. He spoke the language of the people and they loved it. Egyptians in particular and Arabs in general were pleased to hear an Arab leader tell them 'Irfa' Ra'sak ya Akhi' (O brother lift your head up) after centuries of foreign rule. He convinced people that 'imperialists' wanted to get rid of him because he was for the Arabs first. People believed him and some of his charges were true. The Baghdad Pact, the Suez episode, and a host of other events strengthened this belief. He discovered that championing Arab causes was extremely popular among the Arab masses. The union with Syria, for example, came about largely as a result of the force of Nasser's personality. Until the mid 1960s, Nasser's standing was high and Arab leaders could not ignore this in their relations with Egypt. Thus, when an Egyptian case came to the Arab League, the personality factor often worked to the advantage of Egypt against the other League members.

Secondly, Egypt in Nasser's day was able to use the League because of its predominance in the League itself. The most critical and important position in the League, that of secretary-general, was consistently held by an Egyptian citizen. His top assistant and the majority of the staff of the secretariat and the League system as a whole were Egyptian citizens. The allegiance of the League's employees was officially supposed to be to the regional organization. But even if the League's staff and employees wanted to serve the Arab cause first, the Egyptian leaders' pressure would not leave them alone. Experience and the cases examined revealed that their allegiance and services were to their mother country, Egypt. In fact, as the first secretary-general once wrote, 'Egypt is first' regardless of his and others' claim to pan-Arabism. When a member state had a case in the League for consideration, the member often found that the Egyptian view prevailed over the other members. The secretary's actions in the Lebanese case is only one example of the League's employees' allegiance. As a consequence of this predominance, member states voiced doubt over the allegiance of the secretary-general and the League's other officials, and questioned their impartiality in inter-Arab affairs, especially when Egypt was involved.

Another indicator of Egyptian predominance was the substantial Egyptian budget share (until the early 1960s). Due to this factor, Egypt was able to exert heavy influence on the League's deliberations. An illustration of this was the Syrian case when Egypt threatened to withhold its budget share. As a result, the League member states simply submitted to the Egyptian pressure.

The location of the League's headquarters in Cairo gave Egypt considerable leverage in the League's policies. For example, during and after the Shtoura meeting Egypt threatened to break up that organization mainly because it was largely located in the Egyptian capital. Due to these factors, the regional machinery as a whole lost the trust and confidence of member states, and Egypt was often left in that system to act as it pleased.

A third factor which worked to Egypt's advantage was the polarization within the League system itself. Inter-Arab rivalries were skilfully manipulated and exploited by Nasser. For example, until 1956, the Arab League was an arena of balance of power politics due to Arab rivalries. The balance on many occasions was tipped in favour of Egypt. Until then, the League was dominated by two opposing groups: Saudi Arabia, Yemen, and Egypt on one side, the

Hashemite states (Iraq and Jordan) on the other. Majorities were obtained through the votes of Syria and Lebanon. After the 1958 Iraqi revolution there was a realignment which pitted Saudi Arabia against Egypt, as seen in the Yemeni case. Through skilful manœuvres (which included at times threats) Egypt managed to tip the balance in its favour. Egypt led the fight for the League's strong condemnation of, for example, Western-inspired pacts, not only because it regarded them as 'imperialist' plots and designs on the Arab countries, but precisely because Nasser believed they involved other Arab rivals whom he viewed as a threat to his power in the Arab world. For Nasser, the campaign inside (and outside) the Arab League was, in reality, a power struggle, not only against the West, but more importantly against Arab rivals.[4]

Fourth, Egypt exploited anti-Western sentiments which Cairo used to win its fight in the Arab League. Nasser in almost every speech would urge Arabs not to trust Western countries' policies. He constantly reminded Arabs that their miseries and difficulties happened as a result of Western rule over the Arab countries. Nasser insisted that the Arabs, even under Ottoman rule, were one nation until ' "el-Isti'mar" came and divided us to make the Arabs weaker and thus easy to rule and exploit'. The Arabs, the people as well as their leaders, could not contradict what Nasser was saying.

Fifth, Egypt also exploited anti-Israeli feelings which were closely tied to anti-Western sentiments. Since the creation of Israel in their midst, Arabs saw it as a tool of 'Western imperialism' and an offence to their pride. Nasser manipulated this issue of Palestine because of the intense emotionalism attached to it, and the Arab masses supported Nasser, particularly when he spoke of the day of the liberation of Palestine and of other Arab areas dominated by colonialism. To exploit this feeling, Nasser tried to dissuade any League member states from joining the Baghdad Pact. He forcefully argued that the 'ally of Britain is an ally of Israel.' When his contacts with Arab leaders failed, he would go to the public directly through the 'Voice of the Arabs'.

Sixth, Nasser used the issue of pan-Arabism, to which the Arab masses attached great sentimental significance, to enhance Egypt's influence in the Arab League. It was a popular banner and Nasser became its symbol. Since the Arab people see the Arab League as a symbol of Arab unity and since Nasser was the champion of this unity, then, it was felt by the Arab masses, and advanced by the Egyptian propaganda machine, that no League member state should oppose Nasser's foreign policy goals. When the League held its extraordinary session at Benghazi, Egyptian pan-Arabist slogans outweighed the Lebanese appeal for a solution to Egyptian interference in Lebanon's internal affairs.

Comparison with Other Regional Organizations

There are several regional organizations which are viewed as dominated by the most powerful member. The Warsaw Pact and the North Atlantic Treaty Organization are major examples: the Soviet Union is the predominant power in the former and the USA is the predominant power in the latter. These two organizations were created mainly for security reasons. The regional body that most resembles the Arab League, however, is the Organization of American States (OAS) in which the USA is the dominant power. Latin American cases such as the Guatemalan crisis of 1954, the Cuban case of 1960–62, and the Dominican episode of 1965 indicated that the USA did indeed use the OAS to serve American foreign policy interests.[5]

There are similarities and differences between the role of Egypt in the Arab League and the role of the USA in the OAS. Like Egypt, the USA is the major member in the regional machinery. It is militarily the most powerful and it is also the most populous and wealthy member. These capabilities made it easier for the USA to influence other OAS members which ordinarily adopt American foreign policy recommendations without much opposition. Moreover, the USA is the largest financial contributor to the OAS, which is located in Washington, D.C. Furthermore, like Egypt, the USA often finds itself involved in inter-American quarrels and sometimes it gets its way.

However, there are significant differences between the two major members of the League and the OAS. The personality and charisma of Nasser was much more significant in inter-Arab politics than the impact of any US president, including President John F. Kennedy. Nasser's popularity and appeal to the Arab masses surpassed the appeal of any US president. In this regard, Nasser was able to exert much more pressure within the Arab world than any American leader in inter-American politics. Another important difference concerns culture and language. In the Arab League all members are, more or less, homogeneous and Arabic-speaking, which made it easier for

Nasser to address the Arabs directly; in the OAS member states are relatively heterogeneous and speak different languages. Another crucial difference between the roles of Cairo and Washington is the kind of issues involved. In the case of the Arab League the issue of pan-Arabism was the dominant one championed by the major member, Egypt. There is no equivalent broad nationalism in the Western hemisphere. The USA mainly used the OAS to fight the infiltration of extra-regional ideology, such as Communism, into Latin America. In the case of Egypt, Nasser used the Arab League to restrain competing ideologies, such as Ba'athism, within the Arab world. But perhaps the most important difference between Egypt and the USA is that the USA is a superpower, whereas Egypt is only a regional great power, perhaps the greatest regional power. But that latter designation is even contested by rivals such as Saudi Arabia, Syria and Iraq. Therefore, the Egyptian usage of the League was quite different in the sense that the OAS and the Arab League are not really comparable, and the USA and Egypt do not possess similar capabilities in using regional organizations.

On balance, although there are similarities between the use of regional organizations by Egypt and the USA, the differences are greater. In my view this specific study points to the need for further examination in order to make generalizations on the use of regional organizations by their dominant power.

Further research would be fruitful in at least two areas. First, examination of other regional organizations would add to our stock of data on how international organizations serve the interests of their major states. The case of the Organization of African Unity, for example, would provide a contrast to this study, and thereby add to our knowledge of regional organizations, because it does not seem to have only one major power. The Arab League itself in the post-Nasserist era is an example of an organization dominated by more than one power.

Second, it would be helpful to examine the relationship between the use of a regional organization by its hegemonic power and the evolution of that organization. This study has found that the main determinants of Egyptian policy toward the League were its larger national interests. When the League did not serve Egypt's interests, it was effectively paralysed. Other studies perhaps might shed light on whether the dominance of the national interests of the regional major power need paralyze the League in non-conflict areas, such as economic and social progress and constitutional developments. John

G. Stoessinger, in his review of American and Soviet involvement in the UN concluded that 'the dominant role of the national interest in the superpowers' policies in the United Nations has not been, and need not become, an insurmountable obstacle to the growth of the Organization.'[6] It would be interesting to compare this conclusion with studies of regional organizations.

Both kinds of studies — of how regional organizations are used by their powerful members, and of how they function and grow in spite of this — would be important contributions to the study of international organizations in general.

Notes to chapter eight

1   Inis L. Claude, Jr., *Swords into Plowshares: The Problems and Progress of International Organization*, New York, Random House, 4th edn, 1971, p. 105.
2   See Inis L. Claude, Jr., 'The OAS, the UN, and the United States', *International Conciliation*, no. 547 (March 1964), pp. 4–5.
3   Quoted in Lewis Awad, *The Seven Masks of Nasserism* (in Arabic), Beirut, Dar al-Qadaya, 1976, p. 10.
4   Arab rivalries go back to ancient times. For example, the feud between Egypt and Iraq over the Baghdad Pact stemmed from a historical rivalry between the people of the Nile and Mesopotamia going back many centuries.
5   For discussions of these cases see Inis L. Claude, Jr., 'The OAS, the UN, and the United States'; and Minerva M. Etzioni, *The Majority of One*, Beverly Hills, Cal., SAGE, 1970.
6   *The U.N. and the Superpowers*, New York, Random House, 2nd edn, 1970, p. 193.

Appendix A

The Pact of the League of Arab States

HIS EXCELLENCY THE PRESIDENT OF THE SYRIAN REPUBLIC;
HIS ROYAL HIGHNESS THE AMIR OF TRANS-JORDAN;
HIS MAJESTY THE KING OF IRAQ;
HIS MAJESTY THE KING OF SAUDI ARABIA;
HIS EXCELLENCY THE PRESIDENT OF THE LEBANESE REPUBLIC;
HIS MAJESTY THE KING OF EGYPT;
HIS MAJESTY THE KING OF YEMEN;

Desirous of strengthening the close relations and numerous ties which link the Arab States;

And anxious to support and stabilize these ties upon a basis of respect for the independence and sovereignty of these states, and to direct their efforts toward the common good of all the Arab countries, the improvement of their status, the security of their future, the realisation of their aspirations and hopes.

And responding to the wishes of Arab public opinion in all Arab lands;

Have agreed to conclude a Pact to that end and have appointed as their representatives the persons whose names are listed hereinafter, have agreed upon the following provisions:

Article 1 The League of Arab States is composed of the independent Arab states which have signed this Pact.

Any independent Arab state has the right to become a member of the League. If it desires to do so, it shall submit a request which will be deposited with the Permanent Secretariat General and submitted to the Council at the first meeting held after submission of the request.

Article 2   The League has as its purpose the strengthening of the relations between the member states; the coordination of their policies in order to achieve co-operation between them and to safeguard their independence and sovereignty; and a general concern with the affairs and interests of the Arab countries. It has also as its purpose the close co-operation of the member states, with due regard to the organization and circumstances of each state, on the following matters:

A   Economic and financial affairs, including commercial relations, customs, currency, and questions of agriculture and industry.

B   Communications, this includes railroads, roads, aviation, navigation, telegraphs, and posts.

C   Cultural affairs.

D   Nationality, passports, visas, execution of judgments, and extradition of criminals.

E   Social affairs.

F   Health problems.

Article 3   The League shall possess a Council composed of the representative of the member states of the League; each state shall have a single vote, irrespective of the number of its representatives.

It shall be the task of the Council to achieve the realisation of the objectives of the League and to supervise the execution of agreements which the member states have concluded on the questions enumerated in the preceding article, or on any other questions.

It likewise shall be the Council's task to decide upon the means by which the League is to co-operate with the international bodies to be created in the future in order to guarantee security and peace and regulate economic and social relations.

Article 4   For each of the questions listed in Article 2 there shall be set up a special committee in which the member states of the League shall be represented. These committees shall be charged with the task of laying down the principles and extent of co-operation. Such principles shall be formulated as draft agreements, to be presented to the Council for examination preparatory to their submission to the aforesaid states.

Representatives of the other Arab countries may take part in the work of the aforesaid committees. The Council shall determine the conditions under which these representatives may be permitted to participate and the rules governing such presentation.

Article 5   Any resort to force in order to resolve disputes arising between two or more member states of the League is prohibited. If there should arise among them a difference which does not concern a state's independence, sovereignty, or territorial integrity, and if the parties to the dispute have recourse to the Council for the settlement of this difference, the decision of the Council shall then be enforceable and obligatory.

In such a case, the states between whom the difference has arisen shall not participate in the deliberations and decisions of the Council.

The Council shall mediate in all differences which threaten to lead to war between two member states, or a member state and a third state, with a view to bringing about their reconciliation.

Decisions of arbitration and mediation shall be taken by majority vote.

Article 6   In case of aggression or threat of aggression by one state against a member state, the state which has been attacked or threatened with aggression may demand the immediate convocation of the Council.

The Council shall by unanimous decision determine the measures necessary to repulse the aggression. If the aggressor is a member state, his vote shall not be counted in determining unanimity.

If, as a result of the attack, the government of the state attacked finds itself unable to communicate with the Council, that state's representative in the Council shall have the right to request the convocation of the Council for the purpose indicated in the foregoing paragraph. In the event that this representative is unable to communicate with the Council, any member state of the League shall have the right to request the convocation of the Council.

Article 7   Unanimous decisions of the Council shall be binding upon all member states of the League; majority decisions shall be binding only upon those states which have accepted them.

In either case the decisions of the Council shall be enforced in each member state according to its respective basic laws.

Article 8   Each member state shall respect the systems of government established in the other member states and regard them as exclusive concerns of those states. Each shall pledge to abstain from any action calculated to change established systems of government.

Article 9   States of the League which desire to establish closer co-operation and stronger bonds than are provided by this Pact may conclude agreements to that end.

Treaties and agreements already concluded or to be concluded in the future between a member state and another state shall not be binding or restrictive upon other members.

Article 10   The permanent seat of the League of Arab States is established in Cairo. The Council may, however, assemble at any other place it may designate.

Article 11   The Council of the League shall convene in ordinary session twice a year, in March and in September. It shall convene in extraordinary session upon the request of two member states of the League whenever the need arises.

Article 12   The League shall have a permanent Secretariat-General which shall consist of a Secretary-General, Assistant Secretaries, and an appropriate number of officials.

The Council of the League shall appoint the Secretary-General by a majority of two-thirds of the states of the League. The Secretary-General, with the approval of the Council, shall appoint the Assistant Secretaries and the principal officials of the League.

The Council of the League shall establish an administrative regulation for the functions of the Secretariat-General and matters relating to the Staff.

The Secretary-General shall have the rank of Ambassador and the Assistant Secretaries that of Ministers Plenipotentiary. The first Secretary-General of the League is named in an Annex to this Pact.

Article 13   The Secretary-General shall prepare the draft of the budget of the League and shall submit it to the Council for approval before the beginning of each fiscal year. The Council shall fix the share of the expenses to be borne by each state of the League. This share may be reconsidered if necessary.

Article 14   The members of the Council of the League as well as the members of the committees and the officials who are to be designated in the administrative regulation shall enjoy diplomatic privileges and immunity when engaged in the exercise of their functions.

The buildings occupied by the organs of the League shall be inviolable.

Article 15   The first meeting of the Council shall be convened at the invitation of the Head of the Egyptian Government. Thereafter, it shall be convened at the invitation of the Secretary-General.

The representatives of the member states of the League shall alternately assume the presidency of the Council at each of its ordinary sessions.

Article 16   Except in cases specifically indicated in this Pact, a majority vote of the Council shall be sufficient to make enforceable decisions on the following matters:
A   Matters relating to personnel;
B   Adoption of the budget of the League;
C   Establishment of the administrative regulations for the Council, the committees, and the Secretariat-General;
D   Decisions to adjourn the sessions.

Article 17   Each member state of the League shall deposit with the Secretariat-General one copy of every treaty or agreement concluded or to be concluded in the future between itself and another member state of the League or a third state.

Article 18   If a member state contemplates withdrawal from the League, it shall inform the Council of its intention one year before such withdrawal is to go into effect.

The Council of the League may consider any state which fails to fulfill its obligations under this Pact as having become separated from the League, this to go into effect upon a unanimous decision of the states, not counting the state concerned.

Article 19   This Pact may be amended with the consent of two-thirds of the states belonging to the League, especially in order to make firmer and stronger the ties between the member states, to create an Arab Tribunal of Arbitration, and to regulate the relations of the League with any international bodies to be created in the future to guarantee security and peace.

Final action on an amendment cannot be taken prior to the session following the session in which the motion was initiated.

If a state does not accept such an amendment it may withdraw at such time as the amendment goes into effect, without being bound by the provisions of the preceding article.

Article 20   This Pact and its Annexes shall be ratified according to the basic laws in force among the High Contracting Parties.

The instruments of ratification shall be deposited with the Secretariat-General of the Council and the Pact shall become operative as regards each ratifying state fifteen days after the

Secretary-General has received the instruments of ratification from four states.

This Pact has been drawn up in Cairo in the Arabic language on this 8th day of Rabi' II, thirteen hundred and sixty-four (March 22, 1945), in one copy which shall be deposited in the safekeeping of the Secretariat-General.

An identical copy shall be delivered to each state of the League.

[Here follow the signatures.]

1 Annex Regarding Palestine

Since the termination of the last great war, the rule of the Ottoman Empire over the Arab countries, among them Palestine, which had become detached from that Empire, has come to an end. She has come to be autonomous, not subordinate to any other state.

The Treaty of Lausanne proclaimed that her future was to be settled by the parties concerned.

However, even though she was as yet unable to control her own affairs, the Covenant of the League (of Nations) in 1919 made provision for a regime based upon recognition of her independence.

Her international existence and independence in the legal sense cannot, therefore, be questioned, any more than could the independence of the other Arab countries.

Although the outward manifestations of this independence have remained obscured for reasons beyond her control, this should not be allowed to interfere with her participation in the work of the Council of the League.

The states signatory to the Pact of the Arab League are therefore of the opinion that, considering the special circumstances of Palestine and until that country can effectively exercise its independence, the Council of the League should take charge of the selection of an Arab representative from Palestine to take part in its work.

2 Annex Regarding Co-operation with Countries Which Are not Members of the Council of the League

Whereas the member states of the League will have to deal in the Council as well as in the committees with matters which will benefit and affect the Arab world at large;

And whereas the Council has to take into account the aspirations of the Arab countries which are not members of the Council and has to work toward their realisation;

Now, therefore, it particularly behoves the states signatory to the Pact of the Arab League to enjoin the Council of the League, when considering the admission of those countries to participation in the committees referred to in the Pact, that it should do its utmost to co-operate with them and furthermore, that it should spare no effort to learn their needs and understand their aspirations and hopes; and that it should work thenceforth for their best interests and the safeguarding of their future with all the political means at its disposal.

3 Annex Regarding the Appointment of a Secretary-General of the League

The states signatory to this Pact have agreed to appoint His Excellency Abdul-Rahman 'Azzam Bey, to be the Secretary-General of the League of Arab States.

This appointment is made for two years. The Council of the League shall hereafter determine the new regulations for the Secretariat-General.

Appendix B

Pact of Mutual Co-operation Between Iraq and Turkey (The Baghdad Pact)

Baghdad, 24 February 1955

Whereas the friendly and brotherly relations existing between Iraq and Turkey are in constant progress, and in order to complement the contents of the Treaty of Friendship and Good Neighbourhood concluded between His Majesty the King of Iraq and his Excellency the President of the Turkish Republic signed in Ankara on March 29, 1946, which recognised the fact that peace and security between the two countries *is* an integral part of the peace and security of all the nations of the world and in particular the nations of the Middle East, and that it is the basis for their foreign policies;

Whereas article 11 of the Treaty of Joint Defence and Economic co-operation between the Arab League States provides that no provision of that treaty shall in any way affect, or is designed to affect, any of the rights and obligations accruing to the Contracting Parties from the United Nations Charter;

And having realised the great responsibilities borne by them in their capacity as members of the United Nations concerned with the maintenance of peace and security in the Middle East region which necessitate taking the required measures in accordance with article 51 of the United Nations Charter;

They have been fully convinced of the necessity of concluding a pact fulfilling these aims, and for that purpose have appointed as their plenipotentiaries:

His Majesty King Faisal II, King of Iraq;

His Excellency Al Farik Nuri As-Said, Prime Minister;

His Excellency Burhanuddin Bash-Ayan, Acting Minister for Foreign Affairs;

His Excellency Jalal Bayar, President of the Turkish Republic;

His Excellency Adnan Menderes, Prime Minister;

His Excellency Professor Fuat Koprulu, Minister for Foreign Affairs;

who having communicated their full powers, found to be in good and due form, have agreed as follows:

Article 1   Consistent with article 51 of the United Nations Charter the High Contracting Parties will co-operate for their security and defence. Such measures as they agree to take to give effect to this co-operation may form the subject of special agreements with each other.

Article 2   In order to ensure the realisation and effect application of the co-operation provided for in article 1 above, the competent authorities of the High Contracting Parties will determine the measures to be taken as soon as the present pact enters into force. These measures will become operative as soon as they have been approved by the Governments of the High Contracting Parties.

Article 3   The High Contracting Parties undertake to refrain from any interference whatsoever in each other's internal affairs. They will settle any dispute between themselves in a peaceful way in accordance with the United Nations Charter.

Article 4   The High Contracting Parties declare that the dispositions of the present pact are not in contradiction with any of the international obligations contracted by either of them with any third State or States. They do not derogate from and cannot be interpreted as derogating from, the said international obligations. The High Contracting Parties undertake not to enter into any international obligation incompatible with the present pact.

Article 5   This pact shall be open for accession to any member of the Arab League or any other State actively concerned with the security and peace in this region and which is fully recognised by both of the High Contracting Parties. Accession shall come into force from the date of which the instrument of accession of the State concerned is deposited with the Ministry for Foreign Affairs of Iraq.

Any acceding State party to the present pact may conclude special agreements, in accordance with article 1, with one or more States parties to the present pact. The competent authority of any acceding State may determine measures in accordance with article 2. These measures will become operative as soon as they have been approved by the Governments of the parties concerned.

Article 6   A Permanent Council at ministerial level will be set up to function within the framework of the purposes of this pact when at least four Powers become parties to the pact.

The Council will draw up its own rules of procedure.

Article 7   This pact remains in force for a period of five years renewable for other five-year periods. Any Contracting Party may withdraw from the pact by notifying the other parties in writing of its desire to do so six months before the expiration of any of the above-mentioned periods, in which case the pact remains valid for the other parties.

Article 8   This pact shall be ratified by the contracting parties and ratifications shall be exchanged at Ankara as soon as possible. Thereafter it shall come into force from the date of the exchange of ratifications.

In witness whereof, the said plenipotentiaries have signed the present pact in Arabic, Turkish and English, all three texts being equally authentic except in the case of doubt when the English text shall prevail.

Done in duplicate at Baghdad this second day of Rajab 1374 Hijri corresponding to the twenty-fourth day of February, 1955.

NURI AS-SAID
For His Majesty the King of Iraq.
BURHANUDDIN BASH-AYAN
For His Majesty the King of Iraq.

ADNAN MENDERES
For the President of the Turkish Republic.
FUAT KOPRULU
For the President of the Turkish Republic.

Appendix C

Arab League Draft Resolution Concerning Lebanon's Complaint Against the United Arab Republic

4 June 1958

The Council of the League of Arab States, at its extraordinary session held in the city of Benghazi,

Having studied the complaint lodged by the Republic of Lebanon against the United Arab Republic,

Having also heard the statement made by each of the two delegations — that of the Lebanese Republic and that of the United Arab Republic,

Having further, felt the desire of each of the two parties to settle the dispute by peaceful means, within the Arab League and in pursuance of the letter and spirit of the Pact of the League of Arab States,

And being anxious to eliminate the causes and factors disturbing the cordial atmosphere among the sister Arab States,

Has resolved as follows:

First: All (activities) likely to disturb, in any way, the cordial atmosphere among States Members (of the League) should cease;

Second: The Government of the Republic of Lebanon should withdraw its complaint from the Security Council;

Third: An appeal should be addressed to the various Lebanese factions for stopping disturbances and disorders and for working towards the settlement of (their) internal conflicts by constitutional peaceful means;

Fourth: The dispatch of a commission to be appointed by the Council of the League of Arab States from amongst its own members, in order to appease sentiments and to implement the resolution of the Council.

Appendix D

UN General Assembly Resolution on Lebanon and Jordan

21 August 1958

The General Assembly,
Having considered the item 'Question considered by the Security Council at its 838th meeting on 7 August 1958',
   Noting the Charter aim that States should 'practice tolerance and live together in peace with one another as good neighbours',
Noting that the Arab States have agreed in the Pact of the League of Arab States to 'strengthen the close relations and numerous ties which link the Arab States, and to support and stabilize these ties upon a basis of respect for the independence and sovereignty of these States, and to direct their efforts toward the common good of all the Arab countries, the improvement of their status, the security of their future and the realization of their aspirations and hopes',
   Desiring to relieve international tension,

A

1   *Welcomes* the renewed assurances given by the Arab States to observe the provision of Article 8 of the Pact of the League of Arab States that 'Each Member State shall respect the systems of government established in the other Member States and regard them

as exclusive concerns of these States', and that 'Each shall pledge to abstain from any action calculated to change established systems of government';

2   *Calls upon* all Member States to act strictly in accordance with the principles of mutual respect for each other's territorial integrity and sovereignty, of non-aggression, of strict non-interference in each other's internal affairs, and of equal and mutual benefit, and to ensure that their conduct by word and deed conforms to these principles;

B

Requests the Secretary-General to make forthwith, in consultation with the Governments concerned and in accordance with the Charter, and having in mind Section A of this resolution, such practical arrangements as would adequately help in upholding the purposes and principles of the Charter in relation to Lebanon and Jordan in the present circumstances, and thereby facilitate the early withdrawal of the foreign troops from the two countries;

C

Invites the Secretary-General to continue his studies now under way and in this context to consult as appropriate with the Arab countries of the Near East with a view to possible assistance regarding an Arab development institution designed to further economic growth in these countries;

D

1   *Requests* Member States to co-operate fully in carrying out this resolution;

2   *Invites* the Secretary-General to report hereunder, as appropriate, the first such report to be made not later than 30 September 1958.

Appendix E

Provisional Constitution of the United Arab Republic

5 March 1958

PART I
The United Arab State

Article 1   The United Arab State is a democratic, independent, sovereign republic, and its people are part of the Arab Nation.

Article 2   Nationality in the United Arab Republic is defined by law. Nationality of the United Arab Republic is enjoyed by all bearers of the Syrian or Egyptian nationalities; or to those who are entitled to it by laws or statutes in force in Syria and Egypt at the time this Constitution takes effect.

PART II
Basic Constituents of the Society

Article 3   Social solidarity is the basis of society.

Article 4   National economy is organised according to plans which conform to the principles of social justice, and aim at the development of productivity and the raising of the standard of living.

Article 5   Private property is inviolable. The law organises its social function. Property may not be expropriated except for purposes of public utility and with just compensation in accordance with the law.

Article 6   Social justice is the basis of taxation and public imposts.

PART III

Public Rights and Obligations

Article 7   All citizens are equal before the law. They are equal in their public rights and obligations, without distinction of race, origin, language, religion, or creed.

Article 8   There shall be no crime or punishment except on the basis of law. Nor shall there be punishment except for acts (committed) subsequent to the promulgation of the law providing for them.

Article 9   The extradition of political refugees is prohibited.

Article 10   Public liberties are guaranteed within the limits of the law.

Article 11   Defence of the fatherland is a sacred duty, and the fulfilment of military service is an honour for citizens. Conscription is obligatory in accordance with the law.

PART IV

The System of Government

Chapter 1

Head of the State

Article 12   The Head of the State is the President of the Republic. He exercises his powers in the manner prescribed by this Constitution.

Chapter 2

The Legislature

Article 13   The legislative power is vested in an assembly named the National Assembly. The number of the members of the National Assembly and their choice are determined by a decision (qaràr) of the President of the Republic. At least half of the number of members must be members of the Syrian Chamber of Deputies and the National Assembly of Egypt.

Article 14   The National Assembly exercises control over the acts of the Executive in the manner prescribed by this Constitution.

Article 15   To be a member of the Assembly, a person must not be less than thirty years of age according to the Gregorian calendar.

Article 16   The seat of the National Assembly is Cairo. It may be convened elsewhere upon the demand of the President of the Republic.

Article 17   The President of the Republic convokes the Assembly and declares the closure of its session.

Article 18   The National Assembly shall not meet outside its session without convocation. Otherwise its meetings shall be null and void, and decisions taken by it shall be invalidated by law.

Article 19   Before admission to the exercise of their functions members of the Assembly shall take the following oath before the Assembly in public session:
'I swear in the name of Almighty God to preserve faithfully the United Arab Republic and its regime, to watch over the interests of the people and integrity of the fatherland, and to respect the Constitution and the Law'.

Article 20   The Assembly shall elect a President, and two Vice-Presidents at the first ordinary meeting.

Article 21   Meetings of the Assembly are public. Nevertheless, the Assembly can meet *in camera* upon the demand of the President of the Republic or 20 of its members. The Assembly decides thereafter whether the discussion of the question under consideration shall take place at a public or secret sitting.

Article 22   No law may be promulgated unless approved by the National Assembly. No draft law may be adopted unless a vote is taken on each of its articles separately.

Article 23   The Assembly draws up its own internal rules of procedure determining the manner in which it exercises its powers.

Article 24   Every member of the National Assembly is entitled to address to the Ministers, questions or interpellations. Interpellations may not be discussed until after at least seven days from the date of their presentation, except in the case of urgency and with the consent of the Minister concerned.

Article 25   Any twenty members of the National Assembly may ask for the discussion of a general question with a view to ascertaining the Government's policy regarding such a question and exchanging views on it.

Article 26   The National Assembly may express its wishes or proposals to the Government regarding public matters.

Article 27   No tax may be established, modified or abolished except by a law. No one may be exempted therefrom except in the cases specified by the law. None shall be liable to any other tax or duty except within the limits of the law.

Article 28   The law defines the basic rules of the collection of public revenues and the manner of their expenditure.

Article 29   The Government may not contract any loan, nor undertake any project which would entail expenditure from the State Treasury over one or more future years, except with the consent of the National Assembly.

Article 30   No monopoly may be authorized except by law and for a limited duration.

Article 31   The law fixes the fiscal year, prescribes the manner of the preparation of the budget, and its submission to the National Assembly.

Article 32   The draft of the State's General Budget must be submitted to the National Assembly for its discussion and approval at least three months before the end of the fiscal year. Each section of the Budget must be voted separately.

   The National Assembly may not introduce any amendments to the draft budget except with the approval of the government.

Article 33   Every transfer of funds from one section of the Budget to another must be approved by the National Assembly, as well as any expenditure for which no provision is made therein or exceeding the budgetary estimates.

Article 34   Independent and annexed budgets are subject to the rules relating to the General Budget.

Article 35   The law determines the rules regarding the budgets of other public institutions.

Article 36 No members of the National Assembly may, during the session, be subject to a criminal prosecution without the permission of the Assembly except in cases of *flagrante delicto*.

The Assembly must be given notification on any case where prosecution is undertaken while the Assembly is not in session.

Article 37 No member of the National Assembly may be deprived of his mandate except by a decision of a two-thirds majority of the Assembly, upon a proposal of twenty of its members, and this on the ground of loss of confidence.

Article 38 The President of the Republic has the right to dissolve the National Assembly. In this case, a new Assembly must be formed and convened within a period of sixty days from the date of dissolution.

Article 39 When the National Assembly passes a vote of no confidence in a Minister, he must resign.

A motion of no confidence concerning a Minister may not be submitted to the Assembly until after an interpellation has been addressed to him. Such a motion must be proposed by twenty members of the Assembly. No decision may be taken by the Assembly except at least three days after the date of the presentation of the motion.

Withdrawal of confidence is pronounced by the Majority of the members of the Assembly.

Article 40 A member of the National Assembly may not during his mandate, assume any other public office. The law determines the other cases of incompatibility.

Article 41 No member of the National Assembly may be appointed to the board of directors of a company during the period of his mandate except in the cases prescribed by the law.

Article 42 No member of the National Assembly may, during the period of his mandate, purchase or rent any State property; or lease or sell to the State or exchange with it any part of his property.

Article 43 Members of the National Assembly receive a remuneration determined by the law.

Chapter 3

The Executive

Article 44 The executive power is vested in the President of the

Republic, and he exercises it in the manner prescribed by the Constitution.

Article 45   The President of the Republic may not, during his term of office, exercise a liberal profession or undertake any commercial, financial or industrial activity. Nor may he purchase or rent any property belong to the State; or sell to the State or exchange with it any part of his property.

Article 46   The President of the Republic may appoint one or more Vice-Presidents, and may relieve them of their posts.

Article 47   The President of the Republic appoints the Ministers and relieves them of their functions. Ministers of State, and deputy-ministers may be appointed. Each minister supervises the affairs of his ministry, and executes the general policy drawn by the President of the Republic.

Article 48   The Vice-President, or the Minister may not, during his tenure of office, exercise a liberal profession, engage in commercial, financial or industrial activities, nor may he purchase or rent any property belonging to the State, or lease, or sell to the State or exchange with it any part of his property.

Article 49   The President of the Republic and the National Assembly have the right to bring a Minister to justice for crimes committed in the exercise of his functions. The indictment of a Minister by the National Assembly is effected by a proposal submitted by at least one-fifth of the members of the Assembly. No decision of indictment may be taken except by a majority of two-thirds of the members of the Assembly.

Article 50   The President of the Republic has the right to initiate, promulgate and object to laws.

Article 51   Should the President of the Republic object to a draft law, he shall refer it back to the National Assembly within thirty days after the date of its communication to him.

   If it is not referred back to the Assembly within this period, it shall be considered law and promulgated.

Article 52   If a draft law is referred back to the Assembly within the prescribed time, and is voted a second time by a majority of two-thirds of its members, it is considered law and promulgated.

Article 53 While the National Assembly is not in session, the President of the Republic may issue any legislation or decisions originally lying within the competence of the Assembly, should the necessity arise. Such legislation and decisions, must be submitted to the Assembly at its following meeting. If, however, the Assembly opposes them by a two-thirds majority, they are no longer effective from the day of their opposition.

Article 54 The President of the Republic issues the decisions (qaràràt) necessary for the organization of the public service departments and supervises the administration thereof.

Article 55 The President of the Republic is the supreme commander of the Armed Forces.

Article 56 The President of the Republic ratifies treaties and communicates them to the National Assembly. Such treaties will have the force of law after their ratification, sanctioning and publication in conformity with established conditions.

However, peace treaties, treaties of alliance, commercial and navigational treaties as well as all treaties entailing territorial changes or affecting the rights of sovereignty, or those involving expenditure by the Public Treasury for which no provision is made in the Budget, will not be effective unless ratified by the National Assembly.

Article 57 The President of the Republic may declare a state of emergency.

Article 58 The United Arab Republic consists of two regions: Egypt and Syria. In each there shall be an executive council appointed by a decision (qaràr) of the President of the Republic. The Executive Council has the competence to study and discuss matters pertaining to the execution of the general policy in the region.

Chapter 4

The Judiciary

Article 59 Judges are independent. They are, in the administration of justice, subject to no other authority save that of the law. No power in the State may interfere in lawsuits or in the affairs of justice.

Article 60 Judges may not be removed, and this, as provided for by law.

Article 61   The law regulates the various judicial jurisdictions and determines their competence.

Article 62   Sessions of the courts are conducted in public, unless the court decides, in the interest of public order or morality, to sit *in camera*.

PART IV

General Rules

Article 64   The city of Cairo is the capital of the United Arab Republic.

Article 65   The law determines the national flag and the regulations relative thereto.

The law also determines the State emblem and the regulations relative thereto.

Article 66   The provisions of law shall not be applicable except to what occurs after the law becomes effective and this shall have no retroactive effect. Nevertheless, provisions to the contrary may be stipulated in a law except in case of felonies with the approval of the majority of the members of the National Assembly.

Article 67   Laws are published in the Official Gazette within two weeks from the date of their promulgation, and come in force ten days thereafter. Nevertheless this time may be extended or curtailed by a special provision in the law.

PART V

Interim and Final Rules

Article 68   Everything established by legislation in force in each of the two regions of Egypt and Syria at the time this Constitution comes into effect shall remain valid within the regional spheres prescribed for them when promulgated. This legislation may, however, be repealed or amended according to the procedure prescribed in the present Constitution.

Article 69   The coming into effect of the present Constitution shall not infringe upon the provisions and clauses of the international treaties and agreements concluded between each of Syria and Egypt and foreign powers.

These treaties and agreements shall remain valid in the regional spheres for which they were intended at the time of their conclusion, according to the rules of international law.

Article 70   A special budget, alongside the State Budget, shall be drawn up and applied in each of the present regional spheres of Syria and Egypt until the coming into effect of the final measures for the introduction of a single budget.

Article 71   The organization of the public services and the administration systems existing at the time the present Constitution comes into effect shall remain in force in Syria and Egypt until their reorganization and unification by Presidential decision (qaràr).

Article 72   Citizens shall constitute a National Union to work for the realization of national aims and the intensification of the efforts for raising a sound National structure, from the political, social and economic viewpoints. The manner in which such a union is to be formed shall be defined by a decision (qaràr) of the President of the Republic.

Article 73   The present provisional Constitution shall be in force until the announcement of the people's approval of the final Constitution of the United Arab Republic.

Issued on Wednesday, March 5th, 1958.

(Signed) JAMAL 'ABD AN-NASIR

Appendix F

Part of the Address by President Gamal Abdel-Nasser at the Great Popular Rally Held in Suez on the Occasion of its National Day 22 March 1966

For 14 years we have been fighting reaction and imperialism, we have been fighting against the attempt to place us within the spheres of influence. The most outstanding fact in the world today is the intriguing of imperialism which thinks that the opportunity is ripe for it to face the national revolutionary movements especially in the underdeveloped and newly independent countries. We can see that imperialist manœuvres are taking place and this is evident in Asia and Africa. Naturally, we admit that any people have the right to change their government, even if they do so by means of a revolution. When the change, however, is prompted by foreign powers then our suspicions are aroused. All that is happening around us gives rise to suspicions. Imperialism and reaction were forever intriguing; they have paid bribes before, and went as far as to attack us. They got their fleets and armies and they attacked us but they were not successful; of course they cannot forget this. We are a free country, and we can say what we want without heeding anyone. They resent our talking, because it strengthens the other states, and because the geographical position we occupy is one of the most important in the Arab world. Our position is such that we are connected with both Asia and Africa.

If anyone wants to see the jealousy and rancour we are subject to and see the poisoned shafts directed against us, then all he has to do is to read the British newspapers for instance. They are venomous. I read them all; they are furious with us. If they were not furious they would never have been so venomous; their fury means that we are successful in our policy.

Venom and deep hatred are also disseminated by the Israeli broadcasts, the imperialist agent in the zone. There is no country in the Arab world except us, and it is not lying in ambush for any country and harbours no hatred for anything except for Egypt, the Egyptian revolution, and the Egyptian people. It keeps speaking about the Egyptian army, the Yemen, and the Egyptian army in Yemen, and it is greatly concerned with the monarchy and the Imamate in Yemen, and speaks about the Islamic pact. They say that Abdel-Nasser stood against the Islamic pact because it threatens his leadership in the zone. Naturally, it is not Israel's business.

Israel will defend the Islamic pact because we stood against it. If Israel was defending the Islamic pact and did not criticise us because we attacked the Islamic pact, then we become suspicious. As long as the enemy is insulting us, then the imperialist hatred intrigues against us here in Egypt, as well as the Zionist hatred, and the Israeli hatred. Some people, and the imperialist powers, or imperialist agents, take courage when they see that the liberation forces have suffered a setback because they consider this a blow against Abdel-Nasser. Well, anyone who has sufficient courage should try to come near us here. We say to them: 'do not follow a mirage, the imperialist forces, the Zionist forces, and the reactionary forces.' Anything that happens, the Indonesian revolution, the recent events in Indonesia are considered as a setback to Abdel-Nasser. The events of Ghana are a setback to Abdel-Nasser. Anything that happens anywhere is a setback to Abdel-Nasser. The coup d'état which happened is a setback to Abdel-Nasser. Do anything you like, but we shall expose you. We have done it before here and we can do it again outside our country. We follow the road of the revolution, the Arab revolution, which is very strong. We have here the people of the Suez, the people of Port Said, the people of the Suez battle, in which imperialism was defeated. Imperialism had already tried us. Imperialism has tried before with the support of the reactionary forces which it is endeavouring to win to its side once again.

Imperialism constituted a threat in 1956. On the day of the nationalization of the Canal on 26 July, King Faisal, Amir Abdallah, and Nuri al-Said were supping with Mr Eden; and as soon as the news reached Mr Eden, as related in the books, the cup fell from his hand, and King Faisal, Amir Abdallah, and Nuri al-Sa'id plucked up their courage and said to him, 'Here is the opportunity to do away with Abdel-Nasser.' They got up and every one of them returned to his country with a feeling of strength. Where is Eden now? Eden is gone, and the others too are gone; Nuri al-Said is gone; King Faisal is gone; and Amir Abdallah is gone.

Those reactionaries on whom colonialism depended in 1955 and 1956 were cut to pieces in the streets, or dragged along the streets, lost, or disappeared. But the people of Egypt are there, and they developed their income. The Arab people in every Arab country realized their revolution. The occupied Arab south and Aden are in a revolution. The path of the revolution shall never end for the Arab people. Today, imperialism has put forward the Islamic alliance, or the Islamic conference, after the discomfiture of the Baghdad alliance. They seem to understand, jointly with reaction, which is afraid of socialism, which has plundered the funds of the people, the exploiting oppressive reaction which is collaborating with imperialism for a new action, that they might succeed in this new action, and so they come out with this new tune of the Islamic alliance or the Islamic conference.

But I say that the Islamic alliance or conference is dead before it is born, because those who uphold it are two: the Shah of Iran, and we all know that he is the agent of imperialism and Zionism, and Bourguiba who is another agent of imperialism and Zionism. Bourguiba, who is talking today of Islam, who defied Islam in his country, is trying today to plead for Islam. Bourguiba, who brought out a justification for not fasting in Ramadan, and cancelled the Bairam holiday reducing it to a single day, donned a turban today and proclaimed himself Sheikh Bourguiba in the Islamic alliance.

Brethren, imperialism imagined that certain circumstances in the Arab homeland are propitious to it. But this is only an optical illusion. The reactionary forces will not return to dominate in the Arab world. When it started to move, it occurred to it that it held a bridle in its hand. Any movement based on confusion is doomed to failure. Reaction in the Arab world must fall; it is struggling against socialism, against justice and sufficiency; it is struggling under the name of religion. But religion does not sponsor exploitation or oppression. Religion proclaims equality, religion instructs that Muslims' fortunes be for Muslims; whereas reaction claims that the Muslims' fortunes should go for Muslim kings.

Religion says that the Muslims' funds are for the people not for the kings. Socialism goes with religion. Islam is a faith in which the Muslim people believe. Yet reaction is attempting to hide behind Islam, imperialism assisting it in assuming this pretence, just like the Muslim Brothers who are agents of imperialism, and who hid behind Islam; while in fact they received bribes from the Baghdad Pact and from Saudi Arabia. They sold themselves to the highest bidder. But the Arab world is very conscious, and the Arab people are a revolutionary people, and reaction cannot deceive them, however much it masks itself behind Islam, because the people comprehend this message and from where it emanates. If reaction proclaims a message under the name of religion, everyone knows that reaction exploits the efforts of the people; that it enslaves the workmen; that it has kept the people under exploitation and deprived them of their right to life and to dignity. Reaction has never been a doctrine of God; but God's doctrine was that of justice. The doctrine of justice, brethren, is socialism, which prevents the domination of one class over another class and decrees that Muslim kings should not steal the money of Muslims. Socialism is sufficiency and justice, but reaction is exploitation and oppression. Islam does not acquiesce in exploitation, nor in oppression. The doctrine of reaction is against Islam and against religion, however much they feign religion. It is a violation of the religion of God. You look to the first days of Islam, what did the Prophet Muhammad possess? Yet when we look today to the reactionist kings and ask ourselves what they possess, and we look to Abu Bakr and to Omar, these represent true Islam. Are these the fortunes of those kings or the fortunes of Muslims? Reaction is pillaging the fortunes of Muslims and is covering itself with the name of religion. By doing so, they have broken off from the religion of God, because they see that socialism is a doctrine of justice, a doctrine of God, against exploitation and against oppression; they speak of religion and of faith.

But what has religion or faith got to do with the Muslims' money? What role have these in the usurpation of the money of Muslims, the enslavement of Muslims, and their exploitation? Today, reaction plunders the money of Muslims, exploits and enslaves them. If reaction really wanted to prove to the world that it abides by religion, let every one concede his fortunes to the Muslim people. This is God's law, and the law of justice. Let each one cede his plunder and his pillage. The fortunes of Muslims are located in the palaces, in the jewels, in the banks of Switzerland and of Europe; the funds are swallowed up. It is not a matter of religion or of faith, but it is a question of people's rights, of Muslims' rights. They misrepresent the case and say that it is one of Islam and of infidelity to it. They say that there are spiritual cases and material cases. The people are now quite conscious and understanding. They are not dupes, but thinkers. In all Arab countries the Arab people have become aware, the revolution has succeeded here in Egypt in rescuing us from occupation and colonialism; and we have got rid of capitalism and its oppression. Yet, you come and say now that the case is one of Islam and of faithlessness, and we say to you that you are the infidels who plundered the people's money and filled your bellies with it and now assume the pretence of Islam. But the people can never be deceived.

Islam is justice. It means that we should give to Muslims what is due to them, not that we pillage the fortunes of Muslims. You speak of the lack of faith, and we repeat that you are the infidels, the thieves, and the plunderers. It is you who usurped the rights of Muslims; and you come up today and speak of spiritual principles and of faithlessness. But to whom do you say this? The Arab people in every Arab country are in a revolution. They have dragged along the streets Nuri al-Said, King Faisal, and Amir Abdallah; and they did so because they are in a revolution; and they saw who pillaged the Muslims' money and Arabs' money; who are the agents of imperialism; who sold them to imperialism; who bartered with them; they remained silent and mute till they got the chance, and till the day of promise arrived and they got out in the streets, holding the chains, and killing and massacring. Reaction shall never safely escape from the revolution of the people.

If reaction thinks that the revolutionary movements will suffer relapse, we say to it that it is dreaming. The Arab revolution is marching, with liberty, equality, and justice for its goal; it is an Arab revolution, carried out by Muslims and non-Muslims in the Arab world. But is there any one of the reactionaries who recognizes that his religion forbids him to plunder Muslims' money? Or does he know that this religion commands him to observe equality and parity of opportunities. Why did not the Prophet Muhammad proclaim himself king? Why did he not plunder Muslims' money? If this is Islam, our Prophet Muhammad gave us the example. He was the leader of Muslims, and their apostle but he had no wealth; and he once gave his dress in charity. Yet you come today and speak of Islam and of faithlessness. You are the unfaithful; we unmask you, and we continue to expose you until we lay you utterly bare.

Brethren,

There is no doubt that the revolutionary force in the Arab world was taken by surprise in the last few years by worries and problems. The revolutionary force, however, instigated by its honesty during this stage and in these circumstances, defined the steps it was to follow, and it imposed upon its development several ties such as the unified Arab world circumstances, and we find that the subject of controversy in the Arab world now concerns the summit conferences and whether they are worthwhile or not.

You say that Gamal involved us in the summit conferences and caused the revolutionary forces to be silent or quiet. Is it worthwhile or not? They say that the unified Arab world has not yet been realized, they ask if it is worthwhile to proceed in the hope of achieving something, in the hope that he who erred may repent. We hope that there is really a unity of goal for the sake of Palestine. However, when one sees the reactionary movements, one asks how I can risk entering into the Palestine battle with these people when each one of them holds a knife ready and they look upon us as socialists and they want to cut our throats.

It is true that the reactionary forces in the Arab world are afraid of the Arab progressive forces and the Arab revolutionary forces more than they are afraid of the common enemy — Israel. They gather against the Arab revolution and Arab progress all the forces and all the money that could have been gathered for liberation. I say that there is still hope, but if the Arab reactionary forces continue their actions, a decision must be taken for the upsurge of the forces of the Arab revolution for unified Arab work, and we will proceed in the unified revolutionary work. If matters continue as they are at present, it is we who have asked for the unification of the Arab states.

We thought of gathering the Arab countries. After we gathered them and convened, Bourguiba appeared in his true light as an agent of imperialism and Zionism, and the question of reconciliation with Israel came out. Now emerged the question of the Islamic conference or the Islamic pact. Even when the heads of governments convened last week, they discussed everything except the points which matter to the Arabs. No one said a word about the Islamic conference. They did not discuss the Islamic conference, despite the fact that this subject occupies everybody's mind; no one tried to talk of Yemen and what is going on there.

Each one wants to escape and to withdraw. With the reactionary attack and the reactionary grouping, the revolutionary powers should surge forward. I declare that we are about to take a decision on this matter if the reactionary grouping and the reactionary alliance with imperialism remain in the area, otherwise the work for Palestine will be of no avail so long as the reactionary powers are gathering forces against the progressive revolutionary powers and are working against them.

We cannot think of entering the battle of Palestine side by side with the reactionary powers because these would manage to beat the progressive powers if they got involved in a battle against Israel and imperialism which supports Israel. What I want to say is that when we called for the Arab summit conference and for the unity of the Arab action, we thought that there would be goodwill for the unified Arab action, a gathering of all our efforts for the sake of Palestine, and that there would be co-existence among the different Arab regimes for the sake of the Palestine cause. The revolutionary and progressive forces in the Arab world instigated by their honesty to the present stage and circumstances have defined their footsteps for themselves and laid a number of restrictions upon their revolutionary process.

Reaction in the Arab world has exploited the good faith of the revolutionary powers and allied itself to imperialism to destroy the progressive powers in the Arab world. Therefore, if this is allowed to go on, the ultimate result will be a return to the state we were in before the policy of unified Arab action and of summit conferences.

Nevertheless, till this moment we hope that the powers of reaction allied to imperialism will behave with some sense of responsibility — although this is too much to expect — and unite their efforts with regard to the Palestine cause. We have exerted every effort and shut our eyes to every dispute, but reaction is working in all fields in co-operation with imperialism. It is therefore the duty of the progressive and revolutionary powers everywhere in the Arab world to unite and face the alliance between reaction and imperialism. Here in our own country we are today mobilizing our efforts to face the movements of reaction and imperialism in the Arab world. We have to do so and we are sure of ourselves and of our ability. There is one more point I want to talk about, namely our duty in the role imposed upon us by our Arabism and Arab solidarity, the role of defending the Yemeni revolution. Arab struggle has imposed upon us this duty. We have sent armed forces to Algeria, Iraq, and the Yemen, and we shall not hesitate to do so at any time to put into effect the principles we uphold. The Yemen revolution has been faced with conspiracies from imperialism and reaction, and it is a known fact that when the Yemeni revolution took place, Saudi Arabia summoned the uncle of Imam Badr, brought him to the borders, let him enter Saudi Arabia, and gave him arms and money. They started giving money to the tribes, and battles took place, so we sent our armed forces which after a great effort managed to win all the battles they fought and control every region of the Yemen. They have not hesitated to sacrifice the dearest thing they possess. We have sacrificed our lives for the sake of the Yemeni revolution till last summer, and we said then that the situation would lead to a clash with Saudi Arabia. On this basis, we called for peace and I went to Saudi Arabia and we reached the Jiddah agreement. As I have told you, when I went to Jiddah to offer peace I did not at all go to ask them for peace. There was never a question of surrender; we are a strong people and we are patient. We can wait not only one year but five or six years if necessary. However, the Jiddah agreement has not been implemented in the way we had imagined it would be implemented today. Are we going to abandon the Yemeni revolution? Maybe our brethren in Saudi Arabia imagine that we shall tire, that the Egyptian people are grumbling about the Yemeni operation, that we shall tell them good-bye, pack our kit and go, thus letting them have their own way. This is not the way it is going to be. We shall not leave the Yemen till it can stand on its own feet and defend itself against the conspiracies of imperialism and reaction. We shall assist the Yemeni revolution. We are today revising our plans so that we may stay in the Yemen five years or longer if necessary. We shall reduce our forces and our expenditure in the Yemen, but we shall not leave the posts which are of importance. We have actually left some regions such as the Jauf, and we shall adopt a new strategy in the Yemen, the strategy of the long term, the strategy of remaining in the Yemen a long time till the Yemen army can stand on its feet and the Yemeni revolution is able to defend itself.

This is our new plan in the Yemen. Are we going to surrender to Faisal or are we going to stay in the Yemen 10 years? I am saying that we shall stay 20 years and anyone who interferes in the Yemen shall get a hiding from us. This should be quite clear. We are not going to let the bases of aggression alone. We shall strike at them. If anyone crosses into the Yemen with arms from the bases of aggression we shall strike at them.

Brethren, I end my speech by saying that we are, at present, engaged in building our country and bringing about a comprehensive Arab revolution. We are ready to sacrifice what is dear to us. Every one of us is responsible for his country. Everyone is a politician who defends the revolution. Every one of us, indeed every Arab is a defender of the Arab revolution. Thus will the Arab revolution be able to succeed and defeat reaction, imperialism, and the agents of imperialism.

May God grant us success and may His peace be upon you.

Selected Bibliography

Documents

Arab Information Center, New York, 'The Arab League: Its Origin, Purposes, Structure and Activities', 1955.

Documents of the Syrian Complaint against the Nasserist intervention in the Syrian Affair, Shtura (Lebanon) August 22nd–30th, 1962.

Iraq, Embassy, Great Britain, *Iraqi Official Statements of Policy on Internal, Arab, and Foreign Affairs*, London; Office of the Press Attache, Embassy of the Republic of Iraq, 1965.

Iraq, Ministry of Information, *The Unity Agreement Between the United Arab Republic and the Republic of Iraq;* Baghdad, Ministry of Information, 1964.

Joint Defense and Economic Co-operation Treaty Between the States of the Arab League.

League of Arab States: Agreements and Conventions Concluded between Member States within the Framework of the Arab League, n. p., 1955.

League of Arab States, The General-Secretariat, Budgets 1953–1976.

Minutes of the Council of the League of Arab States:

    Extraordinary session at Benghazi, June 1958.

    Extraordinary session at Shtoura, August 1962.

    38th ordinary session, March 1963.

    40th ordinary session, October 1963.

Minutes of the Unity Talks, March–April 1963, Cairo: Moasasat al-Ahram, 1963.

Nasser, Gamal Abdel, *On non-Alignment*, Cairo: Information Administration, 1966.

—, *For the Sake of Truth and For History*, Cairo: Information Administration, 1966.

Pact of the League of Arab States.

President Gamal Abdel Nasser's Statement On the Separatist Rebels in Damascus, Cairo: al-Dar al-Qawmiyyah lil-Nasher, 1961.

Reports of the League Secretary-General to the League Council:
10th–18th ordinary session, March 1949–March 1953.
29th ordinary session, March 1958.
30th ordinary session, October 1958.
39th ordinary session, March 1963.
41st ordinary session, March 1964.
42nd ordinary session, September 1964.
44th ordinary session, September 1965.
46th ordinary session, September 1966.
48th ordinary session, September 1967.

Summit Meetings of Arab Heads of State and Government Resolutions, Cairo, 1964; Alexandria, 1964; Casablanca, 1965; Khartoum, 1967.

United Arab Republic, Bureau of Information, *President Gamal Abdel-Nasser, Efforts Towards World Peace*, Cairo: Information Administration, 1966.

United Nations Documents

General Assembly Official Records, third emergency special session, August 1958.

Security Council Official Records:
13th year, February, May, June, July 1958.
18th year, May, June 1963.

Memoirs

Abdel-Latif al-Baghdadi Memoire, parts I and II, Cairo, Alexandria, al-Maktab al-Misri al-Hadith, 1977.

Abdel-Rahman Azzam Memoire, part I, Cairo, al-Maktab al-Misri al-Hadith, 1977.

Al-Ahram, 'Memoire of an Informed Arab Official', 1977–79 (Anonymous).

King Abdallah Ibn al-Hussein Memoire, Beirut, n. p., 1965.

October (Cairo), 'From President el-Sadat Papers', 1977–78.

Speeches and Statements

The Center of Political and Strategic Studies of al-Ahram (Cairo), *Abdel-Nasser's Documents, 1967–1970*, two volumes.
'Exchange of Letters between King Hussein of Jordan and President Gamal Abdel-Nasser of U.A.R.', *Middle East Affairs*, vol. 12, no. 5 (May 1961).
Maslahat al-Isti'lamat, *Arab Political Encyclopedia Documents and Notes*, Cairo, Documentation Research Center, Information Bureau, 1952–67.
President Gamal Abdel-Nasser Speeches and Press Interviews, Cairo, Information Bureau, six volumes.
Wizarat al-Kharijiyah, Egypt, *White Paper on the Nationalization of the Suez Maritime Canal Company*, Cairo, Government Press, 1956.

Books

Abboushi, W.F., *Political Systems of the Middle East in the 20th Century*, New York, Dodd, Mead, 1970.
Abdallah, Muhamad Anwar, *The Return of the Heroes From Yemen* (in Arabic), Cairo, al-Dar al-Qawmiyyah, 1963.
Abdel-Fadil, Mahmoud, *The Political Economy of Nasserism: A Study in Employment and Income Distribution Policies in Urban Egypt, 1952–1972*, London, Cambridge University Press, 1981.
Abdel-Malek, Anwar, *Egypt: Military Society: The Army Regime, the Left, and Social Change under Nasser*, New York, Random House, 1968.
Abdel-Nasser, Gamal, *The Philosophy of Revolution*, Washington, D.C., Public Affairs Press, 1955.
Abdel-Rahman, Asaad, *Nasserism*, (in Arabic), Beirut, Moasasat al-Abhath al-Arabiyyeh, 1981.
Abu Izzeddin, Najla M., *Nasser of the Arabs*, London, Third World Centre for Research and Pub., 1981.
Abu-'Ouf, Ahmad Shafiq, *The Eternal Principles and Teachings of Gamal Abdel-Nasser* (in Arabic), Cairo, Matba'at al-Amin, 1970.
Adams, Charles Clarence, *Islam and Modernism in Egypt*, New York, Russell and Russell, 1968.
Agwani, M. S., *The Lebanese Crisis 1958: A Documentary Study*, New York, Asia Publishing House, 1965.
Ajami, Fouad, *The Arab Predicament: Arab Political Thought and Practice Since 1967*, London, Cambridge University Press, 1981.
Ali, Ahmad Farid, *The Arab League Between the Reactionary Forces and the Popular Forces* (in Arabic), Cairo, al-Mu'assasah al-Misriyyah al-'Amah, 1972.

Amarah, Mohamed, *The Arab Nation and the Issue of Unity* (in Arabic), Beirut, Dar al-Wihdah, 1981.

Anis, Mohamed, *The Burning of Cairo* (in Arabic), Beirut, al-Moasasah al-Arabiyyah lil-Nashr, 1972.

Ansari, Mohammad Iqbal, *The Arab League, 1945–1955*, Aligarch Muslim University, Institute of Islamic Studies, 1968.

Ashur, Sa'id abdel-Fattah, *A People's Revolution* (in Arabic), Cairo, Dar al-Nahdah, 1964.

Atta, Abdel-Khabir, *The League of Arab States' Communication Function*, Cairo, Mahad al-Bihouth wal-Dirasat al-Arabiyyeh, 1977.

Awad, Lewis, *The Seven Masks of Nasserism* (in Arabic), Beirut, Dar al-Qadaya, 1976.

Awdah, Awdah Butrus, *Abdel-Nasser and World Imperialism*, Beirut, Dar-al-Wihdah, 1975.

Badawi, Muhamad Taha and M. H. Mustafa, *The July Revolution, its Historical Roots and Political Philosophy* (in Arabic), Alexandria, al-Maktab al-Misri, 1966.

Bairis, Dia al-Din, *The July Revolution Secrets* (in Arabic), Cairo, Matba'at al-Ma'rifah, 1976.

—, *Gamal Abdel-Nasser's Personal Secrets* (in Arabic), Cairo, al-Sharikah al-Misriyyah lil-Tiba'ah wal-Nashr, 1976.

Baker, Raymond William, *Egypt's Uncertain Revolution Under Nasser and Sadat*, Cambridge, Mass., Harvard University Press, 1978.

Barrawi, Rashid, *The Military Coup in Egypt*, Westport, Conn., Hyperion Press, 1981.

al-Barudi, Ali, *On Arab Socialism* (in Arabic), Alexandria, Mansha'at al-Ma'arif, 1967.

Bashir, al-Shafi'i Muhamad, *The Theory of Union between States and its Application among the Arab States* (in Arabic), Alexandria, Mansha'at al-Ma'arif, 1963.

Bell, Harold Idris, *Egypt, from Alexander the Great to the Arab Conquest*, Westport, Conn., Greenwood Press, 1977.

Berindranath, Dewan, *Nasser*, New Delhi, Afro-Asian Publications, 1966.

—, *Iraq, the land of Arab resurgence*, New Delhi, Press Asia International, 1979.

Berque, Jacques, *Egypt: Imperialism and Revolution*, transl. from the French by Jean Stewart, New York, Praeger, 1977.

Binder, Leonard, 'Egypt's Positive Neutrality', in M. A. Kaplan, (ed.), *The Revolution in World Politics*, New York, John Wiley and Sons, 1962.

—, *The Ideological Revolution in the Middle East*, New York, John Wiley and Sons, 1964.

—, (ed.) *Politics in Lebanon*, New York, John Wiley and Sons, 1966.

Boutros-Ghali, Boutros Y., 'The Foreign Policy of Egypt', in Joseph E. Black and Kenneth W. Thompson (eds) *Foreign Policy in a World of Change*, New York, Harper and Row, 1963.

—, *The League of Arab States and the Settlement of Regional Disputes* (in Arabic), Cairo, Dar al-Tiba'ah al-Hadithah, 1977.

Burrell, Robert Michael, *Egypt, the Dilemmas of Nation, 1970–1977*, Beverly Hills, Calif., Sage Publications, 1977.

Churchill, Randolph S., *The Rise and Fall of Sir Anthony Eden*, New York, G. P. Putnam's Sons, 1959.

Claude, Inis L., Jr., *Swords into Plowshares*, New York, Random House, 4th edn, 1971.

Cooper, Mark N., *The Transformation of Egypt*, Baltimore, Johns Hopkins Press, 1982.

Copeland, Miles, *The Game of Nations*, London, Weidenfeld and Nicolson, 1969.

Cremeans, Charles D., *The Arabs and the World: Nasser's Arab Nationalist Policy*, New York, Praeger, 1963.

Dann, Uriel, *Iraq Under Qassem*, New York, Praeger, 1969.

Darwin, John, *British, Egypt, and the Middle East*, New York, St. Martin's Press, 1981.

Dawisha, A.I., *Syria and the Lebanese Crisis*, New York, St. Martin's Press, 1980.

—, *Egypt in the Arab World*, London, Macmillan Press, 1976.

el-Dawlih, Ismat Saif, *The Parties and the Problem of Democracy in Egypt* (in Arabic), Beirut, Dar al-Maseerah, 1977.

Deeb, Marius, *Party Politics in Egypt*, London, Ithaca Press for the Middle East Centre, St. Anthony's College, Oxford, 1979.

DeKmejian, R. Hrair, *Egypt under Nasser*, Albany, N.Y., State University of New York Press, 1971.

Dessouki, Ali E. Hillal, *Democracy in Egypt*, Cairo, American University in Cairo, 1978.

DuBois, Shirley Graham, *Gamal Abdel-Nasser, Son of the Nile*, New York, The Third Press, 1972.

Etzioni, Minerva M., *The Majority of One*, Beverly Hills, Cal., Sage Publications, 1970.

Faddah, Mohammad Ibrahim, *The Middle East in Transition: A Study of Jordan's Foreign Policy*, New York, Asia Publishing House, 1974.

Farah, Ilyas, *Arab Revolutionary Thought in the Face of Current Challenges* (in Arabic) S.n., Arab Bath Socialist Party, 1978.

al-Farid, Abdul Meguid, *From the Minutes of Nasser's Arab and International Meetings* (in Arabic), Beirut, Moasasat al-Dirasat al-Arabiyyah, 1979.

Flower, Raymond, *Napoleon to Nasser: The Story of Modern Egypt*, London, Stacey, 1973.

Foda, Ezzeldin, *The Projected Arab Court of Justice*, The Hague, Martinus Nijhoff, 1957.

Ghali, Kamal, *The Pact of the League of Arab States* (in Arabic), Cairo, Matba'at Nahdat Misr, 1948.

Ghanim, Muhamad Hafiz, *Lectures on the League of Arab States* (in Arabic), Cairo, Institute of Higher Arabic Studies, 1960.

al-Ghazzali, Muhammad, *Our Beginning in Wisdom*, New York, Octagon Books, 1975.

al-Ghuneimi, Muhamad Tal'at, *The League of Arab States* (in Arabic), Alexandria, Minsha'at al-Ma'arif, 1974.

Gibbons, Scott, *The Conspirators*, London, Howard Baker, 1967.

Glubb, John Bagot, *Syria, Lebanon, Jordan,* London, Thames and Hudson, 1967.

Gom'a, Ahmad M., *The Foundation of the League of Arab States*, London, New York, Longman Group, 1977.

Gordon, David C., *Lebanon, the Fragmented Nation*, London, Croom Helm, 1980.

Haddad, George M., *Revolutions and Military Rule in the Middle East*, New York, Robert Speller, vol. I, 1965; vol. II, 1971; vol. III, 1973.

Hafiz, Ulwi, *My Secret Mission between Abdel-Nasser and America*, (in Arabic) Cairo, al-Maktab al-Misri al-Hadith, 1976.

Haim, Sylvia G. (ed.), *Arab Nationalism: an Anthology*, Berkeley Cal., University of California Press, 1976.

Hakim, Sami, *The League Pact and Arab Unity* (in Arabic), Cairo, al-Matba'ah al-Fanniyyah al-Hadithah, 1966.

Hammond, Paul Y. and Sidney S. Alexander (eds), *Political Dynamics in the Middle East*, New York, American Elsevier Publishing Company, 1972.

Hamroush, Ahmad, *The Story of the 23 July Revolution* (in Arabic), 3 vols. Cairo, Dar-al-Mawqif al-Arabi, n.d.

Harari, Maurice, *Government and Politics of the Middle East*, Englewood Cliffs, N.J., Prentice-Hall, 1962.

Hashshad, Adli *The Failure of Separation* (in Arabic), Cairo, al-Dar al-Qawmiyyah lil-Nashr, 1963.

Hassouna, Hussein, A., *The League of Arab States and Regional Disputes*, Dobbs Ferry, N.Y., Oceana; Leiden, Sithoff, 1975.

Heikal, Mohamed, *The Cairo Documents: The Inside Story of Nasser and his Relationship with World Leaders, Rebels and Statesmen*, Garden City, New York, Doubleday, 1973.

—, *What Happened in Syria* (in Arabic), Cairo, al-Dar al-Qawmiyyah lil-Tiba'ah wal-Nashr, 1962.

—, *For Egypt, Not for Abdel-Nasser* (in Arabic), s.n., Dar al-Siyasseh, 1976.

—, *The Road to Ramdan*, New York, Quandrangle, 1975.

—, *The Story of Suez* (in Arabic), Beirut, Sharikat al-Matbouat lil-Nashr, 1982.

—, *Autumn of Fury*, London, André Deutsch, 1983.

Hiro, Dilip, *Inside the Middle East*, New York, McGraw Hill, 1982.

Hitti, Philip, K., *History of the Arabs from the Earliest Times to the Present*, London, Macmillan; New York, St. Martin Press, 10th edn, 1970.

Holt, Peter Malcolm, *Egypt and the Fertile Crescent, 1516–1922*, Ithaca, New York, Cornell University Press, 1966.

Hopwood, Derek, *Egypt, Politics and Society 1945–1981*, London, Allen and Unwin, 1982.

Hudson, Michael C., *Arab Politics: The Search for Legitimacy*, New Haven and London, Yale University Press, 1977.

al-Husni, Abdallah, ed., *Haradth Conference: Documents and Minutes*, Beirut, Dar al-Kitab al-Jadid, 1966.

Hussein, Mahmoud, *Class Conflict in Egypt: 1945–1970,* New York, Monthly Review Press, 1973.

Ibrahim, Saad Eddin, ed., *Egypt in a Quarter of a Century* (in Arabic), Beirut, Mahad al-Inma al-Arabi, 1981.

Imam, Abdallah, *Abdel-Nasser's Record* (in Arabic), Cairo, al-Markaz al-Thaqafi al-Jam'i, 1978.

—, *Nasserism, a Documented Study of Nasserite Thought* (in Arabic), Cairo, Dar al-Sha'b, 1971.

Ingrams, Harold, *The Yemen*, New York, Praeger, 1964.

Ismael, Tareq Y., *The U. A. R. in Africa: Egypt's Policy under Nasser*, Evanston, Ill., Northwestern University Press, 1971.

Issawi, Charles, *The Arab World's Legacy*, Princeton, N.J., Darwin Press, 1981.

Izzedin, Nejla M., *The Arab World: Past, Present and Future,* Chicago, Regnery Company, 1953.

Jankowski, James P., *Egypt's young Rebels*, Stanford, Calif., Hoover Institution Press, 1975.

al-Jindi, Anwar, *Get Out of Our Country* (in Arabic), Cairo, Dar al-Nashr al-Islamiyyah, 1946.

Kamel, Mahmoud, *Arab International Law* (in Arabic), Beirut, Dar-al 'ilm lil-Malayeen, 1965.

—, *The Great Arab State* (in Arabic), Cairo, Dar al-Ma'arif, 1967.

—, *Islam and Arabism* (in Arabic), Cairo, al Haiy'ah al-Misriyyah al-'Amah lil-Kitab, 1976.

Karpat, Kemal H., ed., *Political and Social Thought in the Contemporary Middle East*, New York, Praeger, 1982.

Kerr, Malcolm H., *The Arab Cold War, 1958–1964: A Study of Ideology and Politics*, London, Oxford University Press, 1965.

—, *The Arab Cold War: Gamal Abd al-Nasir and his Rivals, 1958–1970*, London, Oxford University Press, 1970.

—, *Egypt under Nasser*, New York, Foreign Policy Association, 1963.

Kerr, Malcolm H. and el-Sayed Yassin, eds., *Rich and Poor States in the Middle East: Egypt and the New Arab Order*, Cairo, The American University in Cairo, 1982.

Khadduri, Majid, *Political Trends in the Arab World; the Role of Ideas and Ideals in Politics*, Baltimore, Md., Johns Hopkins University Press, 1970.

—, *Arab Contemporaries: The Role of Personalities in Politics*, Baltimore, Md., Johns Hopkins University Press, 1973.

Khalid, Sharawi, *Abdel-Nasser and Nasserism* (in Arabic), Dar al-Maseerah, 1979.

Khalil, Muhammad, *The Arab States and the Arab League: a Documentary Record*, vols. I and II, Beirut, Khayats, 1962.

Kirkbride, Sir Alec, *From the Wings: Amman Memoirs 1947–1951*, London, Frank Cass, 1976.

Lacouture, Jean, *Nasser*, transl. from French by Daniel Hofstadter, New York, Knopf, 1973.

—, *The Demigods: Charismatic Leadership in the Third World*, transl. from French by Patricia Wolf, New York, Knopf; London, Secker and Warburg, 1970.

Lenczowski, George, *The Middle East in World Affairs*, Ithaca, N.Y., Cornell University Press, 1962.

Lengyel, Emil, *Egypt's Role in World Affairs*, Washington, D.C., Public Affairs Press, 1957.

Lloyd, George Ambrose, *Egypt Since Cromer*, New York, H. Fertis, 1970.

Long, David E. and Reich, Bernard, eds., *The Government and Politics of the Middle East and North Africa*, Boulder, Westview Press, 1980.

Lonides, Michael G., *Divide and Lose: The Arab Revolt of 1955–1958*, London, G. Bles, 1960.

Love, Kennett, *Suez, the Twice-Fought War*, New York, McGraw-Hill, 1969.

Mabro, Robert, *The Egyptian Economy, 1952–1972*, Oxford, Clarendon Press, 1974.

MacDonald, Robert W., *The League of Arab States: a Study in the Dynamics of Regional Organization*, Princeton, N.J., Princeton University Press, 1965.

Macro, Eric, *Yemen and the Western World, 1571–1964*, New York, Praeger, 1967.

Malone, Joseph J., *The Arab Lands of Western Asia*, Englewood Cliffs, N.J., Prentice-Hall, 1973.

Mansfield, Peter, *The British in Egypt*, New York, Holt, Rinehart and Winston, 1972.

—, *Nasser's Egypt*, Baltimore, Md., Penguin Books, 1969.

Marlowe, John, *A History of Modern Egypt and Anglo-Egyptian Relations, 1800–1956*, Hamden, Conn., Archon Books, 2nd edn, 1965.

—, *Arab Nationalism and British Imperialism*, New York, Praeger, 1961.

Maroon, Fred J., *The Egypt Story*, New York, Abbeville Press, 1979.

Matta, Mitri, *Conference of their Majesties and Excellencies Kings and Presidents of the Arab States in Lebanon, 1956*, Beirut, Jaridatt al-Balagh, 1956.

McClellan, Grant S. (ed.), *The Middle East in the Cold War*, New York, H. W. Wilson Company, 1956.

Muhyi-eddin, Khalid, et. al., *Nasserism* (in Arabic), Beirut, Dar al-Wihdah, 1981.

—, *Egypt, From Revolution to Reversionism* (in Arabic), Beirut, Dar-al-Taleah lil-Nashr, 1981

al-Munajjid, Salah Eddin, ed., *Yemen and the United Arab Republic Between Unity and Separation* (in Arabic), Beirut, Dar al-Kitab al jadid, 1962.

Murad, Mahmoud, *Who was Ruling Egypt?* (in Arabic), Cairo, Matabi' al-Ahram al-Tijariyyah, 1975.

Musa, Ahmad, *The Pact of the Arab League* (in Arabic), Cairo, Matba'at Misr, 1948.

Naguib, Muhamad, *Egypt's Destiny*, New York, Doubleday, 1955.

Nasr, Marlyn, *The Pan-Arab Vision in the Thought of Gamal Abdel-Nasser, 1952–1970* (in Arabic), Beirut, Markaz Dirasat al-Wihdah al-Arabiyyeh, 1981.

Nasr, Salah, *Abdel-Nasser and the Unity Experience* (in Arabic), Cairo, al-Watan al-Arabi, 1976.

Nawwar, Abdel-Aziz Suleiman, *Egypt and Iraq Until World War One* (in Arabic), Cairo, Maktabat al-Anglo Misriyyah, 1968.

Neff, Donald *Warriors at Suez: Eisenhower Takes America into the Middle East*, New York, Simon and Schuster, 1981.

Nofal, Sayed, *The Joint Arab Activities* (in Arabic), Cairo, Institute of Arab Studies and Research, book I, 1968; book II, 1971.

Nuseibeh, Hazem Zaki, *The Ideas of Arab Nationalism*, Ithaca, N.J., Cornell University Press, 1956.

Nutting, Anthony, *Nasser*, New York, E. P. Dutton, 1972.

—, *I Saw For Myself; the Aftermath of Suez*, Garden City, New York, Doubleday, 1958.

—, *No End of a Lesson; the Story of Suez*, New York, C. N. Potter, 1967.

O'Ballance, Edgar, *The War in Yemen*, Hamden, Conn., Archon Books, 1971.

Oudeh, Muhamad, *The Fabrication of Nasserism and the Ignorance of Marxism* (in Arabic), Cairo, Matabi' Rose el-Youssef, 1977.

Oudeh, Oudeh Boutros, *Gamal Abdel-Nasser: his Role in the Arab Struggle* (in Arabic), Cairo, al-Matba'ah al-Fanniyyah al-Hadithah, 1971.

Perlmutter, Amos, *Egypt, the Praltorian State*, New Brunswick, N.J., Transaction Books, 1974.

—, *Political Roles and Military Rulers*, Totowa, N.J., Frank Cass, 1981.

Peterson, John, *Yemen, The Search for Modern State,* Baltimore, Johns Hopkins University Press, 1982.

Petran, Tabitha, *Syria: A Modern History*, London, Ernest Benn, 1978.

Pye, Lucian W. and Sidney Verba (eds), *Political Culture and Political Development*, Princeton, N.J., Princeton University Press, 1965.

Qayyum, Shah Abdul, *Egypt Reborn*, New Delhi, S. Chand, 1973.

Radwan, Arwa, *The Political Committee of the League of Arab States* (in Arabic), Beirut, Dar al-Nahar lil-Nashr, 1973.

Rahmy, Ali Abdel-Rahman, *The Egyptian Policy in the Arab World: Intervention in Yemen, 1962–1967*, Washington D.C., University Press of America, 1983.

Ramazani, R. K., *Iran's Foreign Policy, 1941–1973: A Study of Foreign Policy in Modernizing Nations*, Charlottesville, Va., University Press of Virginia, 1975.

Razzaq, Munir, *Abdel-Nasser's Conspiracy* (in Arabic), Baghdad, Dar al-Bilad lil-Nashr, 1959.

al-Razzaz, Munif, *The Evolution of the Meaning of Nationalism*, transl. from Arabic by Ibrahim Abu-Lughod, Garden City, New York, Doubleday, 1963.

Rejwan, Nissim, *Nasserist Ideology: Its Exponents and Critics*, New York, Wiley, 1974.

Richmond, John C.B., *Egypt, 1798–1952*, New York, Columbia University Press, 1977.

Rida, Adel, *An Attempt to Understand the Yemeni Revolution* (in Arabic), Cairo, Alexandria, al-Maktab al-Misri al-Hadith lil-Tiba'ah wal-Nashr, 1974.

Rifa'i, Muhamad Ali, *The Arab League and the Liberation Causes* (in Arabic), Cairo, al-Sharikah al-Misriyyah lil-Tiba'ah wal-Nashr, 1971.

Rif'at, Kamal, *Nasserites Yes* (in Arabic), Cairo, al-Matba'ah al-'Arabiyyeh al-Hadithah, 1976.

Rousan, Mamdouh, *Iraq and the East Arab Issues* (in Arabic), Beirut, al-Moasasah al-Arabiyyeh lil-Dirasat wal-Nashr, 1979.

el-Sadat, Anwar, *Secrets of the Egyptian Revolution* (in Arabic), Cairo, al-Dar al-Qawmiyyah lil-Tiba'ah wal-Nashr, 1965.

—, *In Search of Identity*, New York, Harper and Row, 1978.

—, *Revolt on the Nile*, New York, John Day Company, 1957.

—, *O My Son this is Your Uncle Gamal* (in Arabic), Cairo, Maktabat al-'Irfan, n. d.

—, *The Full Story of the Revolution* (in Arabic), Cairo, Maktabat al-Irfan, n.d.

al-Saifi, Abdel-Fatah Mustafa, *The Arab National Society: Its Potential, Capabilities and Problems* (in Arabic), Alexandria, al-Maktab al-Misri al-Hadith, lil-Taba'ah wal-Nashr, 1969.

el-Sakit, Muhamad Abdel-Wahab, *The Secretary-General of the League of Arab States* (in Arabic), Cairo, Dar al-Fikr al-Arabi, 1974.

Salameh, Ghassan, *The Saudi Foreign Policy Since 1945* (in Arabic), Beirut, Mahad al-Inma al-Arabi, 1980.

Salibi, Kamal Suleiman, *Cross Roads to Civil War*, Delmar, N.Y., Caravan Books, 1976.

Sawant, Ankush B., *Egypt's Africa Policy*, New Delhi, National, 1981.

Sayegh, Fayez A., *Arab Unity: Hope and Fulfilment*, New York, Devin-Adair, 1958.

Sbaih, Muhamad, *Days and Days* (in Arabic), Cairo, Matba'at al-'Alam al-Arabi, 1967.

Schmidt, Dana Adams, *Yemen: the Unknown War*, New York, Holt, Rinehart and Winston, 1968.

Seale, Patrick, *The Struggle for Syria: A Study of Post-war Arab Politics, 1945–1958*, London, New York, Toronto, Oxford University Press, 1965.

al-Shahari, Mohamed Ali, *Abdel-Nasser and the Yemeni Revolution* (in Arabic), Cairo, Maktabat Madbouli, 1976.

Sharabi, Hisham, B., *Nationalism and Revolution in the Arab World*, Princeton, N.J., D. Van Nostrand, 1966.

Shazly, Saad, *The Crossing of Suez*, London, Third World Centre for Research and Publishing, 1980.

Shehab, Mufid Mahmoud, *The League of Arab States* (in Arabic), Cairo, Mahad al-Buhouth wal-Dirasat al-Arabiyyah, 1978.

al-Shuqairi, Ahmed, *The Arab League* (in Arabic), Tunis, Dar Bu Salameh lil-Nashr, 1979.

al-Shuqairi, Jamil, and Mitri Matta, *The National and International Objectives of the League of Arab States* (in Arabic), Beirut, Jaridat al-Balgh, 1953.

Sid-Ahmad, Mohamed, *After the Guns Fall Silent*, London, Croom Helm, 1976.

Simari, Muhyi, *Egypt 21st Century,* Cairo, s.n., 1980.

Stephens, Robert Henry, *Nasser: a Political Biography*, New York, Simon and Schuster, 1972.

St. John, Robert, *The Boss: The Story of Gamal Abdel-Nasser*, New York, McGraw-Hill, 1960.

al-Taah, Saad, *Egypt Between Two Periods 1952–1970, 1970–1981*, (in Arabic), Beirut, Dar al-Nidal, 1983.

Taha, Riad, *Minutes of the Unity Talks*, Beirut, s.n., 1963.

Taylor, Alan R., *The Arab Balance of Power*, Syracuse, Syracuse University Press, 1982.

Tibi, Bassam, *Arab Nationalism*, Trans. Marion Farouk-Sluglett and P. Sluglett, London, Macmillan, 1981.

The International Secretariat of the Future, London, Royal Institute of International Affairs, 1944.

Thompson, Kenneth, James Rosenau, and Gavin Boyed (eds), *World Politics*, New York, The Free Press, 1976.

Torrey, Gordon S., *Syrian Politics and the Military*, Columbus, Ohio State University, 1964.

Trevelyan, Humphrey, *Diplomatic Channels*, London, Macmillan, 1973.

al-Tubji, Ahmad Kamal, *The Arab Armed Forces in Yemen* (in Arabic), Cairo, al-Dar al Qawmiyyah lil-Nashr, 1966

Tütsch, Hans E., *Facets of Arab Nationalism*, Detroit, Wayne State University, 1965.

Uthman, Uthman Ahmad, *Pages from my Experience* (in Arabic), Cairo, al-Maktab al-Misri al-Hadith, 1981.

Vatikiotis, P. J., *The Modern History of Egypt*, New York, Praeger, 1969.

—, *Nasser and his Generation*, New York, St, Martin's Press, 1978.

Vocke, Harald, *The Lebanese War, Its Origins and Political Dimensions*, New York, St. Martin's Press, 1978.

Waterbury, John, *Egypt, Burdens of the Past, Options for the Future*, Washington and London, Indiana University Press, 1978.

—, *The Egypt of Nasser and Sadat*, Princeton, N.J., Princeton University Press, 1983.

Wenner, Manfred, *Modern Yemen, 1918–1966*, Baltimore, Md., Johns Hopkins University Press, 1967.

Wien, Jake, *Saudi-Egyptian Relations*, Santa Monica, Calif., Rand Corp., 1980.

Wynn, Wilton, *Nasser of Egypt*, Cambridge, Mass., Arlington Books, 1959.

Zabarah, Mohamed Ahmad, *Yemen, Traditionalism Vs. Modernity*, New York, Praeger, 1982.

Zaboob, Adel, *The Arab Pact* (in Arabic), Beirut, Dar al-Maseerah, 1979.

Zaqlamah, Anwar, *Great Egypt*, Cairo, Maktabat al-Anglo al-Misriyyah, 1955.

Zayid, Mahmud Y., *Egypt's Struggle for Independence*, Beirut, Khayats, 1965.

Zeine, Zeine N., *The Emergence of Arab Nationalism*, Beirut, Khayats, rev. edn, 1966.

Articles

For contemporary works (Arabic) on Pan-Arabism and President Gamal Abdel-Nasser see the numerous publications of Markaz Dirasat al-Wihdah al-Arabiyyeh (Centre for Arab Unity Studies) of Beirut which also publishes the monthly journal *al-Mustaqbal al-Arabi* (The Arab Future).

Also the League of Arab States publishes materials related to the League in its own journal, *Shóun Arabiyya* (Arab Affairs).

Abada, Fikri, 'The League of Arab States', *al-Mussawar* (Cairo), March 1964.

Abdel-Malek, Anouar, 'The Crisis in Nasser's Egypt', *New Left Review*, vol. 45 (September–October 1967).

Abdel-Nasser, Gamal, 'The Egyptian Revolution', *Foreign Affairs*, vol. 33, no. 2 (January 1955).

Abdul Aziz, Mohamed, 'The Origin and Birth of the Arab League', *Revue Egyptienne de Droit International*, vol. 11 (1955).

A. D., 'The Arab League: Development and Difficulties', *World Today*, May 1951.

Abu-Jaber, Faiz S., 'The Egyptian Revolution and Middle East Defense: 1952–1955', *Middle East Forum*, vol. 45, no. 4 (1969).

Anderson, Totton, J. 'The Arab League', *World Affairs Interpreter*, vol. 23 (autumn 1952).

'Arab Nationalism and "Nasserism",' *World Today*, vol. 14 (December 1958).

Ashford, Douglas E., 'Contradictions of Nationalism and Nation-building in the Muslim World', *Middle East Journal*, vol. 18, no. 4 (1964).

Badeau, John, 'The Revolt Against Democracy', *Journal of International Affairs*, vol. 13, no. 2 (1959).

al-Bouni, Afif, 'In the Pan-Arabism Identity', *al-Mustaqbal al-Arabi*, November 1983.

Boutros-Ghali, Boutros Y., 'The Arab League 1945–70', *Revue Egyptienne de Droit International*, vol. 25 (1969).

—, 'The Arab League 1945–1955', *International Conciliation*, no. 498 (May 1954).

—, 'The Joint Arab Activities in the Arab League' (in Arabic), *al-Siyyassah al-Dawliyyah*, (Cairo), no. 20, (April 1970).

—, 'Nasserism and Egyptian Foreign Policy' (in Arabic), *al-Siyyassah al-Dawliyyah*, (Cairo), no. 23 (January 1971).

—, 'Loss of Membership in the League of Arab States' (in Arabic), *Revue Egyptienne de Droit International*, vol. 11 (1955).

Chejne, Anwar G., 'Pan-Arabism in the Light of Recent Developments', *Islamic Literature*, vol. 10 (August–September 1958).

—, 'Egyptian Attitudes toward Pan-Arabism', *Middle East Journal*, vol. 11, no. 3 (summer, 1957).

Claude, Inis L., Jr., 'The OAS, the UN, and the United States', *International Conciliation*, no. 547 (March 1964).

Cleland, Wendell, 'The League of Arab States after Fifteen Years', *World Affairs*, vol. 123, no. 2 (summer, 1960).

Coury, Ralph M., 'Who Invented Egyptian Arab Nationalism?' (Two Parts) *International Journal of Middle Eastern Studies* Vol. 14, nos. 3 and 4, (August and November 1982).

Cox, Robert W., 'The Executive Head', *International Organization*, vol. 23, no. 2 (spring, 1969).

Dawisha, A. I., 'Intervention in the Yemen', *Middle East Journal*, vol. 27, no. 1 (winter, 1975).

Denny, L. M., 'The Goal of Arab Unification', *International Journal*, vol. 19, no. 1 (winter, 1963/64).

'Egypt since the Coup d'état of 1952', *World Today*, vol. 10 (April 1954).

Farrukh, Omar A., 'Arabism: A Concise and Objective History from 850 B.C. to Early 1963 A.D.', *Islamic Studies*, vol. 3, no. 1 (March 1964).

Fatemi, Nasrallah S., 'The Roots of Arab Nationalism', *Orbis*, vol. 2, no. 4 (winter, 1959).

Fay, Sidney B., 'Egypt and the Arab League', *Current History*, (August 1947).

G. E. K., 'Cross Currents within the Arab League', *World Today*, vol. 9, no. 1 (January 1948).

—, 'Iraq, Egypt and the Arab League', *World Today*, Vol. 11, no. 4 (April 1955).

Guldescu, Stanko, 'Yemen: The War and the Haradth Conference', *Review of Politics*, vol. 28, no. 3 (July 1966).

Hammad, Majdi, 'Israel . . . In the Realization of Abdel-Nasser, 1952–1970', *al-Mustaqbal al-Arabi*, (October 1980).

Hanna, Paul L., 'The Anglo-Egyptian Negotiations, 1950–52', *Middle Eastern Affairs*, vol. 3, nos. 8–9 (August–September 1952).

Harbison, Frederick, 'Two Centers of Arab Power', *Foreign Affairs*, vol. 37 (July 1959).

Heikal, Muhamed, 'Egyptian Foreign Policy', *Foreign Affairs*, vol. 56, no. 4 (July 1978).

Hourani, Albert, 'The Anglo-Egyptian Agreement: Some Causes and Implications', *Middle East Journal*, vol. 9, no. 3 (summer, 1955).

Hourani, Cecil A., 'The Arab League in Perspective', *Middle East Journal*, vol. 1, no. 2 (April 1947).

Howard, Harry N., 'Middle East Regional Organization: Problems and Prospects', *Proceedings of the Academy of Political Science*, vol. 24 (January 1952).

Hussein, Adel, 'Abdel-Nasser and the Economic System', *al-Mustaqbal al-Arabi*, (January 1982).

Hussein, Mahmoud, 'Nasserism in Perspective', *Monthly Review*, vol. 23, no. 6 (November 1971).

Ismael, Tareq Y., 'The United Arab Republic in Africa', *Canadian Journal of African Studies*, vol. 2, no. 2 (autumn, 1972).

Issawi, Charles, 'The Bases of Arab Unity', *International Affairs*, vol. 31, no. 1 (January 1955)

—, 'Crusades and Current Crises in the Near East, a Historical Parallel', *International Affairs*, vol. 33, no. 3 (July 1957).

Jamati, Habib, 'The Birth and Growth of the Arab League', *al-Mussawar* (Cairo), March 1964.

al-Kadhem, S. J., 'The Role of the League of Arab States in Settling Inter-Arab Disputes'. *Revue Egyptienne de Droit International*, vol. 32 (1976).

Kelidar, Abbas, 'The Struggle for Arab Unity', *World Today*, vol. 23, no. 7 (July 1967).

Kenny, L. M. 'Sati' al-Husri's Views on Arab Nationalism', *Middle East Journal*, vol. 17, no. 3 (summer, 1963).

Kerr, Malcolm H., 'Notes on the Background of Arab Socialist Thought', *Journal of Contemporary History*, vol. 3, no. 3 (July 1968).

—, 'Lebanese Views on the 1958 Crisis' (book review), *Middle East Journal*, vol. 15, no. 12 (spring, 1961).

—, 'Coming to Terms with Nasser: Attempts and Failures', *International Affairs*, vol. 43, no. 1 (January 1967).

Khadduri, Majid, 'The Arab League as a Regional Arrangement', *American Journal of International Law*, vol. 40, no. 4 (1946).

—, 'Toward an Arab Union: The League of Arab States', *American Political Science Review*, vol. 40 (February 1946).

—, 'Governments of the Arab East', *International Affairs*, vol. 6 (winter, 1952).

Khoury, Nabeel A., 'The Pragmatic Trend in Inter-Arab Politics', *The Middle East Journal* Vol. 36, no. 3 (summer 1982).

el-Kodsy, Ahmad, 'Nationalism and Class Struggles in the Arab World', *Monthly Review*, vol. 22, no. 3 (July–August 1970).

Little, Tom R., 'The Arab League: A Reassessment', *Middle East Journal*, vol. 10, no. 2 (spring, 1956).

Maglad, Ismail, 'The Arab League', *al-Ahram el-Iqtisadi*, no. 543 (April 1978).

Major, John, 'The Search for Arab Unity', *International Affairs*, vol. 39, no. 4 (1963).

Malone, Joseph, 'The Yemen Arab Republic's Game of Nations', *World Today*, vol. 27, no. 12 (December 1971).

Mansfield, Peter, 'Nasser and Nasserism', *International Journal*, vol. 28, no. 4 (1973).

Masannat, George, 'Nasser's Search for New Order', *Muslim World*, vol. 56 (April 1966).

McKay, Vernon, 'The Arab League in World Politics', *Foreign Policy Reports, I,* vol. XXII, no. 17 (15 November 1946).

Moore, Clement H., 'On Theory and Practice among Arabs', *World Politics*, vol. 24, no. 1 (October 1971).

Naf'a, Hasan, 'Pan-Arabism and the Disentanglement in the Arab Nation', *al-Mustaqbal al-Arabi* (January 1982).

Newman, K. J., 'The New Monarchies of the Middle East', *Journal of International Affairs*, vol. 13, no. 2 (1959).

Nolte, Richard H., 'Arab Nationalism and the Cold War', *Yale Review*, vol. 49, no. 1 (autumn, 1959).

Palmer, Monte, 'The United Arab Republic: An Assessment of its Failure', *Middle East Journal*, vol. 20, no. 1 (winter, 1966).

Parker, J. S. F., 'The United Arab Republic', *International Affairs*, vol. 38, no. 1 (January 1962).

Perlmutter, Amos, 'Sources of Instability in the Middle East: Two Decades of Nationalism and Revolution', *Orbis*, vol. 12, no. 3 (1968).

al-Qazzaz, Ayad, 'Political Order, Stability and Officers: A Comparative Study of Iraq, Syria, and Egypt from Independence till June 1967', *Middle East Forum*, vol. 45, no. 2 (1969).

Raleigh, J. A., 'Ten Years of the Arab League', *Middle Eastern Affairs*, vol. 6 (March 1955).

Range, Willard, 'An Interpretation of Nasserism', *Western Political Quarterly*, vol. 12 (December 1959).

Rizk, Edward A., 'The Arab League', *Asian Review*, vol. 59, no. 217 (January 1963).

Salem, Elie, 'Arab Nationalism: A Reappraisal', *International Journal*, vol. 20, no 3 (summer, 1962).

Salim, Mohamed el-Sayed, 'The Nasserist Analysis of Foreign Policy', *al-Mustaqbal al-Arabi* (October 1980).

Sayegh, Fayez A., 'The Theoretical Structure of Nasser's Arab Socialism', *Middle Eastern Affairs*, vol. 4., St. Antony's Papers 17 (1965).

Seabury, Paul, 'The League of Arab States: Debacle of a Regional Organization', *International Organization*, vol. 3, no. 4 (November 1949).

Seale, Patrick, 'The Break-up of the United Arab Republic', *World Today*, vol. 17 (November 1961).

—, 'The United Arab Republic and the Iraqi Challenge', *World Today*, vol. 16 (July 1960).

Sharabi, Hisham, B., 'Power and Leaders in the Arab World', *Orbis*, (fall, 1963).

Siegman, Henry, 'Arab Unity and Disunity', *Middle East Journal*, vol. 16, no. 1 (winter, 1962).

Silbermann, Gad, 'National Identity in Nasserist Ideology, 1952–1970', *Asian and African Studies*, vol. 8 (1972).

'The Arab League: Development and Difficulties', *World Today*, vol. 7, no. 5 (May 1951).

'The Meaning of the United Arab Republic', *World Today*, vol. 14 (March 1958).

Watt, D.C., 'The Postponement of the Arab Summit', *World Today*, vol. 23, no. 9 (September 1966).

Weinryb, Bernard D., 'The Arab League: Tool or Power?', *Commentary*, vol. 1, no. 5 (March 1946).

Wilkenfeld, Jonathan, *et al.*, 'Conflict Interactions in the Middle East, 1949–1967', *Journal of Conflict Resolution*, vol. 16, no. 2 (July 1972).

Wright, Esmond, 'Defense and the Baghdad Pact', *Political Quarterly*, vol. 28 (April–July 1957).

Newspapers and Periodicals

al-Ahram, 1954–79.
al-Mussawar, 1964–78.
Keesing's Contemporary Archives, 1958–70.
Rose el-Youssef, 1977.

Index

Hassan, Prince of Yemen, 138
Hassan, Saif al-Islam, 80
Hassouna, Abdel-Khaliq, 20,
    23–4, 29, 42n, 44n, 53, 56;
    against Baghdad Pact, 73, 74–5;
    Lebanon crisis 1958, 102–3,
    106–8; reappointed 1962, 130,
    165; Shtoura Meeting, 119;
    Yemeni conflict, 144, 145,
    147
Hassouna, Hussein, 14n, 15n,
    16n, 43n, 85n, 109n, 110n,
    111n, 134n, 159n, 161n
Haykal, Dr Muhammad Hussein,
    3
Heikal, Mohamed Hassanein, 55,
    62, 65n, 113, 116, 133n,
    135n
Hijaz, Sherif Hussein of, 2
Hitti, Philip K., 13n
Hourani, Cecil A., 12, 15n, 16n
Hurani, Akram, 117
Hurewitz, J.C., 109n
al-Husri, Sati, 42n
Hussein, King of Jordan, 39, 58,
    61, 116; Baghdad Pact, 80,
    84; dismissal of Glubb, 56, 81;
    Yemen conflict and, 145, 148,
    150, 154
Hussein, Kamal al-Din, 157
Hussein al-Kibsi, Sayed, see al-
    Kibsi, Sayed Hussein

Ibn Khaldun, see Khaldun, Ibn
Ibrahim, General Muhamad, 72
Iglimiyyah, 2
Infisal, see secession from UAR
Ingrams, Harold, 158n
Iran, Shah of, 152, 153
Iraq: Baghdad Pact, 68–88, 163,
    168; monarchy overthrown,
    79, 81, 82, 84, 99; revolution
    1921, 3; sided with Lebanon
    1958, 98
Iraqi-Kuwaiti dispute 1961, 23

al-Islam Hassan, Saif, *see*
    Hassan, Saif al-Islam
Israel, 168; diversion of Jordan
    river, 60, 146, 147, 148; Gaza
    raid, 34, 35–6; June war 1967,
    39–40, 154; manoeuvres
    1950s, 56
Issawi, Charles, 45n
al-Ittihad al-'arabi, 4

al-Jabri, Sa'adallah, 8
Jackson, Judith, 41n
al-Jamali, Fadil, 22, 71, 76, 93,
    98
Jamati, Habib, 15n
Jiddah agreement 1965, 150–1
Joint Saudi-Syrian-Egyptian
    Command, 81
Jordan: British troops in, 100–2,
    104; criticism of Azzam, 21–2;
    destabilization by Nasser, 82;
    diplomatic relations broken off,
    116; UN resolution on, 184–
    5a; *see also* Hussein, King of
    Jordan
Jordan River, 60, 146, 147, 148
Junblatt, Kamal, 90, 91, 92
June war 1967, 39–40, 154

al-Kaillany, Rashid Ali, 4, 5
Kallas, Khalil, 120–1
Kamal al-Din Hussein, 157
Kamel, Mahoud, 13n, 16n, 43n,
    64n, 66n, 88n
Kamil, Muhamad Ibrahim, 129
Karami, Rashid, 91, 92, 99, 104
Kennedy, John F., 139, 140,
    156, 169
Kerr, Malcolm, 46n, 55, 65n,
    66n, 67n, 109n, 133n, 134n,
    135n, 160n
Khadduri, Majid, 14n, 15n, 16n,
    54, 65n, 86n
Khaldun, Ibn, 33, 54
Khalil, Muhammad, 16n, 41n,

225